DOGS
OF THE WORLD

Translated by Julie Almond
Copyright © 1982 Arnoldo Mondadori Editore S.p.A., Milan
English translation copyright © 1983
Arnoldo Mondadori Editore S.p.A., Milan
First British edition 1983

Printed and bound in Italy by
Officine Grafiche di Arnoldo Mondadori Editore, Verona
for the publishers, W.H. Allen & Co. Ltd
44 Hill Street, London W1X 8LB

ISBN 0 491 03481 4

Maurizio Bongianni & Concetta Mori

DOGS
OF THE WORLD

Illustrations by Piero Cozzaglio

Foreword by Mrs Catherine G. Sutton,
member of the Kennel Club of Great Britain,
a judge and presenter at Crufts,
and an international judge

W.H. ALLEN · LONDON
A Howard & Wyndham Company
1983

CONTENTS

FOREWORD

This is a well-illustrated book with just over 270 colour pictures of the different breeds of dog that inhabit the world. It is a complete book on the dog and apart from the excellent colour illustrations there are nearly 100 black and white drawings of other breeds seen in Europe, Asia, America and Australasia and detailed descriptions of all the breeds illustrated.

This is probably the most up-to-date book of its kind and should be a very valuable addition to the connoisseur's library as well as a wonderful introduction for those seeking to learn about the more unusual breeds not generally seen outside one's own country.

The table at the back of the book listing the qualities and defects of nearly 300 breeds is a very good quick reference guide.

It is my pleasure to recommend this book thoroughly to all dog enthusiasts.

Mrs Catherine G. Sutton

INTRODUCTION

The dog, man's companion since ancient times, needs no introduction to the reader, but not everybody may be acquainted with its "natural history", which is much more interesting than history in the usual sense of the word.

There are approximately 5000 species of mammals – classified under eighteen different categories, the family *Canidae* being close in number to the family *Felidae* – and, of them all, the dog is unique in the relationship of trust and co-operation it has built up with man, its friend and master. The long process of domestication of the dog has been achieved, as has that of all other domesticated animals, by virtue of two important developments:

1) changes in external appearance (phenotype) and hereditary composition (genotype) due to variations in environmental conditions;

2) a change in the breeding pattern, brought about by man substituting artificial selection for natural selection.

As a consequence of man's intervention, the evolution of the dog has followed a set pattern, leading, on the one hand, to the development of numerous characteristics typical of the species, and on the other to a kind of morphological affinity with other domestic animals.

For instance, the drop ear found in many dogs (hounds for example) is also a feature of goats, sheep and cattle; the coat-type with light and dark markings typical of the Dutch breeds (Wetterhoun, Stabyhoun) is found in cattle as well as in dogs; the flattened skull, due to an uneven development of the different parts of the skeleton, is a characteristic of the pig as well as the dog.

In addition to these modifications, which are gradually absorbed until they become hereditary, the influence of the environment also has a subtle and penetrating effect on the psyche of the domestic animal. Life under the protection of man makes fewer demands on the dog than the uncertainty of life in the wild. This narrowing of experience causes a 20 to 30 per cent reduction in brain capacity, mainly in the areas of the brain concerned with optical and acoustic stimulation, and is so pronounced as to be already observable in the first generation of wild animals to be held in captivity. To the degree that "stress" factors are absent, the level of hormonal production is also reduced and instinctive behaviour is modified. As a result, instinctive actions are no longer governed by the fixed and ritualized patterns found in wild animals, so that the seasonal mating rhythm, for instance, is no longer the same. Some forms of domestication (specifically pet dogs) often lead to such clear alterations in behaviour that it is not unusual to find that certain characteristics of human behaviour have been transmitted to the dog.

Scientific research into breeds is based on the study of the frequency with which certain genes (submicroscopic particles responsible for the transmission of hereditary characteristics) appear in the entire genetic equipment of the individual. To facilitate research, this study is carried out on genes responsible for characteristics which are easy to study, such as the colour of the coat or the shape of the eyes. However, since it is not always easy to classify morphological differences according to scientific criteria, researchers are not always in agreement as to which breed a given individual should be attributed to, and it is therefore possible for it to be classified differently. Some animal experts would deny the existence of separate breeds in the genetic sense of the word on the grounds that all breeds are the result of crossbreeding.

Therefore the term "breed" is merely a convenient expression used to identify a group of animals which have been selectively bred for a specific purpose, and which can be divided into geographical units according to their ability to adapt to certain environmental conditions. The origin of different breeds can probably be attributed to the very gradual emergence, over thousands of years, of a few "natural breeds" from an undifferentiated canine population distributed over a large area, as a result of the evolutionary process induced both by environmental factors, such as geographical isolation or climate, and by gene-changing factors (pervasive radiation, chemical substances), which bring about changes at a genetic level. These natural breeds probably survived through natural selection, providing the human race with a reserve from which they could select and interbreed the desired types.

It is not therefore scientifically correct to refer to the primitive dog as a "bastard", with all the negative implications contained in the term.

To discover the origins of the dog, one must go back into the distant past, to the so-called Lower Tertiary age, which spans a period of time from approximately 63 to 23 million years ago. It was then that an undistinguished animal – massive in appearance, with non-retractable claws, a long tail and teeth with no specialist function – made its appearance. The Creodont, for such was its name, is considered by palaeontologists to be the precursor of all carnivores and therefore also of our *Canis familiaris*. There is a very long interlude between the appearance of Creodont and the *Canis familiaris*, not always accounted for by fossilized remains, which gives scope for different phylogenetic theories.

One ancestor of the modern dog was, without any doubt, the Hesperocyon, with a long body and short legs like all primitive carnivores. It hunted on the ground but still had retractable claws, enabling it to climb trees. Two separate species emerged from this animal. The first, the Temnocyon, represents an important step in the evolutionary chain which leads down to the Lycaon of South Africa, also known as the Cape Hunting Dog, which differs from the domestic dog by virtue of its long legs, large ears and hyena-like coat. The second, the *Cynodesmus*, is considered the forerunner of the large and diversified *Canidae* family.

About 15 million years ago another predator, the *Tomarctus*, appeared, again, with a long body and short legs but of a slimmer and sturdier build, adapted to running and predation. The *Tomarctus*, already very similar to the modern dog, further evolved to give rise to dogs, wolves, foxes, coyotes, fennecs and jackals. Some considerable time was still to elapse between the appearance of the *Tomarctus* and the *Canis familiaris* (the first modern dog as we know it). The *Canis familiaris* has roamed with man for approximately 10,000 years, leaving traces of its presence in the form of the skulls of *Canis palustris* found in Neolithic remains. The *Canis matris optimae* which, crossed with the *palustris*, gave us the *Canis intermedius* belongs to the Bronze Age. After this period, there is again a gap in our knowledge of the subsequent evolutionary stages which led to the development of the numerous breeds of dog which exist today.

The classification of dogs into separate breeds and no longer into types is an innovation of the last hundred years, before which time dogs were grouped into four main categories:
1) herding dogs,
2) sporting dogs and terriers,
3) Spitz dogs and toy dogs,
4) guard dogs.

When this method of classification proved inadequate, it was replaced by a wider range of categories which corresponded more closely to the different characteristics of present-day canine breeds.

The dog is a lively, intelligent and sociable animal, of not very large dimensions (it tends to stand between 18 and 80 cm [7 and 31 in] tall at the withers). Its head is long and the muzzle generally slim and on a lower level than the forehead. It has between 42 and 44 teeth, sometimes even less. The pupils of the eyes are round. The size of the ears and tail varies and this same variability is found in the shape of the body, the texture and colour of the coat and the shape of the limbs. Because of this great variability, some dogs bear a greater resemblance to the wolf and others to the jackal, and it is not easy to detect clear differences between these species.

The study of hybrids has shown that a dog bitch can be successfully mated with a male wolf and (less easily) vice versa. Mating is also accomplished fairly easily with a jackal and, in both cases, the offspring of the union seem to be fertile. On the other hand, it is extremely unusual for a dog to mate with a fox, which leads one to assume that the dog is much more similar to the wolf and the jackal than to the fox.

On the basis of these findings, the ethologist Konrad Lorenz reaffirms the theory already put forward by Charles Darwin that the dog is descended from both the wolf and the jackal. It follows therefore than our dogs have jackal blood (*canis aureus*) or wolf blood (*canis lupus*) in varying proportions, accounting for differences not only in appearance but, even more important, also in character, the *aureus* type being docile, submissive, obedient and free with its affections, and the *lupus* proud, independent and faithful to only one master.

The muscles of the dog are generally strong and long-reaching, located mainly in the upper half of the body to allow freedom of movement. It has slim legs and short toes with hard, non-retractable nails. The body combines with the other characteristics to endow the dog with a physical framework specially adapted for running, over prolonged periods if necessary. Unlike the family *Felidae*, which uses the technique of stealthy pursuit and ambush in hunting, the dog relies on speed and will hunt either alone or in a pack. Speed of movement depends on the degree of flexibility of the spine. If this is relatively rigid, as in the horse, the impetus comes almost exclusively from the leg muscles, but if it is more arched, as in the *Canidae* and *Felidae* families, the hind legs move forward with every bound, causing the body to shorten considerably. The rapid straightening of the back gives further impetus to the body, reinforcing that provided by the hind legs.

This kind of spinal flexibility reaches the maximum degree of efficiency in greyhounds and, among wild animals, in the cheetah which, although resembling the cat in the shape of its head, is in other respects (long legs, semi-fixed claws) much closer to the dog. Extreme flexibility of the spine does, however, have its drawbacks, in that the high energy output entailed in producing this spring-like movement cannot be sustained over long distances.

Special attention is paid nowadays to dog psychology and behaviour, taking for granted that its gregariousness is a vestige of its ancestral past retained through the ages. The dog has transferred the attachment it once had for the leader of the pack to man, receiving understanding, affection and protection in return. The ancient pact contracted freely with man has enriched the dog's psychological and emotional life, which has developed in accordance with its social nature. All other domestic animals, with the exception of the cat which cannot truly be called domestic, are really slaves; only the dog is a friend.

The descriptions of the different breeds of dog are grouped into a classification, suggested by the dogs' respective aptitudes and the uses to which they have been put. This classification is fairly close to those adopted by the international canine organizations, although a few breeds have been placed in a different group where this has been considered more in keeping with its present role. The dogs have been divided into rescue breeds, working dogs (sheepdogs, cattle dogs, sledge dogs), guard and watch dogs, hunting breeds (gundogs, earth dogs, hounds and greyhounds), and companion dogs.

It is inevitable that such specific classifications based on the most striking quality of various dogs tend to overshadow their many other aptitudes which make them particularly versatile. For example, there are hunting dogs used to pull sledges, guard or sheepdogs suitable for training as guide dogs for the blind, dogs of different groups used as personal guard and watch dogs, as well as the ever increasing use being made by the police force of a variety of different breeds. Similarly the group of so-called "companion dogs" includes breeds originally created for a specific purpose, which has become obsolete or irrelevant, or breeds with no distinctive characteristic corresponding to the groups mentioned above. But ultimately almost all dogs may be considered companions and the trend is that even breeds with specific functions are kept purely as pets.

It is also true that not only "pedigree" dogs know how to serve man; those dogs belonging to no particular breed which are given the name of mongrels also make good hunters or guard dogs, in addition to being man's faithful companion. As an illustration of the wide range of their activities, some dogs, usually mongrels, are used for sniffing out truffles. What is more, the moral or physical qualities of these dogs which are often quite wrongly maligned, such as intelligence, loyalty, obedience, liveliness, strength, hardiness, sense of smell and an affectionate nature are very often on a par with, or even superior, to those of their more aristocratic high-ranking cousins.

RESCUE DOGS

This group of dogs contains some of the largest of all the canine breeds. They are powerfully built, strong, sturdy animals, resistant to fatigue and severe weather conditions, and are also excellent swimmers. They have a natural instinct to retrieve both people and objects, and a very sensitive nose which enables them to sniff out people buried beneath snow or wreckage. They are intelligent and very easy to train.

Leonberger

This magnificent dog owes its name to its creator, Heinrich Essig of Leonberg in Württemberg. In appearance it has many of the characteristics of the St Bernard and the Newfoundland, from which the Leonberger was bred, with a possible contribution from the Pyrenean Mountain Dog. Its classification as a separate breed did not happen overnight, partly because it was not developed in accordance with a strict breeding programme. The definition of its official standard therefore dates from little more than thirty years ago. The Leonberger has a coat of long, thick, soft and quite oily hair, reinforced by a very dense, waterproof undercoat. Despite this abundant coat, the lines of the body are clearly distinguishable, revealing a strong and muscular but well-proportioned frame, which lends the Leonberger an air of elegance. The head is considerably smaller than that of the St Bernard,

and the skin of the skull is normal, without the characteristic wrinkles of the St Bernard. Around its neck, which is free of dewlap, there is a wide collar of very thick, long hair, quite different from that on the chest. The tail is long, very hairy, with a fine plume. The forelegs are straight, while the shape of the hind ones, with short, muscular thighs and long hocks, is a characteristic of the breed. The feet are webbed. The Leonberger has an excellent character, is very intelligent and easily trained for water rescue, good-natured, faithful, affectionate, patient with children and makes a good companion.

Weight: 40–50 kg (88–110 lb). Height: 70–80 cm (27½–31½ in). Colour: fawn, reddish, with or without black (wolf-like) markings.
Country of Origin: Germany.

St Bernard

The national dog of Switzerland, its origins lie in the Tibetan Mastiff which, once domesticated, spread to Nepal, India and China. The Molossus, a derivate of the Mastiff, was first introduced into Greece and then into ancient Rome, and finally into the country that was to become its homeland. From 1659 onwards, the monks of the St Bernard pass took charge of this splendid dog which by then had lost some of the aggressiveness and ferocity typical of the Mastiff. They initiated a highly selective breeding programme which brought about changes both in physical appearance and in temperament. The aim of the monks was to create a sturdy animal, resistant to cold and fatigue, suited originally to transporting foodstuffs in the mountains, later promoted to the rank of "rescuer" of men.

They also wished to eliminate its negative character traits, gradually replacing them with qualities of intelligence, kindness, selflessness, obedience, loyalty and judgement. The first official mention of alpine rescue was in 1707, a date which marks the beginning of a vast number of rescue operations – of which the undisputed champion is the famous Barry, who alone was responsible for finding and rescuing at least forty-four people. Towards 1820, the breed came close to complete extinction, because the monks were more concerned with developing the qualities of strength and stamina than with preserving the characteristics peculiar to the breed. Selective breeding was then taken up both by specialized Swiss breeders, with excellent results, and by the English and Americans, who concentrated their efforts, however, mainly on developing the size of the breed producing animals a metre (39 in) high and weighing 100 kg (220 lb). Nowadays there are two types of St Bernard, the long-haired and the short-haired variety, the advantage of the latter being that the snow clings less to its coat, allowing it greater freedom of movement. The coat of the long-haired is flat or slightly wavy, but never curly, longer on the thighs and tail, whereas that of the short-haired is dense, smooth and strong, without any appreciable variations in length on the different areas of the body. Typical of the St Bernard is its enormous head with the slightly arched skull, covered in skin which forms characteristic wrinkles, particularly noticeable when the animal assumes an air of alertness or absorption. This makes it look rather sad, an impression accentuated by the upper eyelid falling well over the eye which often has part of the haw exposed. The bridge of the nose is straight, the stop clearly defined and the muzzle full and not too long. The upper lip is pendant, while the lower one is normal-sized; the ears also hang down, are relatively small and set high on the head. The strong neck, with dewlap, fits into the well-rounded, but not too prominent, chest. Its massive, muscular body is supported by straight legs, also heavily muscled, and large, compact feet which prevent the dog from sinking into the snow. Nowadays its role as a rescue dog has been rendered almost, though not entirely, obsolete by the use of much more efficient technical equipment.

Short-haired Saint Bernard

Long-haired Saint Bernard

Weight: 55–80 kg (121–176½ lb). Height: the English Standard states: "the taller the better, provided that symmetry is maintained". Colour: white and red, grey with brown and white, various shades of red. Mask often black; sometimes black markings on ears, chest and collar.
Country of Origin: Switzerland.

Newfoundland and Landseer

The Newfoundland is a large, powerful example of the rescue and working breeds. Its origin is much disputed. It is called after the island of the same name, but does not seem to have originated there. It may have been brought there by Basque fishermen or by the English, who concentrated on breeding very large dogs specially trained for guarding and sea rescue work. The Newfoundland is equally at ease in the water and on dry land, where it is useful for transporting loads over reasonably even ground, its wide, well-shaped, webbed feet being more suited to swimming than to running. The Newfoundland used to be an habitual boat dweller, responsible for retrieving objects which had fallen overboard, as well as rescuing people. Such behaviour does not come completely naturally, and a suitable period of training is required although the dog's love of water and swimming is a great asset. The retrieving instinct on the other hand is deep-rooted, and the dog can even dive and swim under water. The Landseer (from the name of its breeder) is a variety of Newfoundland and shares many of the black dog's general characteristics. The main difference lies in the colour of the coat; in addition, the Landseer has a less massive head, their hair tends to curl, and it is often bigger. There are no psychological differences, both dogs having excellent characters – good-natured, faithful, patient with children, calm and intelligent. In spite of its size, the Newfoundland conveys an impression of harmonious proportions and elegance. The broad, massive head, the short, square muzzle, the small, deeply set eyes, the small ears lying close to the head and the soft but not pendulous lips create the Newfoundland's characteristic expression: kindly, friendly, vaguely thoughtful and at times melancholy. The broad, muscular body, supported by strong legs, is agile, nimble and swift in movement. The coat is dense, flat, smooth or slightly wavy, long, coarse and oily so that the dog can stand lengthy immersions even in icy water. In the very cold season the coat is kept waterproof by the formation of a dark, oily undercoat, which tends to disappear in dogs who live a long way from the water.

Weight: dogs 60–65 kg (132–143 lb); bitches 50–55 kg (110–121 lb). Height: 70–75 cm (27½–29½ in). Colour: jet black (turns dull and brown during moulting and with age) in the Newfoundland; pure white with black markings and black mask (in the Landseer).
Country of Origin: Canada (Newfoundland); Northern Europe (Landseer).

Landseer

Newfoundland

Pyrenean Mountain Dog

This immense, majestic dog, not to be confused with the Berger des Pyrénées, seems made for life in the mountains. Found in large numbers in Andorra, it is a valuable asset to the peasant farmers, protecting flocks and herds against wolves and even bears. Obedient and adaptable, it is easy to train for mountain rescue work. The Pyrenean Mountain Dog is a very intelligent, good-natured animal, and exceptionally devoted to its master, whom it will defend to the last. Because of its physical beauty and admirable character, it has been used in cross-breeding to improve the St Bernard and Newfoundland dogs. It is closely related to the Hungarian Kuvasz and the Maremma Sheepdog, but is much more elegant and magnificent, and indeed enjoyed a period of splendour at the court of Louis XIV in the dual role of guard dog and companion. Its coat is thick, flat and long all over the body but particularly on the neck, tail and back of the thighs. The head is large but in proportion to the body, with a slightly domed skull and a wide muzzle ending in a pointed nose. The lips, palate and eye-rims are edged in black. The eyes themselves are rather small, dark rich brown in colour and slightly oblique. The lips never droop. The ears are small, triangular, set high, and carried low and close to the head. The sturdy neck has a hint of dewlap, continuing on to the broad, deep chest.

Weight: 45–55 kg (99–121 lb). Height: dogs 70–80 cm (27½–31½ in); bitches 65–72 cm (25½–28½ in). Colour: white, sometimes with light yellow or grey markings on the head.
Country of Origin: France.

GUARD AND WATCH DOGS

This is another group of dogs which have served man well and continue to do so. Usually of medium to large size, but occasionally small, they are characterized by a solid but not heavy build and a highly-developed, streamlined musculature. They are hardy, agile, swift and alert, and possess a set of very strong teeth. Intelligent, easy to train, faithful and very attached to their owners, they are naturally very courageous and aggressive towards any person behaving suspiciously.

Boxer

The modern Boxer is a recent breed, developed in Munich in 1896 and still evolving. Its official standard, first drawn up in 1905, has been altered several times. Its ancestry can be traced back to the Bulldog and the Bullenbeisser (Bull-baiter), which was very common in Germany and Holland where it was used for hunting wild boar, deer and bears. However, as with many other dogs, its oldest forebear is the Tibetan Mastiff. The aim of Boxer breeders was not only to reduce the physical deformities of its predecessors but also to diminish the excessive aggressiveness present in the early strains. The careful, patient work of professional breeders has been rewarded with a dog in which unquestionable beauty is combined with an extraordinary temperament, unique among guard and watch dogs. The Boxer distrusts strangers and tolerates no intrusion into what it considers its property. Intelligent and responsible, it is also very tractable and can therefore be trained as a police dog and a guide dog for the blind. It is a naturally clean animal, well behaved, quiet, modest, tolerant and loves to play, making an ideal companion, perfectly suited to apartment living provided that it is often taken for long walks to enable it to give free rein to its boisterous nature. It has an extraordinary agility and a very keen sense of smell. It has a hardy constitution and is resistant to fatigue, but is prone to rheumatism and tends not to live very long,

sometimes not beyond the age of twelve. Being a relatively young breed and continually developing, the standard cannot always be relied upon to provide a definitive guide to the evaluation of a dog's merits in the show ring, and the competition judges may not always reach an agreement on the dog in question. The skull is slightly arched, neither flat nor too prominent, and narrow, in line with the cheek-bones. The large, dark eyes are not therefore too far apart and there is a mere suggestion of a furrow down its forehead.

The ears, set high on the head, are cropped in some countries to about a third of their length to make them stand erect, thereby reinforcing the noble, elegant appearance of the head. The skin on the skull shows no wrinkles in repose, only when the dog is alert or absorbed. The muzzle is short and square, with the lower jaw protruding significantly and bending slightly upwards. The thick, padded upper lip droops down to cover the lower jaw completely but does not extend below it; seen from the front, the border of the lip forms the shape of an upside-down U with the arms extended. The teeth should not be visible. The nose is set high and back in relation to the jaws and the topline of the muzzle is straight, never sloping. The neck – round, strong but not thick, of medium length and powerful – arches elegantly down to the back, which is muscular and shapely,

sloping gently to the hindquarters. The tail attachment is high and the tail docked short. The stomach line is lightly tucked up, blending into a graceful and elegant curve to the rear. The forelegs are straight and not very wide apart, whereas the hind legs are well angulated. The feet are normal-sized with arched toes. The coat is short, smooth, shiny and even.

Weight: dogs 30–32 kg (66–70½ lb); bitches 25–28 kg (55–62 lb).
Height: dogs 56–61 cm (22–24 in); bitches 53–58 cm (21–23 in).
Colour: brindle (sometimes with white chest and feet), all one colour, from light yellow to fawn, with black mask.
Country of Origin: Germany.

Dobermann
Dobermann Pinscher

As a guard and watch dog the Dobermann has no peer. It is of fairly recent origin and made its first official appearance only in 1876. Developed in Germany by a breeder called Dobermann, it is still not known for sure which breeds contributed towards its creation, but the Thuringian shepherd dogs, the Black and Tan Terrier, the Beauceron, the Greyhound and the Schnauzer are thought to have formed part of its basic stock. However the end result of this hypothetical miscellany has turned out to be so attractive and well formed, combining strength with elegance, that it has gained rapidly in popularity not only in its country of origin but also in Europe and America. The Dobermann is a very intelligent animal with a good memory; it is faithful and very courageous, even risking its life to protect its owner. Resistant to fatigue and adverse weather conditions, easy to train because of its extraordinary powers of understanding, it makes an ideal police or war dog. Although generally good-natured, patient and affectionate towards its owner, it is suspicious of strangers whom it tends to treat with watchful wariness which, particularly in the male of the species, often borders on aggressiveness. Its agility and speed of movement make it a fearsome guard dog, equipped as it is with a set of very strong teeth with a scissor-like bite. Artificial selection has, in the case of the Dobermann, produced a particularly fine physical specimen, whose body, while strong and powerful, is never thickset or massive, neither is it too thin like that of the Greyhound. The head is long, bony and well chiselled, with only a very slight stop. The eyes are of medium size, with a lively, proud expression and are dark in colour and bright. The ears are either dropped or cropped – though this is not allowed in Britain – not too short and carried erect, adding to the proud expression of the head. The neck is long and dry, and completely free from dewlap, not cylindrical but widening gradually towards the body. The back extends in a straight line from the withers to the strong, thick tail, which is docked very short. The legs are straight and perfectly parallel, with short feet well suited to jumping because of their compact, well-arched toes. The nails are strong and resistant to the impact of the dog landing after the jump. The coat is short, hard, close-lying and gleaming, preferably without any undercoat which, when present, should not be visible.

Weight: 30–40 kg (66–88 lb). Height: dogs 62–68 cm (24½–27 in); bitches 58–65 cm (23–25½ in). Colour: black, brown, grey blue, with sharply defined rust-red markings. Country of Origin: Germany.

Schnauzer

The Schnauzer – so called because its characteristic beard draws attention to its muzzle – was, for a long time, known by the name of Stable Griffon because of its affinity with horses, which it used to accompany on long, hard journeys by stage-coach, on rides with its noble owners and on beatings with the hunt. This breed of dog is known to have existed in Germany for a very long time, and its origins are very similar to those of the terrier breeds, with which it shares not only a good many physical characteristics but also many psychological ones. Although too tall to be used as a burrowing dog, the Schnauzer is very good at catching mice, polecats and martens. It was also known and bred in France, Switzerland and Italy, but it was not until the start of the twentieth century that the breed was subjected to strict selection and therefore in its definite form it is a fairly recent breed. There are three types of Schnauzer: large or giant, standard and miniature. All three are very robust and hardy dogs, strongly muscled, agile and quick, energetic and always alert. The Giant Schnauzer, known as the Riesenschnauzer, has been used for police and war work,

in addition to its role of guard and watch dog, for which it is ideally suited due to its size and its proud, awe-inspiring appearance; but its size and need for physical exercise and open spaces make it a poor candidate for apartment living. The Standard Schnauzer, known as the Pinscher Schnauzer, has, in the past, been used largely to catch rats and other vermin, thus making a valuable contribution towards the protection of the harvest, hen-houses and rabbit-runs. Nowadays its main role is as a guard dog and companion, being well suited to life in the home. The Miniature Schnauzer, known as the Zwergschnauzer, differs from the other two only in size, which in no way detracts from its proud and fearless nature. Although nowadays considered largely a pet and lap dog, its natural guarding instinct makes it an able guard dog of its master's person. The physical characteristics of the three varieties of Schnauzer are basically the same and are covered by the same standard. The dog is fairly heavy set, presenting a nearly square appearance. The head is strong and long, quite large but not massive or broad. The muzzle is almost in line with the flat forehead, and there is not sufficient

Standard Schnauzer

Miniature Schnauzer

play of skin on the head to allow for the formation of wrinkles. The eyes – neither large nor small – are dark and oval beneath thick, bushy brows. The ears are set high on the head and docked to make them stand erect, or drop forward in a V-shape in countries where ear-cropping is not permitted. Both neck and body are fairly short, but not disproportionately so. The tail is set high and docked very short. Both fore and hind legs have a strong bone structure, strong muscles and are parallel to each other, with round cat-like paws. The coat is of medium length, rough, hard and wiry, fairly sparse, neither curly, wavy, nor too close to the body, and forming the characteristic beard and moustache on the muzzle. The Schnauzer's coat is normally stripped in order to emphasize the elegance of the body outline. To gain the full effect the coat should be clipped to different lengths.

Weight: Giant: 35 kg (77 lb); Standard 15 kg (33 lb); Miniature 5 kg (11 lb). Height: Giant 65–70 cm (25–27 in); Standard 45–50 cm ($17\frac{1}{2}$–$19\frac{1}{2}$ in); Miniature 30–35 cm (12–14 in). Colour: identical for the three sizes: black, pepper-and-salt.
Country of Origin: Germany.

Great Dane

Harlequin Great Dane

The Great Dane – a misleading name in itself – also has a variety of other misnomers, including Deutsche Dogge and German Mastiff (perhaps because the breed is in fact German in origin). However, the term mastiff is inappropriate as it has a long, rectangular muzzle rather than the short, square muzzle of the mastiff, though the breed may indeed be the result of crossing powerful mastiffs – brought to Germany at the beginning of the fifth century by Eastern invaders – with greyhound-type dogs. Despite repeated attempts on the part of Danish breeders to lay claim to the Great Dane, the evidence is more in favour of it originating in Germany. The Great Dane is considered the giant of the canine breeds, combining great size and a powerful, well-formed body with natural elegance and great nobility of bearing. It should never appear stocky or massive, like the mastiff, nor too thin

and light, like the greyhound. Its beauty lies in the exact balance between its various characteristics, in its proud, dignified bearing, and its easy, smooth, springy gait and long stride. The Great Dane is a very intelligent dog, quick to learn and has a good memory, which makes it easy to train. It has had a variety of roles in the past – war dog, hunting dog, personal guard and watch dog; but nowadays it is essentially a guard dog, also providing a regal addition to the household. The Great Dane is good-natured, docile and affectionate but, because of its size, cannot indulge in the great shows of affection typical of other dogs. It is very fond of children and will automatically look after them. Like all guard dogs it is somewhat wary of strangers and ready to attack at the first sign of suspicious behaviour. Because of its size the Great Dane is not at all suited to apartment living. Its coat is very short, thick, strong,

25

Brindle Great Dane

Fawn Great Dane

close-lying and glossy. The head is longer than it is broad, with a flat or slightly domed skull and a barely pronounced furrow between the eyes. The muzzle is long like the head, and straight or slightly convex with a black nose and dilated nostrils. The eyes are round and preferably dark, the colour varying according to that of the coat, and with a serious, knowing expression. The ears, set high on the head and not too far apart, are sometimes docked and carried erect; in countries such as Great Britain where ear-cropping is prohibited, the ears hang close to the cheek. The neck is long, lean and muscular, free from dewlap and broader at the base. The back is straight, relatively short and strong, with arched loins. The tail is set high and carried like a sabre, level with the line of the back when running, and low when not in action. There is considerable tuck-up at the loins, but not so much as in the greyhound.

The legs are long and well muscled, with rounded, compact feet, turned neither inwards nor outwards; they have strong nails curved downwards. There are different varieties of Great Dane, distinguished predominantly by the colour of their coat, which can either be self-coloured, brindle or harlequin. The differences between them are only very slight, both in appearance and temperament. The fawn and brindle Great Danes tend to have a slightly slimmer build than the self-coloured blacks and blues, and a more lively disposition. But the harlequin Great Dane is the most majestic of them all, with a somewhat heavier build and rather aloof disposition, less eager to please.

Weight: approximately 60 kg (132 lb). Height: dogs minimum 78–80 cm (31–$31\frac{1}{2}$ in); bitches minimum 72 cm ($28\frac{1}{2}$ in). Colour: self-coloured: all shades of fawn, blue, black, white; brindle: yellow or fawn base colour with well-defined stripes; harlequin: pure white background with irregular black markings.
Country of Origin: Germany.

Black Great Dane

Hovawart

The Hovawart is indigenous to Germany and its origins are probably linked to those of the Pyrenean Mountain Dog, the Hungarian Kuvasz and the Bernese Mountain Dog. Known in Germany since ancient times, it was practically unknown elsewhere, so much so that it was in danger of extinction when other dog breeds were more in fashion and monopolized the attention of dog-lovers. Fortunately, thanks to a number of devotees, the breed was salvaged by cross-breeding and restored to its original form on the basis of drawings and other available information. The Hovawart is not only an excellent guard and watch dog, but also a fine sheepdog, having an exceptional nose and an instinct for guarding, which dispenses with the need for extensive training. It is a very intelligent animal, alert and responsive, faithful and very attached to its owner, affectionate, calm and patient. If it needs to be trained for a specific purpose, this is best started after the age of two, because the Hovawart retains its juvenile characteristics for a long time, and its puppy-like temperament prevents it from taking any instructions it may be given seriously. The Hovawart is very resistant to both bad weather and tiredness, never flagging even over the most impassable ground, and will warn its owner of danger by its characteristic piercing and persistent bark, hence it is extremely useful. It has a solid, agile and sturdy frame, which is neither heavy nor thick-set. Bitches are considerably smaller and look much more elegant. The head is powerful, with a slightly rounded skull and strong jaws. The eyes are amber and the ears flat, set high and pendant. The length of the strong neck is in proportion to the body, which looks slightly longer than it is high, with powerful hindquarters, wide hocks and hard but elastic pads. The coat is long and thick, with a slight wave, not woolly, forming feathering on the legs, and the tail slightly upturned.

Weight: dogs 30–40 kg (66–88 lb); bitches 25–30 kg (55–66 lb). Height: dogs 60–70 cm (24–27½ in); bitches 55–65 cm (21½–25½ in). Colour: black, black and tan, light or deep (preferable) gold.
Country of Origin: Germany.

Rottweiler

The Rottweiler, a breed of ancient lineage developed in Germany, owes its name to the town of Rottweil, south of Württemberg. It may be descended from the Neapolitan mastiff, brought to Germany by the Roman legions. For a long time it was known by the name of Metzgerhund (Butcher's Dog) and used largely as a cattle dog, for it was always very common wherever there were herds to guard. Its reputation as a good and courageous herder led it to being used as a personal guard and watch dog. As it is also endowed with great intelligence, tractability, obedience, strength and courage, it is often trained as a police dog, mainly in its country of origin. Its steady, unexcitable nature and natural cleanliness also make it a suitable pet for the home. The Rottweiler's skull is broad and rounded, with a well-defined stop. The muzzle is fairly short and the eyes large, round and dark. The ears are comparatively small, triangular in shape, and hang down slightly away from the head. The neck is strong, very muscular and rather short, and may sometimes have a slight dewlap. The Rottweiler is powerful and massive of build, with a broad, deep chest and little tuck-up of the belly. The tail is set high and should ideally be short. The legs are straight and muscular; the feet of average length with compact, well-arched toes.

Weight: 40–50 kg (88–110 lb). Height: dogs 60–68 cm ($23\frac{1}{2}$–$26\frac{1}{2}$ in); bitches 55–65 cm ($21\frac{1}{2}$–$25\frac{1}{2}$ in). Colour: black and tan.
Country of Origin: Germany.

Dogue de Bordeaux

The Dogue de Bordeaux is a very ancient breed, mentioned in writings dating back to the first century BC. It may be considered a French breed, although its origins are somewhat obscure. Some would say that, like all mastiffs, it is descended from the great Tibetan Mastiff, others that its progenitor is a Spanish animal, the Dogue de Burgos, brought to France across the Pyrenees, and the theory favoured by the English is that it is a cross between the Old English Mastiff and the Bulldog. The Dogue de Bordeaux is not common in Europe, not even in France. It enjoyed a period of great popularity about a century ago, but then public interest waned and its numbers have decreased markedly. This may have come about because the Dogue de Bordeaux – used initially as a fighting dog, then for hunting large animals

such as bears and wild boar, and finally as a guard and watch dog – has retained, despite careful selective breeding, a considerable degree of aggressiveness and ferocity. A fearsome guard, it is not suitable for training as a police dog as, once roused, it loses all control and unleashes its relentless fury on the unfortunate victim. However, if it is raised with patience and kindness it is capable of demonstrating affection and devotion. Although not very tall, the Dogue de Bordeaux is a veritable giant with its massive, muscular, powerful and fearsome appearance. Physically, it is very similar in many respects to the Old English Mastiff, but the head is not so massive, the muzzle is slightly slimmer, and the forehead slopes much more steeply from the bridge of the nose, which lies almost at a right angle. However, the head is still broad and short, with a flat skull and substantial muzzle. The lower jaw should extend at least one centimetre ($\frac{1}{4}$ in) beyond the upper jaw. The eyes are large and dark, not prominent, with no haw visible and a rather dull expression. The ears are small, set high and hang close to the head. The neck has a slight dewlap, and the long, powerful body rests on legs which are relatively short, making it rather low. The coat is short, fine and smooth, not rough as in the Bulldog.

Weight: large animals (dogues) dogs 50 kg (110 lb) and over; bitches 45 kg (99 lb) and over; medium-sized animals (doguins) dogs 38–45 kg (84–99 lb); bitches 35–40 kg (77–88 lb). Height: 58–66 cm (23–26 in) (bitches smaller). Colour: mahogany, fawn, golden, with black points.
Country of Origin: France.

Bulldog

The Bulldog, as its name implies, was bred for the sport of bull-baiting. With the decline of this brutal form of entertainment, the Bulldog was in danger of extinction by 1835, but the breed was saved thanks to the efforts of English breeders. Like all mastiffs, the Bulldog is also descended from the Tibetan Mastiff which the Phoenicians are said to have brought to Britain, where it developed into a powerful, aggressive, ferocious animal, used in war as a fighting dog. Despite the inevitable controversies over the parentage of the Bulldog, it has symbolic significance for the English. Beauty played no part in the development of this breed: abnormalities which happened to appear in the breeding of the mastiff were bred into the Bulldog as hereditary characteristics. By the process of artificial selection a series of "deformities" affecting practically the whole body have been incorporated in a single animal. These deformities were sometimes magnified by unscrupulous breeders, who inhibited the growth of puppies by shutting them in low places, or increased the deformity of the skull by making them wear stiff masks. They also fostered the aggressiveness and ferocity of the Bulldog by ill-treatment and torture in order to create specimens fierce enough to withstand even the most painful punishment the opponent could hand out. Even later on, when it was used only as a guard and watch dog, it was still very dangerous because of its ferocious, bloodthirsty character. Over the years the Bulldog has gradually been transformed into the essentially docile and good-natured, lovable, patient beast we know today; yet it is still a splendid guard and watch dog. The most remarkable aspect of the Bulldog's appearance is the lack of proportion between the various parts of its body. The head is very large, with prominent orbital arches and a deep furrow between the eyes. The stop is very broad and deep, and the muzzle short and clearly turned upwards, squashed back towards the head. There is an abundance of skin on the skull, forming deep folds on the muzzle and between the eye-sockets. The flews hang down over the lower jaw at each side but meet the under lip in front, covering the teeth when the mouth is closed. The eyes are dark, small and very wide apart; the medium-sized ears are set high and curved over, but not pendant. The jaws are heavily undershot, with the lower jaw projecting considerably beyond the upper so that the teeth close in a *morsus inversus* bite. The short, massive, muscular neck with heavy folds of skin forming a dewlap, and the very broad, full chest give the Bulldog an appearance of width rather than length. The body narrows considerably at the loins, causing the female considerable problems when giving birth, the pelvis being too narrow to accommodate the large head safely; so much so that the bitch may sometimes die while the puppies are being delivered. The forelegs are set wide apart and are curved, very stout and slightly shorter than the hind legs, which are also much lighter in structure. These various anomalous bodily features combine to give the Bulldog a characteristic gait. The coat is thick, even, short and rough.

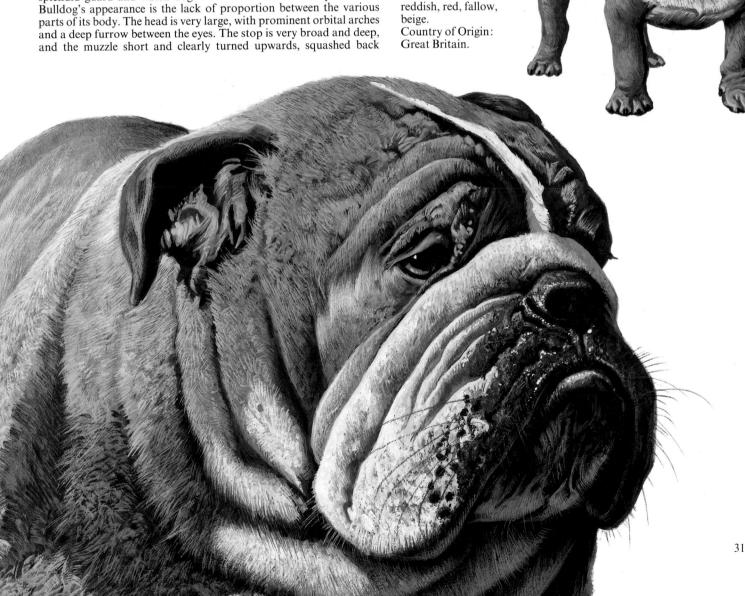

Weight: 22–25 kg
(48½–55 lb). Height:
30–35 cm (12–14 in).
Colour: white, brindle,
reddish, red, fallow,
beige.
Country of Origin:
Great Britain.

Mastiff
Old English Mastiff

The Old English Mastiff is a magnificent animal, a giant among the canine population, which has been known to weigh up to 90 kg (200 lb). Its name – from the latin *massivus* (massive), or from the Celtic *mas* and *tuin* (in old English the name was "mastyne") meaning "home" and "watch" respectively – is a reflection of the dog's characteristics. A very ancient breed, it is generally looked upon as a typically English dog. In common with so many of the large breeds, its ancestry can be traced back to the Tibetan Mastiff (nowadays almost extinct in its place of origin, where only a few specimens still remain, ferocious and aggressive in temperament and almost untrainable). The theory that the Old English Mastiff is descended from the Molossus of Epirus is not so well founded but is not contradictory, the Molossus also being an offshoot of the ancient Asian mastiffs. If this is the case, the Mastiff would have been brought to England by the Romans, who used Molossian dogs for fighting in the arenas and in war (*Canis pugnacis*). The Old English Mastiff – particularly common in the British Isles during the Middle Ages – was used for big game hunting, but the role for which it was destined was that of guard and watch dog. It was also cruelly employed to bait lions, bears and leopards, and gained an infamous reputation when it was exported to America by the English and used for a time to track down negro slaves who had escaped from the cotton plantations. Ever since this practice became obsolete, the Old English Mastiff has been selectively bred to diminish its traditional aggressiveness and to develop an animal which, though huge and somewhat forbidding in appearance, is a valuable asset to man. Faithful to its owner, towards whom it is even capable of displaying affection, it is suspicious of strangers and will turn ferocious if attacked. The head of the Old English Mastiff is massive and broad rather than long, with prominent brows – separated by a furrow – above small, dark, wide-set eyes. The ears are also small, set high and wide apart and hang close to the head, The jaw is only slightly undershot. The skin on the head forms wrinkles when the dog is alert. The muzzle is deep and short, the neck very muscular, the chest powerful and the legs sturdy. The coat is very short, dense, coarse and close-lying.

Weight: 70–90 kg (154–200 lb). Height: 75–80 cm (29½–31½ in). Colour: gold or silver shades of fawn, light fawn, reddish, brindle (ears and muzzle black, with black round the orbits).
Country of Origin: Great Britain.

Bullmastiff

This breed has a very recent history and was officially recognized in 1924. It was created by the English breeder Moseley from the union between a Mastiff bitch and a male Bulldog, whose first generation were then crossed with Mastiffs or with other cross-breeds of subsequent generations, until the required combination was obtained making the Bullmastiff 40 per cent Bulldog and 60 per cent Mastiff. Prior to this, other dogs such as the Great Dane and the Wolfhound had also been used, but the results were not always satisfactory or predictable. The Bullmastiff incorporates the characteristics of both its ancestors, being a guard dog of considerable size but not so large as the Mastiff, endowed with the power, courage and resistance to tiredness and pain characteristic of the Bulldog. It was formerly used by the English police, who trained it to bring a man down and hold him without mauling him. Nowadays it is essentially a guard and watch dog. Being a very intelligent, obedient and affectionate animal, whose natural instinct is to carry out faithfully the duties entrusted to it, it automatically assumes the role of protector of its master and guardian of his property. The head is broad and large, but not out of proportion to the massive, muscular body. The lower jaw juts out less noticeably than in the Bulldog and the flews are not too pendulous but sufficient to give the muzzle a squarish appearance. The forehead is slightly wrinkled and the ears are pendant, but not close to the head as in the Old English Mastiff. The hindquarters are in proportion to the rest of the body, creating an overall impression, despite the powerful build, of elegance and harmony. The forelegs are straight and not very wide apart, and the feet are strong and slightly rounded. The coat is very short, smooth and dense.

Weight: 40–58 kg (88–128 lb). Height: dogs 63–68 cm (25–27 in); bitches 61–66 cm (24–26 in). Colour: any shade of fawn or brindle. Country of Origin: Great Britain.

Airedale

Official recognition of the Airedale, which looks like a large Wire-haired Fox Terrier, came in 1880; its birthplace was the Aire Valley in Yorkshire, in the north of England. The Bull Terrier, the Scottish Terrier and the Otterhound are thought to have contributed to the development of this breed. Its name, which refers to the Aire River, is an apt reminder of the natural affinity between this dog and water, and of the aptitude of the Airedale for the demands of marsh hunting. It is a dog of rare intelligence, with great resistance to tiredness, strong and courageous, able to adapt to any climate, even the least favourable, without any trouble. The Airedale is a dog of amazing versatility which, over the years, has been used for many different purposes – ratting, otter-hunting, retrieving ducks, as tracker and gun dog – and excelled at them all. Furthermore it is an excellent guard and watch dog, and is also easily trained for police work. Its extreme loyalty, its affectionate nature, particularly where children are concerned, and its calm, unruffled nature also make it a much sought-after pet and companion. Although not massive in appearance, the Airedale is a solidly built dog, with a sturdy frame and powerful muscles. The characteristic and unmistakable rectangular shape of the head is greatly accentuated by its thick whiskers. The ears are V-shaped and set high and back on the head. The eyes are small, oval rather than round in shape, deep-set, dark and very expressive. The neck is long and not thick-set, though muscular, forming an angle with the straight line of the body. The tail is a very characteristic feature: it is docked to a third of its length and is carried vertically. The Airedale has a characteristic swinging gait, the legs should be carried straight forward, the forelegs being perpendicular and parallel with the sides. This motion requires the body to be perfectly balanced. The body is covered in very hard, dense, stiff, not wavy hair, with an oily undercoat which is waterproof and makes the dog resistant to cold.

Weight: 18–25 kg (39½–55 lb). Height: 56–61 cm (22–24 in). Colour: black or dark grizzle with a few red hairs and tan markings on the head, ears and legs up to the thighs and elbows.
Country of Origin: Great Britain.

This dog of ancient origin has been known in the Campania region of Italy for about 2000 years, but has only recently achieved recognition outside its native country. Its first official appearance, at the Naples dog show in 1946, aroused considerable interest and so impressed the breeders present that within the space of four years an official standard was drawn up for it. The ancestors of this mastiff can once again be traced to the Tibetan Mastiff, while its nearest forebear is thought to be the Molossus of Epirus. The Neopolitan Mastiff was originally a highly aggressive dog, but this aggression has been toned down over the years through selective breeding to make it suitable for different purposes. Its strength equips it for use as a draught dog or even as a police dog, but it is mainly a guard dog, defending its owner and his property. The Neapolitan Mastiff has a large, massive head with a wide, flat skull. The stop is well defined and the muzzle short and straight, ending in a broad nose with open nostrils. The flews are very large and pendulous, with the bottom edges turned up to reveal the gums where the upper lips join the lower lips. The skin on the head is very abundant and wrinkled and the large, dark, deep-set eyes with protuberant upper lids have an attentive, thoughtful expression. The ears may be left to hang naturally but are usually cropped to a point in the dog's native country. The neck is a distinctive feature of the breed, being thick, strong, heavy and very muscular, with an abundance of loose skin forming a voluminous dewlap. The body of the Neapolitan Mastiff is very strongly built with heavy, powerful muscles. There is only very slight tuck-up of the belly, and the tail should be docked if it reaches below the stifle joint. The legs are fairly long and strong, with large, compact feet, and the elbows tend to be turned slightly outwards. The coat is smooth, dense and very shiny.

Weight: 50–70 kg (110–154 lb). Height: 60–72 cm (23½–28½ in). Colour: black, grey, lead, fawn, brindle (occasionally with white markings on the chest and toes).
Country of Origin: Italy.

Neapolitan Mastiff

Chow Chow

A native of China, the Chow Chow arrived in Europe relatively recently. It was towards the end of the eighteenth century that the first pair of these dogs was brought to England by the British ambassador to China. The Chow Chow is a very ancient breed of dog whose ancestral origins are so remote they remain a mystery to this day. The majestic and elegant appearance of this dog with its characteristic lion-like face makes it a very popular pet and show dog. But the Chow Chow is an extremely versatile and useful animal, and has been variously employed as a hunting or guard dog or for pulling sledges. It was and still is bred in China for its flesh and for its fur, which means that breeders tend to concentrate more on this aspect rather than on preserving the actual characteristics of the breed. The powerful head with its broad, flat skull, short muzzle, small, dark, half-closed eyes and wrinkled forehead give the Chow Chow a scowling, gloomy expression. The gums, lips and roof of the mouth are black and the tongue a deep inky blue, a characteristic unique among the canine breeds. The short, strong neck is well covered with a collar of long, thick hair. The coat on the rest of the body is not quite so long but is still dense and abundant, covering a thick, woolly undercoat. The body is strong and fairly short and the underline not very well defined. The legs are long in relation to the body, strong, solidly built, and the feet small, round and cat-like.

Weight: 20–22 kg (44–48½ lb). Height: from 45–52 cm (18–20½ in) (up to 60 cm (23½ in) in some specimens). Colour: black, red, fawn, blue, cream, silver, rarely white.
Country of Origin: China and the Far East.

Dalmatian

Despite its name, it is unlikely that this dog is a native of Dalmatia. It is believed by some to have its origins in the East – a direct descendant of the now extinct Hound of Bengal – and by others to be a native of Denmark, where it is found in large numbers and known also by the name of Small Dane. One of the reasons why it is difficult to verify the origins of this dog is that the selection of stock for breeding proved particularly difficult, and present-day breeding is still not without problems. The development of the Dalmatian represents a complicated process of artificial selection; breeders, whose intention it was to create a dog with a white coat with small, very distinct black markings, often found that puppies of subsequent generations were being born with coats of all kinds which apparently bore no relation to that of their parents. This is because physical characteristics (in this case, the colour of the coat) are controlled by numerous pairs of correlated, interacting genes, none of which is completely dominant. Because of these objective difficulties, the Dalmatian has a relatively recent official standard (end of the eighteenth century). It has long been

highly prized as a pet and show dog. In Victorian England it came to be known by a second name – the Carriage Dog – because groups of these dogs used to be trained to accompany the carriages of aristocrats. However, in earlier times because of its extremely keen nose the Dalmatian was for long periods popular as a sporting dog, and as a guard and watch dog, being endowed with great courage and a strong attachment to its owner. Its independent character can make it disobedient at times, but it is very intelligent and sensitive, has a good memory, is clean and loves company. The Dalmatian strongly resembles the Pointer both in the shape of the head and the lines of the slim and elegant body.

Weight: approximately 22–25 kg (48½–55 lb). Height: 50–60 cm (19½–23½ in). Colour: pure white with black spots, bigger on the body; white with dark brown spots in the liver spotted variety.
Country of Origin: Yugoslavia.

Austrian Pinscher

Ainu Dog

Japanese Akita

Sanshu

Kyūshū

Tosa

Aidi

Portuguese Water Dog

Fila Brasileiro

Spanish Mastiff

Tibetan Mastiff

Pyrenean Mastiff

Other Guard and Watch Dogs

Breed: Austrian Pinscher – *Origin*: Austria – *Height*: average 40 cm (16 in) – *Weight*: 12–18 kg (26½–39½ lb) – *Colour*: fawn, light or pale yellow, black and tan, stag red, brindle; often white markings on muzzle, collar, chest, feet and tip of the tail – *Physical characteristics*: pear-shaped head; fairly well-developed nose; various ear conformations; barrel chest; tail curled over the back (generally docked); short coat.

Breed: Kyūshū – *Origin*: Japan – *Height*: dogs 48–54 cm (19–21½ in); bitches 42–48 cm (16½–19 in) – *Weight*: approximately 30 kg (66 lb) – *Colour*: grey and white – *Physical characteristics*: small, pointed ears; tail curled over the back; short, rough coat.

Breed: Ainu Dog (Hokkaido Dog) – *Origin*: Japan – *Height*: 41–50 cm (16–19½ in) – *Weight*: around 25 kg (55 lb) – *Colour*: red, black, white, pepper and salt – *Physical characteristics*: triangular eyes; erect, pointed ears; tail feathered and curled; hard, shaggy coat with thick, soft undercoat.

Breed: Tosa – *Origin*: Japan – *Height*: dogs over 60 cm (23½ in); bitches over 54 cm (21½ in) – *Weight*: dogs over 37 kg (81½ lb); bitches over 30 kg (66 lb) – *Colour*: all red or red flecking on white base, dark red markings on lighter base – *Physical characteristics*: well-developed, black nose; powerful jaws with strong teeth; dark eyes; drop ears; smooth, hard coat.

Breed: Japanese Akita – *Origin*: Japan – *Height*: dogs 64–70 cm (25–27½ in); bitches 57–63 cm (22½–24½ in) – *Weight*: 35–40 kg (77–88 lb) – *Colour*: pepper and salt, red pepper, black pepper, brindle, white – *Physical characteristics*: dark eyes; triangular, erect ears; tail curled over the back; hard coat.

Breed: Sanshu – *Origin*: Japan – *Height*: dogs over 50–55 cm (20–22 in); bitches 45–50 cm (18–20 in) – *Weight*: 20–25 kg (44–55 lb) – *Colour*: rust red, grey – *Physical characteristics*: dark, almond-shaped eyes; triangular, erect ears; tail curled over the back; strong coat of moderate length.

Breed: Aidi – *Origin*: Morocco – *Height*: dogs 52–62 cm (20½–24 in); bitches 45–58 cm (18–23 in) – *Weight*: around 30 kg (66 lb) – *Colour*: sandy, fawn, white, tricolour, speckled, black and white, fawn and white – *Physical characteristics*: semi-drop ears; tail carried well and reaching down to the hocks; well-developed muscles; thick coat approximately 6 cm (2¼ in) long.

Breed: Tibetan Mastiff – *Origin*: Tibet – *Height*: dogs 64–69 cm (25–27 in); bitches 56–61 cm (22–24 in) – *Weight*: 65–95 kg (143½–209½ lb) – *Colour*: black, black and tan, golden fawn, russet with black mantle – *Physical characteristics*: black nose; dark eyes; medium drop ears; tail curled over the back, long, profuse coat.

Breed: Pyrenean Mastiff (Mastin de los Pirineos) – *Origin*: Spain – *Height*: 70–80 cm (27½–31½ in) – *Weight*: 55–70 kg (121–154½ lb) – *Colour*: black and white, white with flecking, white with golden or grey markings on the sides of the head and the start of the neck (sometimes on other parts of the body) – *Physical characteristics*: small, drop ears; tail carried low and feathered; thick, coarse coat.

Breed: Spanish Mastiff (Mastin Español) – *Origin*: Spain – *Height*: 65–70 cm (25½–27½ in) – *Weight*: 50–60 kg (110–132½ lb) – *Colour*: fawn, black and white, grey and white, wolf grey – *Physical characteristics*: small, lively eyes; drop ears of modest size; tail carried low and well feathered; coat not long.

Breed: Portuguese Water Dog (Cão d'Agua) – *Origin*: Portugal – *Height*: dogs 50–57 cm (19½–22½ in); bitches 43–52 cm (17–20½ in) – *Weight*: dogs 19–25 kg (42–55 lb); bitches 16–22 kg (35–48½ lb) – *Colour*: black, white (black nose, mouth, eyelids), brown (various shades), black and white, brown and white – *Physical characteristics*: ears set high and hanging close to the head; tail held high and curled, tapering to the tip; curly or wavy coat.

Breed: Fila Brasileiro – *Origin*: Brazil – *Height*: approximately 65 cm (25½ in) – *Weight*: not specified – *Colour*: very varied (any allowed) – *Physical characteristics*: drop ears; long tail, curved at the tip; smooth coat.

WORKING DOGS

Shepherd Dogs, Cattle Dogs and Sledge Dogs

These dogs, which the English classify with the rescue dogs in one large "working group", are of great assistance to man, whom they have helped from the time when he was a mere hunter through his development into a breeder and farmer, when he needed the dog to protect his property and help him guard the animals he was rearing. They are predominantly large animals, solidly built and well muscled, sturdy and resistant to both fatigue and extremes of the weather. Their appearance has gradually been refined with the progressive change of function that many of them have undergone over the years. They have thick coats of varying lengths, providing good protection against the cold and damp. They are very intelligent, easy to train and capable of acting independently.

German Shepherd Dog
Alsatian

The German Shepherd or Alsatian is the undisputed king among dogs, the best known representative of the canine species. This large, noble and proud animal has only existed in its present form since 1889, when a stricter and more scientific breeding programme was undertaken by a group of German breeders from Württemberg. The first definition of its official standard dates back to 1899. Known also by the name of "Wolf Dog", it is the dog which resembles the wolf most closely in the shape of its head and body. A number of experts are of the opinion that spontaneous cross-breeding with the wolf may have taken place before man embarked on the process of artificial selection, and it is a well-known fact that matings between dogs and wolves produce mutually fertile offspring. The German Shepherd has much to recommend it – undeniable beauty, combining elegance and harmony of form with a solid, powerful frame, rare intelligence and the ability to adapt to any climatic environment – qualities which ensure it is very popular throughout the world. Alsatians are renowned for their ability to learn and their good memory, which mean that they may be trained for many different kinds of work, always with excellent results. They are famed for their activities as police dogs, trained to track down lost or wanted people or to sniff out drugs, as messengers and couriers in war, as guide dogs for the blind, as mountain rescue dogs and as guard and watch dogs. They are rarely found nowadays in their original role of sheepdog, being required for more demanding tasks to which their great intelligence and extraordinary character well suits them. In addition to all its other qualities, the German Shepherd also possesses an ideal temperament. It is cheerful, obedient, sensitive, affectionate, friendly with children, tolerant, faithful and so devoted to its master that it has been known to pine away if separated from him. The German Shepherd is slightly larger than the average dog, but should not be too big as this would create an effect of heaviness and destroy the overall proportion and balance. Correctly proportioned, its gait is supple, quick and smooth, seemingly light and effortless. The head is long and lean, broader between the ears, with only a slight stop and a straight muzzle. The dark, almond-shaped, slightly oblique eyes show a lively, proud expression reinforced by the high-set ears, broad at the base and pointed at the tips, carried erect and parallel. The neck is muscular and strong and free from dewlap. The body is slightly longer than it is high, giving an overall impression of length. The long, flowing stride is achieved by the extension of the forelegs, the impetus given by the long, powerful thighs and strong hocks. The feet are short, arched and rounded. There are three varieties of German Shepherd, which are distinguished by their coat. The fairly rare variety has very short, rather thin hair lying very close to the body; the most common has a coat of medium length, with hair approximately 5–6 cm (2–2½ in) long, thick, dense, straight and rough to the touch, with a woolly undercoat if the animal lives out in the open. The Old German Shepherd has a long, wavy and woolly coat.

Weight: 35–40 kg (77–88 lb). Height: dogs, 61–66 cm (24–26 in); bitches, 56–61 cm (22–24 in). Colour: black, wolf-grey or iron-grey, fawn with or without black cape, or white only in the woolly-haired variety.
Country of Origin: Germany.

Belgian Shepherd Dog (Groenendael)

Groenendael

The Belgian Shepherd Dog is, in many respects, similar to the German Shepherd. It emerged as a result of a strict selective breeding programme undertaken towards the end of the last century in an attempt to create a definite type out of the multitude of shepherd dogs, very different both in appearance and temperament, which were to be found in Belgium at that time. This process, involving carefully chosen blood-relations indigenous to the region, gave rise to the numerous varieties of Belgian Shepherd Dog which, differentiated only by the length, colour and texture of their coat, all share a common official standard. The most popular variety is the Groenendael, named after the castle which was the home of its creator, Nicolas Rose, who chose not to give his own name to this jet-black animal. The Belgian Shepherd Dog is of medium size, slightly smaller than the German Shepherd, combining power and strength with considerable elegance and harmony of form. Bred as a sheep herder, a task it performs admirably, it also has a wider application as a police dog, a war dog, a guard and watch dog, and companion. However, compared with the German Shepherd, it is difficult to train because of its nervous temperament. The Belgian Shepherd Dog is highly intelligent, very lively, responsive, watchful, tireless and always alert, but because of its great capacity for action it is often over-excitable, edgy and nervous, and if it is not trained with skill, affection, kindness and patience, it can turn aggressive and vicious. The head is well chiselled and long, with a pointed muzzle and a slight but definite stop. The dark, obliquely set eyes are lively and alert, and the small, triangular ears are carried high and erect. The muscular neck and powerful body are reminiscent of the German Shepherd, but the Belgian Shepherd Dog is shorter in the back with a square rather than rectangular body outline. The height at the withers should approximately equal the length from point of breast bone to point of rump. The belly is moderately developed, neither drooping nor unduly cut up; the legs are long and sturdy; the fore-feet rounded and short and the hind ones slightly longer, but still compact. The tail, which reaches down to the hocks, is always carried low but not between the thighs. The Groenendael, the Tervueren and the other long-coated Belgian Shepherd Dogs have very abundant, sleek coats, long all over except on the ears and lower part of the legs, and plumed

Malinois

tails. The smooth-coated variety, including the Malinois and the other short-haired members of the breed, have thick, dense coats, short all over but longer on the neck and tail, with slight feathering on the hindquarters. The wire-coated variety, including the Laekenois and the other coarse-haired Belgian Shepherd Dogs, have rough, shaggy coats, short all over, with plumed tails.

Weight: approximately 28 kg (62 lb). Height: dogs approximately 62 cm (24½ in); bitches approximately 58 cm (23 in: 4 cm [1½ in] over and 2 cm [¾ in] under allowed). Colour: long-coated Groenendael: jet black; Tervueren: fawn with black overlay and black mask; other colours: grey, light fawn. Smooth-coated Malinois: fawn with black overlay and black mask; other colours: black. Wire-coated Laekenois: fawn, with traces of blackening on muzzle and tail; other colours: grey brindle, dark ash grey.
Country of Origin: Belgium.

Tervueren

43

Briard
Chien Berger de la Brie

The Chien Berger de la Brie has been known for centuries, though not quite in its present form. It undoubtedly shares some common ancestry with the Bergamasco, given the strong similarity between the two dogs. According to some dog-fanciers they are actually one and the same breed and merely developed along different lines rather than one being the offshoot of the other. The Briard made its first official appearance in 1886. Originally a shaggy, ungainly sheepdog, which ably performed its task of guarding the flocks with dedication and efficiency, it has been improved over the years both in appearance and character through selective breeding. Although it has lost none of its physical qualities of strength, resistance to bad weather, tirelessness and love of water, its shape and its character have been refined to give it an elegant and well-proportioned appearance, and turning it into the docile, affectionate, patient and good-natured animal we know today which at times is even a little timid and diffident. These new characteristics have made the Briard into a suitable pet, although it is really too big to keep in a flat. Very intelligent and an excellent swimmer, it has also been used for sea rescue work and, because of its keen hearing, also for use on sentry duty. The head of the Briard is substantial, with a well-marked stop half way between the top of its head and the tip of its nose. The large, round eyes have a calm, intelligent expression. The ears are placed high and in France are generally cropped to a rounded shell shape and carried erect. The neck is strong, muscular and fairly long, and the back straight with only slight tuck-up of the belly. The legs are set true and are very straight and muscular. The feet are compact with tightly-closed toes. The characteristic appearance of the Briard is created by the coat which is long (approximately 7 cm [2¾ in] on average), stiff, coarse and like that of a goat, evenly distributed over the body, with a waterproof undercoat. It has long whiskers, a beard and long eyebrows which fall over the eyes. The ears are also well feathered and when cropped, the hair falls forward, adding to the distinctive appearance of the head.

Weight: approximately 30 kg (66 lb). Height: dogs 62–68 cm (24–26½ in); bitches 56–64 cm (22–25 in). Colour: all black, any single dark colour, fawn and champagne with gradual transition from one colour to another, never white.
Country of Origin: France.

Beauceron
Beauce Shepherd Dog

The Beauceron is another typically French dog, an ancient but only recently recognized breed, which made its first public appearance in 1897. Little is known of its forebears, though some dog-fanciers suggest a possible relationship with the Dobermann in view of a certain resemblance between the two dogs. The Beauceron was originally a very aggressive sheepdog, valiantly defending its flock and obedient only to its master, which made it very dangerous with any strangers regardless of their intentions. Indeed this negative characteristic motivated breeders to undertake a selective breeding programme aimed both at refining its appearance and improving its temperament. Nowadays the Beauceron is a large, strong, powerful and muscular dog but not thick-set nor massive. Intelligent and alert, it will make an excellent guard and watch dog if trained to curb its aggressiveness. It is not suited to life in the home. The head is long and thin, the eyes small and dark, and the ears (usually cropped) are carried erect. It has a strong frame and fairly long legs, making it taller than most sheepdogs. The hair is very short, thick and close to the body.

Weight: 30–35 kg (66–77 lb). Height: dogs 63–70 cm (25–27½ in); bitches 61–68 cm (24–27 in). Colour: black, black and tan (bas-rouge), grey, grey with black and tan markings, fawn with black overlay.
Country of Origin: France.

Picardy Sheepdog

This sheepdog, though of very ancient origin and already known in the Middle Ages, has remained within the confines of Picardy, its native region of northern France which extends from the English Channel to the Belgian border. Here the supremacy of the Picardy was almost unchallenged; it was the classic sheepdog, cattle dog and a superb guard, just aggressive and fierce enough to keep marauders away. Nowadays, because its unsociable habits and its need for open spaces make it unsuitable for city life, and possibly also in view of its rather unattractive appearance, its decline is so grave that the breed is in danger of extinction. The Picardy is a very sturdy animal, resistant both to tiredness and bad weather, being protected by its thick, untidy, shaggy coat of medium length; the hair is coarse, neither smooth nor wavy, and waterproof. The head is in proportion to the body, with a broad, slightly domed skull, a very slight stop and a muzzle which is thin without being long or pointed. The dark eyes are of normal size and the high, erect ears, wide at the base and pointed, are slightly larger than average. The neck and the body are strong and muscular. The back is level and there is considerable tuck-up of the belly. The legs are relatively long and the feet round and compact, with dew-claws. The overall appearance is of a medium-sized dog of light and muscular build, whose most striking feature is its unusual coat.

Weight: 19–23 kg (42–51 lb). Height: dogs 60–65 cm (23½–24½ cm); bitches 55–60 cm (21½–23½ in). Colour: light or dark grey, reddish, light or dark fawn (not always solid), never white.
Country of Origin: France.

46

Pyrenean
Berger des Pyrénées

Considered the most ancient of the French sheepdogs, the Pyrenean originated in the mountainous region between Lourdes and Gavarnie. It is not known how it is related to the other French sheepdogs (although some claim it to be derived from the Briard) nor who its ancestors were. The Pyrenean was officially recognized as a breed in 1921, when its standard was ratified. This recognition came as a result of the Pyrenean, scarcely known outside its native mountains, being used in the 1914–18 war to carry messages and to search for the wounded, many dogs in fact being killed as a result. Yet the Pyrenean is still a little-known dog, despite its undoubted qualities. It is very alert and has an excellent memory, it is faithful, cunning, attentive, devoted and loyal, with great courage. Small and agile, with great speed of movement and quick reflexes, it not only makes an excellent mountain sheepdog, but also a good guard dog and defender of the home, where it is useful in catching mice. Its fine character, combined with a most enchanting appearance, also make it a desirable pet. Capable of withstanding most kinds of weather, it can adapt to any climate and is particularly resistant to the more serious illnesses, such as distemper. Finally, it is capable of going without food for some time since it can also eat grass. The head of the Pyrenean is somewhat reminiscent of the brown bear, both in the flat skull with its barely visible stop and in the straight, short, wedge-like muzzle. The eyes are dark and round with black rims. The ears may either be left to hang naturally, or be cropped very short and carried erect. The neck is long and muscular, as is the body. The legs are fairly short, ending in oval feet which often have two sets of dew-claws, particularly on animals born and bred in the mountains. The coat is long in one variety and slightly shorter in the other, but always abundant and close-lying, slightly wavy and thicker and woollier on the rump and haunches. The smooth-headed variety differs only in its longer, more pointed muzzle and the shorter, finer hair on the head.

Weight: 20–25 kg (44–55 lb). Height: 40–50 cm ($15\frac{1}{2}$–$19\frac{1}{2}$ in) (bitches up to 38 cm [15 in]). The smooth-headed variety 2–4 cm ($\frac{3}{4}$–$1\frac{1}{2}$ in) over the maximum limit. Colour: various shades of fawn, smoky grey, harlequin.
Country of Origin: France.

Smooth-headed Pyrenean

Bergamasco Sheepdog

The Bergamasco Sheepdog is closely related to the Briard, and it is widely thought that the two breeds have a common origin. They are probably both derived from long-haired shepherd dogs brought over to Italy by the Phoenicians, where they became acclimatized and spread first to the central regions (giving rise to the Maremma Sheepdog) and then to the north where the Bergamasco was born. They later spread beyond the Alps, finally giving rise to the Briard. This is the most reliable theory, although French breeders like to claim that their Briard came first. The home of the Bergamasco Sheepdog is the Val Imagna, but it is found all over northern Italy. It is a dog of medium size, solid and sturdy but well proportioned, and of shaggy, untidy appearance. It is a very intelligent animal, docile and courageous, friendly and obliging with an alert, keen expression and proud bearing. It will persevere with its tasks until they have been accomplished, with courage, energy and tirelessness which is quite exceptional considering its size. It also makes a popular pet, capable of gentleness and affection, but should not be kept in a flat. The Bergamasco is very resistant to bad weather, and is also suitable for training as a personal guard and watch dog. Its characteristic feature is its coat, which is long and profuse all over the body, the strong, wavy tufts of hair parted down the middle of the back. The hair is also abundant on the muzzle, covering the eyes, where it is less coarse. The hair on the legs hangs down in tufts, but without forming feathering. The undercoat is short and very thick, completely hides the skin, and is oily to the touch and completely waterproof. The head is large, with a broad, slightly domed skull, pronounced stop, blunt muzzle and black nose. The eyes are large and dark with a calm, lively expression, and the ears are soft and fine, hanging close to the head, well feathered, and prick up when the dog is alert. The neck is strong, not long, with a thick collar. The solid, sturdy body is square in outline, and is set on massive, solid legs. The tail reaches down to the hocks and is carried like a sabre in repose.

Weight: dogs 32–38 kg (70½–84 lb); bitches 26–32 kg (57½–70½ lb). Height: dogs 60 cm (23½ in); bitches 56 cm (22 in) – 2 cm (¾ in) either way allowed. Colour: solid grey or spotted, light smoky grey, isabella or pale fawn, never white.
Country of Origin: Italy.

Maremma Sheepdog

The Maremma, together with the Bergamasco, is the oldest Italian sheepdog, found in large numbers all over central Italy, from the Abruzzi to Tuscany. There were originally two varieties – the Maremma and the Abruzzi – which were made into one breed in 1950, because the differences between them were too slight to warrant any such division. The remaining variations are the coat, which is less curly and abundant in the Maremma; the colour, which is pure white in the Abruzzi and shaded in the Maremma; and the visible mucous membranes (lips, eyes, nose), which are black in the Abruzzi and lighter in the Maremma. However, the official standard, drawn up in 1958, is identical for the two varieties. The Maremma Sheepdog was developed as a fierce adversary of the wolf, from whose bite it was protected by a spiked metal collar. This sheepdog is massive and majestic in appearance, but not heavy, being agile, elegant and graceful. Calm, reflective and docile, it is nevertheless a fearsome foe when needs be, not only rounding up and driving its flock but also defending it with its life. An invaluable asset to man, it is also his faithful and devoted friend. Its many qualities, combined with intelligence and alertness, have earned it admirers beyond its country of origin. In England it is also a popular, much-loved pet but should not be made to live in cramped conditions. The coat of the Maremma is, except on its head, thick and rather coarse, with a profuse collar of longer hair (up to 8 cm [3 in]) extending to its chest, giving it a bear-like appearance, and with fringes on the belly and legs. The long tail, which reaches to below the hocks, is carried low at rest. In winter an abundant undercoat forms. The head is large and bear-like, the skull domed and broad between the ears, the stop not very well defined and the muzzle straight. The eyes are almond-shaped and ochre or brown in colour, and the small, triangular ears should be left to hang naturally, not cropped. The body is solid, with a wide, deep chest, broad croup and slight tuck-up at the loins. The legs stand perfectly square, have tight rounded front feet, with hind feet more oval, and toes close together.

Weight: dogs 35–45 kg (77–99 lb); bitches 30–40 kg (66–88 lb). Height: dogs 65–73 cm (25½–29 in); bitches 60–68 cm (23½–27 in). Colour: pure white or with shadings of ivory, isabella, pale orange.
Country of Origin: Italy.

49

Karst

Like its close relative, the Sar Planina, the Karst is considered a native of Yugoslavia, although like most herding dogs it is descended from the ancient dogs brought from the East. It belongs to the group of wolf-like sheepdogs, with rough, shaggy coats, often impressive in size and found practically throughout the whole of Europe, from Portugal to Russia. Officially recognized as a breed around 1940, under the name of Kraški Ovčar, it is better known by the easier name of Karst. This sheepdog is a sturdy, medium-sized animal, less massive in build than the Sar Planina, but with the same remarkable ability to defend and control the flock and the courage to attack intruders and assailants. Intelligent, brave and very loyal, it makes a highly dependable guard dog, and will not allow the slightest harm to come to its owner or the flock, which it regards as its personal property. Unlike the Sar Planina, the Karst has a less aggressive, more thoughtful and demonstrative nature; it is capable of establishing a deeply affectionate relationship with man, providing companionship for its master through the long, cold and lonely winters. It is very resistant to bad weather, thanks to its long coat and the thick, woolly, waterproof undercoat which forms in severe weather. The Karst is also extremely resistant to fatigue, being used to running over difficult, stony ground in search of lost sheep. Its feet are particularly well suited to this, being strong and round with solid, elastic pads like leather. The Karst has a fairly large, broad head in relation to its body, and a set of very strong teeth with scissors bite. The eyes are slanting and dark, with a proud expression, and the ears are set high and hang close to the head. The neck is strong and moderately long; the body is solidly built with a level back, sturdy croup, and slightly drawn-up belly. The tail reaches down to the hocks, is slightly curved at the tip and covered in long hair.

Weight: 25–40 kg (55–88 lb). Height: dogs 55–60 cm (21½–23½ in); bitches 52–56 cm (20½–22 in). Colour: iron grey with shading. Country of Origin: Yugoslavia.

Sar Planina

The Sar Planina is the most common and carefully bred sheepdog of Yugoslav nationality. The breed was defined in 1939 under the name of Ilirski Ovčar, which was later changed to Sar Planina. Its characteristic appearance is somewhat similar to the Belgian Tervueren, but with stronger bone and a much more profuse coat. Very strong, courageous to the point of recklessness, intelligent, alert, serious and disinclined to show affection, it guards the flock with great dedication and is a fearless enemy of wolves. It is completely dependable, cannot be approached by strangers, and faithful to only one master, towards whom it shows an extraordinary loyalty. It can also be trained to guard and defend the home, but is rarely used for this because of its aggressive tendencies, size and way of life, which make it unsuitable for living in society. Its coat is coarse, up to 10 cm (4 in) in length, shorter on the head and legs and feet. A thick, woolly undercoat which forms in severe weather provides even greater protection from the rigours of the climate. In appearance it is sturdy, sound and well proportioned. The skull is slightly domed, with a slight stop and rounded muzzle, and it has a particularly strong set of teeth. The brown, slanting eyes have a calm but determined expression; the ears are high, V-shaped and pendant, sometimes cropped so that there is nothing for an opponent to hold on to in a fight. The neck is free from dewlap, with a thick collar of longer hair. The back is straight, the croup broad and well muscled, the brisket wide and the belly slightly drawn up. The tail reaches down to the hocks. The legs are sound and muscular, with strong, oval feet, suited to the uneven ground on which it lives.

Weight: dogs 35–45 kg (77–99 lb); bitches 30–40 kg (66–88 lb). Height: dogs 55–60 cm ($21\frac{1}{2}$–$23\frac{1}{2}$ in); bitches 50–55 cm ($19\frac{1}{2}$–$21\frac{1}{2}$ in). Colour: iron grey, dark grey. The Krachevatz variety has a maximum height of 65 cm ($25\frac{1}{2}$ in). The Sar Planina variety exceeds 65 cm ($25\frac{1}{2}$ in) in height.
Country of Origin: Yugoslavia.

Rough Collie

Collie
Scotch Collie

The name Collie is derived from the fact that the first representatives of the breed were known as Colley Dogs, from the Anglo-Saxon *Col*, meaning black, which was the original colour of the coat. The Collie is the best known British sheepdog and its popularity has spread beyond the confines of Great Britain. The breed was standardized in the seventeenth century in Scotland, where this dog had long been used for guarding and herding sheep. Because it is unusually slim and elegant in appearance compared to the more massive structure of other sheepdogs, it has been suggested that it might be the product of a cross between the Scottish Deerhound and the Old English Sheepdog. But the Collie actually belongs to the group of wolf-like sheepdogs that spread from the East, its early, coarser characteristics having been refined by careful selective breeding and by crossing it with the Borzoi (Russian Wolfhound). In addition to an overall sophistication, the effect of this was a slimming down and lengthening of the skull. In the second half of the nineteenth century, mainly as a result of the passion Queen Victoria had for this breed, the Collie abandoned its age-old work as a sheepdog to become an aristocratic and show dog. The Collie is an intelligent, docile, good-natured, somewhat melancholy dog, which responds quickly and easily to training if treated with kindness, but will obstinately resist it if abused. An excellent guard dog, affectionate and faithful, it can easily live in a flat provided that it is taken for frequent long walks. There are two types of Collie, the long-haired, known as the Rough Collie, and the short-haired variety, known as the Smooth Collie, the only difference between them being the length and texture of the hair. The Rough Collie has a very dense coat, a soft undercoat and a harsh outer coat, with an abundant mane and frill, smooth mask and ears, and well-feathered forelegs, whereas the Smooth Collie has a harsh, dense, smooth coat. Because of its attractive appearance, the Collie is often used in crosses to create new breeds. The Collie has a flat skull with a very slight stop and a thin muzzle, dark, almond-shaped eyes and small ears slightly drooping at the tips when the dog is at rest. The strong, sturdy body is never cloddy or massive, and the legs are short in relation to the height, but not so as to detract from the impression of harmony. The tail reaches below the hocks.

Weight: dogs 20.5–29.5 kg (45–65 lb); bitches 18–25 kg (40–55 lb). Height: dogs 56–61 cm (22–24 in); bitches 51–56 cm (20–22 in). Colour: sable and white, tricolour, blue merle (silvery blue marbled with black with or without tan shadings), all with white markings.
Country of Origin: Great Britain.

Smooth Collie

Shetland Sheepdog

The Shetland Sheepdog or Sheltie is a miniature version of the Collie, which it closely resembles both in body structure and coat. The size of this sheepdog from the Shetland Isles is well suited to the size of the small native sheep with their long, silky fleeces and characteristic black mask. The name Collie has its origins, some would say, in the name of these sheep rather than in the Colley Dog. The Shetland cannot be classed as a toy relation of the Collie, because there is none of the disproportion between parts of the body characteristic of the toy breeds. It may be the result of crossing the Collie with the Yakki or Iceland Dog, or possibly the result of crossing the Border Collie with the Greenland dogs, with a contribution from various members of the Spitz family and the Scotch Collie. The Sheltie was introduced to England towards the end of the nineteenth century, where it became very popular as a companion. The official standard was only brought out in 1914, and there is still some controversy over its classification because there is very little difference between the Sheltie and the Scotch Collie other than size, making it necessary to impose very stringent restrictions on size. The Sheltie is a small dog, well made and balanced, a very fine sheepdog despite its size, lithe and agile, resistant to bad weather, strong and active. It does not long miss the harsh life of the country and soon adapts to a soft, comfortable life in the home. Affectionate and responsive towards its owner, it shows reserve, even wariness, towards strangers, but not to the point of nervousness or aggression. It is intelligent and eager to learn, with a good memory, and makes an excellent playmate for children. The head of the Shetland is long, with a very flat skull, moderately wide between the ears, a mere suggestion of stop and a long muzzle. Both neck and body are long and muscular, combining an overall elegance and grace with a solidly built frame, perfectly proportioned in every respect. Its elastic gait is graceful and powerful, quick and smooth. The coat is of medium length, soft and thick, with an abundant mane and frill and legs well feathered. The tail is not very long.

Weight: 10–18 kg (22–40 lb). Height: maximum 38 cm (15 in). Colour: sable, light and deep mahogany, blue merle (marbled silver) with or without white markings, tricolour.
Country of Origin: Great Britain.

Bearded Collie

Close parallels may be drawn between the Bearded Collie and the French Briard, the Hungarian Puli and Komondor and the Italian Bergamasco Sheepdog, in terms of body structure and coat type. The Bearded Collie is, like the classical Collie, a native of Scotland, but is more massive and less refined in appearance than its aristocratic relation, lacking the height and characteristic tapering muzzle of the Scotch Collie. Yet before selective breeding and crosses with the Borzoi gave the Collie its present appearance, the two must have been very much alike in these respects. The Bearded Collie is also closely related to the Bobtail, with whom it shares many characteristics. At one time very popular all over Britain, this medium-sized sheepdog is nowadays diminishing in number and is scarcely known outside its own country. Highly resistant to bad weather and tiredness, an indomitable and courageous guardian and protector of cattle, it was particularly proficient at rounding up the herd and was therefore used to drive cattle in search of new pastures. Intelligent, good-natured, active, eager to learn, agile, docile and affectionate, the Bearded Collie makes a good guard and watch dog and also an ideal family pet, provided that it is not kept cooped up in a small flat. The head is broad, with prominent, arched eyebrows, a moderate stop and a fairly long foreface. The eyes, hidden by the long hair, are large, wide apart and bright, with a keen, enquiring expression. The drooping ears, covered in long hair, blend in with the hair on the head. The neck is fairly long, strong and muscular. The body is long, with a deep chest, straight back and little belly tuck-up. The legs are short in relation to the length of the body, making the Bearded Collie appear elongated, without, however, creating an impression of disharmony. The tail may reach below the hocks and in repose is carried low with an upward swirl at the tip. One of the distinctive characteristics of the Bearded Collie is its coat, the whole of its body being covered with long, coarse hair over a very thick undercoat of fine, soft, furry hair. Only the hair on the bridge of its nose is short, in contrast to the long beard which hangs down either side and gives this beautiful dog its name.

Weight: approximately 30 kg (66 lb). Height: dogs 53–56 cm (21–22 in); bitches 51–53 cm (20–21 in). Colour: slate grey, all shades of grey, reddish fawn, black, brown, sandy, with or without the characteristic white markings of the Collie.
Country of Origin: Great Britain.

Old English Sheepdog
Bobtail

The Bobtail, or to be more precise, the Old English Bobtailed Sheepdog, is, without any doubt, the oldest of the English sheepdogs. A native of the West Country of England, where it is still very popular, this dog is closely related to the French Briard and the Bergamasco sheepdog, to which it bore a strong resemblance until fifty years ago. Its name is a reflection of the fact that the Bobtail is often born tail-less, a much prized feature for a variety of reasons which has led to the automatic docking of the tail at the root where necessary. The Old English Sheepdog was mainly used for guarding flocks and herds, to which it was well suited thanks to its resistance to bad weather and fatigue, its intelligence, calm, docile, patient temperament and even-temper. All these qualities, combined with its obedience and friendliness towards children, have also made it a much loved pet. Its characteristic appearance – somewhat comical and at the same time attractive – is created by the profuse, shaggy coat covering the whole of the body. The hair is long and coarse in texture, harsh, with a slight wave, and covers a thick, waterproof undercoat. Other characteristics of the Old English Sheepdog are its ambling gait – due to the dog's habit of moving front and back right legs together, followed by front and back left legs – and its bark, which is hoarse and cracked like the sound of a pot breaking. The mats which form in the coat should be disentangled either with the fingers or with a very wide-toothed comb, not with a brush or a fine-toothed comb. The Bobtail is a sturdy, medium-sized dog of attractive appearance, agile and with an elastic gallop. The dark, almost black eyes are covered by its long hair, which also hides the flat, drop ears. The neck is a good length and the body leans slightly forward, the dog standing lower at the shoulders than at the loins. The back is gently arched, the hindquarters are muscular and there is little tuck-up of the belly. The legs are straight, pillar-like, solid and muscular, with small, round compact feet.

Weight: 25–30 kg (55–66 lb). Height: 50–60 cm (19½–23½ in). Colour: any shade of grey, blue, blue merle, with or without white collar, muzzle, legs and chest.
Country of Origin: Great Britain.

Welsh Corgi

Welsh Corgi (Pembroke)

Welsh Corgi (Cardigan)

This small dog, originally a cattle herder and long used for this purpose, has evolved into a good companion dog, and a delightful playmate for children. The Welsh Corgi is distinctive in appearance and seems to have undergone selective breeding only fairly recently. A native of Wales, it may have sprung from a union between the Welsh Sheepdog and the Nordic dogs such as the Buhund and the Vallhund. Others claim that it emerged from a union between the Shetland and the Sealyham Terrier. Although it has been known for a long time, the Welsh Corgi only attracted the attention of dog-fanciers at the end of the last century, when it was officially exhibited for the first time in a dog show. Despite being small, the Welsh Corgi is a sturdy and energetic dog, lively and agile, resistant to bad weather, fatigue and disease. It is intelligent and easy to train, good-natured, cheerful, affectionate, high-spirited and loves to play. There are two quite separate varieties of Welsh Corgi, namely the Cardigan and the Pembroke and, although considered a single breed, there is sufficient disparity between them to warrant two different official standards. The most striking similarity between them is the long body resting on short legs, reminiscent of the dachshund. The Cardigan is the older variety, and has a fox-like head with a wide skull, flat between the ears, and a long muzzle. The eyes are fairly large, round and preferably dark, and the ears are also rather large, well back on the head and pricked. The neck is long and muscular and the body very long (91 cm [36 in] from nose to tip of tail) and strong, with broad, arched hindquarters and slight tuck-up of the belly. The tail is long and sweeps downwards almost to the ground in a manner reminiscent of the fox. The forelegs are curved forwards slightly and the feet large and round. The Pembroke variety is more recent than the Cardigan and its body is more cylindrical in appearance, the forelegs are straight, the feet oval with the centre toes longer than the outer ones, the tail naturally short or docked and its coat is slightly longer.

Cardigan. Weight: 9–12 kg (20–26½ lb). Height: approximately 30 cm (12 in). Colour: any colour except white.
Pembroke. Weight: 8–11 kg (17½–24 lb). Height: 25–28 cm (10–11 in). Colour: red, sable, fawn, black and tan, black with white chest, legs and neck.
Country of Origin: Great Britain.

Swedish Vallhund
Västgötaspets

Puli and Pumi

The Puli and the Pumi are two Hungarian sheep-dogs, smaller in size than the Kuvasz and the Komondor. The Puli is an excellent sheep herder, also used in hunting, particularly as a water retriever, which has earned it the title of "Hungarian Water Dog". The first standard of the Puli was drawn up in 1905, but was then revised several times, mainly with regard to the colour of its coat. Lively, agile, intelligent, energetic, good-natured and affectionate, it is easily trained as a guard and watch dog and will adapt to family life, provided there is plenty of open space at hand. The head is large but in proportion to the body, which is massive, cobby and square in outline. It has dark, bright eyes and hanging, V-shaped ears. The neck, body and legs are all muscular. The whole of the body is covered in a dense coat – 8 – 18 cm (3–7 in) long, and corded or matted – which almost reaches the ground when the dog is standing. The Pumi is an offshoot of the Puli which evolved from a crossing of the latter with French and German shepherd dogs. Similar in size to its relative, the Pumi has a shorter and less profuse coat but otherwise the two dogs are very much alike, particularly in the general structure of the body. The Pumi also makes an excellent guard and defender of the flock, but is more aggressive in character and inclined to bark a lot. It is independent and tends to lead a nomadic life, so that it is not unusual for some of them to revert to their wild state.

Puli. Weight: dogs 13–15 kg (29–33 lb); bitches 10–13 kg (22–29 lb). Height: dogs 37–47 cm (14½–18½ in); bitches 34–44 cm (13½–17 in).
Pumi. Weight: 8–13 kg (17½–28½ lb). Height: 33–44 cm (13–17 in). Colour: black, reddish black, slate grey, silver grey, light grey, white.
Country of Origin: Hungary.

The Swedish Vallhund is a small, attractive dog which, at first glance, seems far removed from the usual herding dog. Despite its appearance, however, the Swedish Vallhund makes an excellent herder, being of proud and fearless character, full of stamina – enabling it to run about from morning till night – and extremely resistant to bad weather, so that it is able to stay out in the open all night keeping a vigilant watch. The breed is native to Sweden, and has a fairly recent official standard (1948). It is difficult to identify it with the majority of European herding dogs not only because of its small size but also because of its long body and short legs. These characteristics link it closely with the Cardigan variety of Welsh Corgi which was also originally a cattle dog, but is nowadays most common as a family pet because of its cheerful and affectionate nature. The Västgötaspets also has an affectionate and docile temperament and, like its Welsh cousin, is often kept as a town dog, a companion and pet. However, it has a closer affinity with the country and is therefore less able to adapt to living in a confined space, having for centuries been used to working off its abundant energy in running about in the open. The Swedish Vallhund is a sturdy, solidly built, muscular dog. The head is large, with a flat or slightly arched skull, broad between the ears, a moderately long muzzle and a pointed nose. The eyes are dark and oval in shape, and the triangular ears pointed and erect. The neck is strong, of moderate length, with a profuse collar and frill of longer hair than the rest of its coat. Its long body, with a level back and slightly tucked-up belly, is supported by short, strong legs, the front ones straight and the back ones with powerful, wide, solid thighs. The large feet are rounded and compact, adapted to the hard work the dog is called upon to perform. The tail is very short, no more than 10 cm (4 in) in length, and is carried horizontal in repose. The coat is of medium length, thick, fairly close to the body, and coarse in texture with a full, woolly winter undercoat.

Weight: 9–14 kg (20–30 lb). Height: 33–40 cm (13–15½ in). Colour: grey with a darker area on the back.
Country of Origin: Sweden.

Puli

Kuvasz

The Kuvasz is very similar in appearance to the Maremma Sheepdog and is one of the most ancient sheepdogs of its native Hungarian steppe. It was certainly one of the sheepdogs imported from the East, which spread throughout Europe, developing into separate local breeds. The name itself, which in Turkish means "guardian of the peace", gives a clue to the origins of this extraordinarily beautiful dog. It is a first-class sheepdog, whose size and powerful appearance are combined with an air of grace, harmony and great nobility of bearing. The Kuvasz is excellent at herding and guarding cattle, courageous and fearless in warding off attackers, brave and indomitable and yet at the same time docile, faithful, devoted to its owner and affectionate. Such splendid qualities, combined with undeniable beauty and a sharp and lively intelligence, make it an easily trained dog which may also be kept as a family pet, provided that it does not have to live cooped up in a flat. Its large head is in proportion to the rest of the body; it is not very broad, fairly long, and the muzzle tapers but does not end in a point. These characteristics, together with the less pronounced stop, distinguish it in appearance from the Maremma Sheepdog. It is also lighter in build, lacking that marked bear-like quality of its Italian relation. The body is solidly built, its bone structure strong but not heavy, with fine joints. The eyes are dark and almond-shaped, with a friendly but alert expression, and the medium-sized ears, set low and well back, are folded over at the base and hang down. The neck is powerful without being thick-set and has no dewlap. The back is slightly curved and there is moderate tuck-up of the belly. The forelegs are straight and the hind legs sturdy and perfectly balanced, ending in strong, compact feet with resistant, elastic pads. The coat is thick, rough to the touch, with plenty of wave, very long all over (up to 10–15 cm [4–6 in]) except on the head and lower legs and feet. The fairly long tail (reaching at least to the hocks) is set low and the tip curves slightly upwards.

Weight: dogs 40–52 kg (88–115 lb); bitches 30–42 kg (66–92½ lb).
Height: dogs 71–75 cm (28–29½ in); bitches 66–70 cm (26–27½ in).
Colour: pure white, ivory allowed.
Country of Origin: Hungary.

Komondor

The Komondor is the "King of Hungarian Sheepdogs". It was officially presented as a breed in its own right in 1920, and since then it has gained in recognition and popularity beyond its country of origin. It is a big dog, with a strong, powerful build and a solid, muscular frame. Unsociable and somewhat hostile by nature, it is very devoted to its master whom it blindly obeys, and woe betide anybody foolish enough to threaten its master or the flock entrusted to it. Intelligent, lively and quick to learn, it also makes a good house guard and protector of property, but is not suited to apartment living. The distinctive characteristic of the Komondor is its coat, which is dense and corded or matted. It is long all over the body but particularly on the hindquarters, where it may reach 20–27 cm (8–10½ in) in length, whereas on the head, neck and legs it ranges from 10–18 cm (4–7 in), and is approximately 10 cm (4 in) long on the feet. It also has a thick undercoat. The head is broad and in proportion to the rest of the body, the skull is arched and the muzzle fairly short and not pointed. The teeth are strong with a scissors bite. The eyes are dark brown and the ears hang down in the shape of a U. The powerful neck has no collar or dewlap. The back is slightly curved and a parting runs along it so that the long coat falls either side of the body. There is little tuck-up at the loins. The tail is quite long and hangs down in repose. The legs are sturdy and straight, and the feet large and compact.

Weight: dogs 50–61 kg (110–135 lb); bitches 40–50 kg (88–110 lb).
Height: dogs 65–80 cm (25½–31½ in); bitches 55–70 cm (21½–27½ in).
Colour: white.
Country of Origin: Hungary.

Rafeiro do Alentejo
Alentejo Herder

The Rafeiro do Alentejo, a native of Portugal, is a large, rugged, majestic animal of great versatility, used not only as a sheepdog but also as a guard and watch dog, a sledge dog and a rescue dog. This adaptable and intelligent animal, whose name is derived from the Portuguese province of Alentejo on the Spanish border, is a very hardy, tireless worker, resistant to any kind of climate and the most debilitating fatigue, and even to temporary lack of food. Heavy and massive, bearing a certain resemblance to the St Bernard, it has a large, bear-like head, a wide skull, flat between the ears, and a clearly visible stop. The bridge of the nose is straight and the muzzle long but not narrow. The dark, almond-shaped eyes have a gentle, calm expression. The short, powerful neck, with a slight dewlap, continues into the line of the back, which is solid with strong hindquarters. The tail, which reaches down to the hocks, is slightly curved upwards and carried low in repose. The legs are quite long in relation to the rest of the body, giving the dog an imposing air. Because it is so big and used to open spaces, the Rafeiro does not make a suitable household pet. The coat may be short or of medium length, smooth and dense, and evenly distributed over the body.

Weight: 35–50 kg (77–110 lb). Height: dogs 66–75 cm (26–29½ in); bitches 64–70 cm (25–27½ in). Colour: black, fawn, yellow, wolf, grizzle, brindle, spotted.
Country of Origin: Portugal.

Appenzell Mountain Dog
Appenzell Sennenhund

The Appenzell Mountain Dog belongs to a close-knit group of Swiss dogs of similar characteristics and origins, used for herding and guarding cattle. It is one of the sheepdogs of the Molossian type which basically developed along parallel lines, giving rise to two varieties – a larger one, to which the Great Swiss Mountain Dog belongs, and a smaller one, to which the Appenzell belongs. The Appenzell Mountain Dog, which has been common throughout German-speaking Switzerland since the last century, has retained all of its original characteristics, being by far the most popular mountain dog in this area and therefore mating with other herding breeds is an unlikely occurrence. Smaller than average, this noble animal is an excellent guard and herder of cattle; it is agile, courageous and untiring, resistant to weather extremes, intelligent and responsive. It is capable of rounding up as many as 200 head of cattle, including recalcitrant bulls, on its own but is not very good at controlling sheep. Because of its extrovert, noisy character and love of freedom, it is not to be recommended as a pet, although it is not lacking in gentleness and affection. A close relative of the Appenzell Mountain Dog is the Entlebuch Mountain Dog, found in the cantons of Berne and Lucerne, and the two are so alike that the latter is not considered a separate breed by some dog-fanciers but merely a variation of the Appenzell. The differences in the standards are in fact so negligible that it is sometimes difficult to differentiate between the two dogs. The head of the Appenzell is in proportion to its body, with a broad skull, flat between the ears, which are set high and hang down when not pricked. The small, dark, slanting eyes give the dog a keen and lively expression. The sturdy, muscular neck is moderately long and forms a graceful extension of the body which, because of the lack of belly tuck-up, is cylindrical in shape. The legs are solidly built, with round, cat-like feet. The tail is set high and carried curled over one side of the back when the dog is in action. The coat is short, thick, shiny and lies close to the body, over a black or brown waterproof undercoat.

Weight: approximately 20–25 kg (44–55 lb). Height: dogs 52–58 cm (20½–23 in); bitches 48–54 cm (19–21 in). Colour: black with regular tan and white markings.
Country of Origin: Switzerland.

Great Swiss Mountain Dog

Great Swiss Sennenhund

The Great Swiss Mountain Dog is the largest of the closely related group of Swiss dogs, and it too has been known and made use of since ancient times. It was very widespread and popular until the middle of the last century, when it suffered a decline in numbers because, being such a large dog, it was causing considerable damage to vineyards and orchards as it hunted its staple diet of game; the resulting damage to the latter also caused concern. Its size and build curtail speed and ease of movement, so it is not ideally suited to herding and droving, and even small animals such as sheep prove problematic. Its main role has therefore always been that of guard and watch dog in the Zürich countryside, where no farm was without at least one of these dogs. With its great physical strength, it has also proved its worth to man as a draught dog, being able to haul very heavy loads. Good-natured, affectionate, intelligent, courageous and faithful to the point of utter dedication, it also makes an excellent companion for man provided that it has plenty of space. It was not only the peasants who valued the Great Swiss Mountain Dog so highly but also the shopkeepers (butchers, cheese-mongers etc.) whose merchandise it ably guarded. Despite its massive, robust physique, it is well proportioned so that its overall appearance is rather attractive. The head is large, powerful and in proportion to the rest of the body, the skull flat and broad between the ears, the stop not very well defined and the muzzle of medium length, with powerful jaws. The eyes are medium-sized, alert and watchful, and hazel or nut-brown in colour. The ears are set high and pendant. The neck is strong, sturdy, muscular and relatively short. The body is compact, fairly short and powerful, with a straight back and slight tuck-up of the belly. The legs are fairly long, well-boned, muscular and straight and the feet round with closely-set toes. Dew-claws, if any, should be removed. The coat is fairly short (from 3–5 cm [1–2 in]), hard, smooth and thick, with a dense undercoat. The tail reaches down to the hocks and has a slight upward curve.

Weight: 40 kg (88 lb) and over. Height: dogs 65–70 cm (25½–27½ in); bitches 60–65 cm (23½–25½ in). Colour: black with symmetrical white and tan markings.
Country of Origin: Switzerland.

Bernese Mountain Dog
Bernese Sennenhund

The Bernese Mountain Dog is between the Great Swiss and the Appenzell Mountain Dogs in size, and shares their ancient Molossian ancestry. Indeed images of dogs very like the present-day Sennenhunde (mountain dogs) have been found on clay objects from the time of the Roman invasions. The Bernese Mountain Dog has a robust constitution, and is well known outside its country of origin, for instance in the United States of America and in Holland, Belgium and Germany, where it is used more as a guard and watch dog than for cattle herding and droving. The popularity it enjoys is due both to its magnificent, attractive appearance, and to its considerable intelligence and aptitude for learning, which make it easy to train. It is also affectionate, docile and very attached to its master, so that it is very reluctant to change owners. But its size and need of exercise make it impossible to keep in a flat. Its coat is long, thick and abundant, sometimes wavy but never curly, and soft to the touch. It is shorter on the head, with slight feathering on the forelegs, and the dog has a

beautiful, bushy tail of medium length. The head is well proportioned, short and massive, with a flat or slightly arched skull, sloping gently down to join the fairly long muzzle. The neck is strong and muscular, of medium length, and the body relatively short, well ribbed-up and powerful, with a straight back and moderate belly tuck-up. These characteristics make the body more or less square in outline and the dog is a good height. The legs are strong, straight and solidly built, well suited to the amount of running and hard work entailed in being a draught and mountain dog. The feet are round and compact, with strong, elastic pads.

Weight: 35–40 kg (77–88 lb). Height: dogs 64–70 cm (25–27½ in); bitches 58–66 cm (23–26 in). Colour: jet black with deep tan markings over the eyes, on the cheeks and legs. White blaze down the forehead and white chest.
Country of Origin: Switzerland.

Bouvier des Flandres

A native of Flanders, and thus Franco-Belgian in origin, this dog was once found throughout the region but did not conform to any particular type, and it was not until 1910 that a standard was drawn up for the breed. After the 1914–18 war, the Bouvier des Flandres was on the brink of extinction, and the few remaining specimens were carefully and selectively bred in an attempt to rebuild the breed. In subsequent years a new standard was devised, which combined the two main varieties of this cattle dog – the Paret of French Flanders and the Belgian Bouvier of Rouliers. The two are by no means identical, in that the Rouliers is slightly heavier than its French counterpart, its head is marginally longer, the torso a different shape and the coat always black with lighter overlay. The unification of the standards has not pleased all dog-fanciers, and indeed there are some who would like to see them separated again. Originally a drovers' dog, the Bouvier des Flandres currently serves as a guard and watch dog, a police dog and a draught dog, particularly in Holland. It has a determined character and an exceptional sense of smell, it is alert and responsive, faithful and affectionate in spite of its size, a one-person dog, and patient with children. It can be kept as a family pet but should not be cooped up in a flat. The Bouvier des Flandres is a rugged, solidly built animal, with a massive, compact body and powerful presence. The head is large but in proportion to the rest of the body, with a wide, flat skull, shallow stop and prominent arched, shaggy brows over dark, oval eyes, which have a calm but lively expression. The ears are set high, and cropped to a point on the Continent. If the dog is born with a tail, it too is docked very short, to the second or third joint. The neck is long, strong and free from dewlap. The back is short, broad and muscular, with only slight tuck-up of the belly. The legs are strong, but with low hocks and short pasterns, which makes the dog slightly smaller than one would expect. The feet are short with arched toes. The coat is rough and tousled, up to 6 cm ($2\frac{1}{4}$ in) in length, shorter on the head which has characteristic eyebrows and moustache. The thick undercoat makes the topcoat stand out.

Weight: dogs 35–40 kg (77–88 lb); bitches 27–35 kg ($59\frac{1}{2}$–77 lb). Height: dogs 62–68 cm ($24\frac{1}{2}$–27 in); bitches 59–65 cm (23–$25\frac{1}{2}$ in). Colour: fawn, grey with black points, pepper and salt, brindle, black.
Country of Origin: France/Belgium.

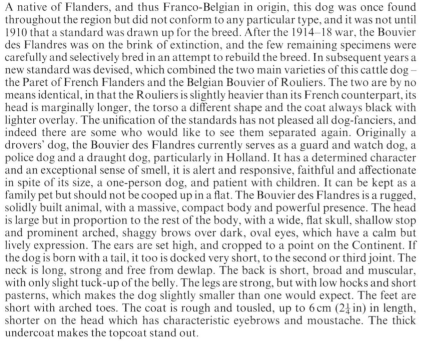

Eskimo Dog

The Eskimo Dog is one of the Spitz dogs which inhabit the Arctic regions. Siberia, Lapland, Greenland, Iceland and Alaska are the domain of this clearly-defined group of dogs, which are closely related not only to each other but also to the Arctic wolf, although the connection with the latter is not now so apparent, there having been no evidence of interbreeding for a very long time. These powerfully-built dogs are used for pulling sledges and have great powers of endurance, being capable of covering up to 80 km (50 miles) in a day, and 15,000–20,000 km (9,000–12,000 miles) in a winter season. They have a highly developed sense of direction, which makes them invaluable to man when there are no other means of transport and communication. The Eskimo Dog is the sledge-dog of the Canadian territory, a descendant, in common

with all the other Arctic dogs, from dogs brought over from Asia which grew accustomed and adapted to life in regions with rigorous climates through strict natural selection which eradicated all the physically unsuitable or defective specimens. The local population, the Eskimos, added artificial selection to the culling process, killing the weak specimens since the inhospitable environment and the problems of providing food mitigate against feeding an animal which cannot earn its keep. As a result the Eskimo dog is a magnificent, sturdy animal, resistant to both cold and illness. Its chief function is to act as a draught dog, but it is also often used for hunting bear and caribou. It feeds mainly on fish. Its profuse coat is of hair 7–15 cm ($2\frac{3}{4}$–6 in) long, shorter only on the head, covering a dense, oily undercoat, which enables it to endure temperatures of up to 60–70°C (76–94°F) below zero. The head is broad, with a tapering, wolf-like muzzle and powerful jaws. The deep-set, slanting eyes and in particular their penetrating gaze, and the small, triangular ears also recall the similarity with the wolf. The likeness is even more pronounced when the dog lifts its upper lip in its characteristic "laugh". The neck is powerful, muscular and rather short, and the massive, sturdy body with its heavy bone structure is set on strong, straight legs with very powerful low hocks. Its splayed feet prevent the dog from sinking into the snow. The bushy tail is carried curled over the back.

Weight: 30–50 kg (66–110 lb). Height: 56–60 cm (22–24 in). Colour: white, grey, dark brown, blue, black, or combinations of these colours.
Country of Origin: Canada.

Siberian Husky

The Siberian Husky is another Spitz breed of wolf-like appearance, a native of Siberia, which spread to Alaska towards the start of the twentieth century. In overall appearance it is not very different from the other dogs who live in the Arctic regions. It too is a close relation of the wolf, which it resembles both facially and in body structure, and is the smallest and most refined in build of all the sledge dogs. It owes its name to the indigenous Husky tribe, among whom it has dwelled since ancient times. Its size – slightly smaller than its nearest relative, the Eskimo dog – gives it greater agility and quickness of movement, although its considerable speed is at the expense of endurance. It is, however, a very strong, sturdy, solidly built dog, lively, intelligent and faithful, very devoted to its owner, sociable and affectionate. All these qualities and the fact that it is a reasonable size have combined to ensure its popularity even outside its natural habitat. It has a fairly wide following in France, having been brought back there from polar expeditions. Like the other Arctic dogs it is an able hunter and happily eats fish, which tends to constitute its staple diet. Its physical characteristics reveal its common ancestry with both the Eskimo Dog and the Alaskan Malamute. It resembles the latter more closely in the length and texture of its coat, which is of medium length and soft, covering a dense, woolly undercoat that is oily to the touch and completely waterproof. Like the other Spitz breeds, it is also capable of enduring temperatures ranging far below zero. The head is wolf-like in appearance with brown or blue, slightly slanting eyes, which have a friendly expression. The high, erect ears give the dog an air of nobility. The tail is fox-like, carried over the back in a sickle curve. Both the body and the legs are well muscled and solidly built, more powerful than they might appear given the moderate size of the dog. The feet have the typical broad, compact shape which comes from constantly walking on snow.

Weight: dogs 20–27 kg (44–59½ lb); bitches 16–22 kg (33–48½ lb).
Height: dogs 53–60 cm (21–23½ in); bitches 51–56 cm (20–22 in).
Colour: all colours from wolf grey to silver grey, and from light sable to black with white points.
Country of Origin: U.S.A.

Alaskan Malamute

The Alaskan Malamute is the largest and heaviest of all the Spitz breeds, and also one of the most ancient. Its origins are obscure, but the breed has been known and used by natives of Alaska for many centuries. It was named after the Alaskan tribe of the Mahlemuts, who used this splendid animal not only for pulling sledges but also to provide valuable assistance in hunting and fishing. It is by far the hardiest of all the Northern dogs, with exceptional powers of endurance over long distances, and amazing strength and courage. It is very popular in America, where it is greatly valued as a guard dog and companion, as it is intelligent, faithful, docile, affectionate, devoted and loyal, exceptionally clean and not at all noisy. It has an excellent nose and an astonishing sense of direction. The Alaskan Malamute has been made famous all over the world through the tales of Jack London and Rudyard Kipling. The Malamute is a powerful-looking dog, substantially built, well proportioned and balanced, not thick-set. The large, broad, powerful head narrows from between the ears to the eyes. The muzzle is wide but suitably long; the profile is soft, the stop clearly visible but forms a gentle curve. The dark, almond-shaped eyes have a calm, proud expression, and the rather small, pointed ears are set back and carried erect. The neck is strong, powerful and fairly long. The back is straight, the chest wide and deep, and the belly moderately tucked up. The tail is of medium length and carried high, curled well over to one side in repose. Both fore and hind legs are straight and solid, with very strong hocks. The wide, compact, solid feet support the weight of the dog well, preventing it from sinking into the snow. The coat is of medium length, somewhat coarse, standing away from the body and covering a very dense, woolly, oily undercoat, which provides the skin with complete protection against the external environment and enables the dog to withstand temperatures of up to 70°C (94°F) below zero. The hair is longer around the neck, forming a profuse collar, and on the tail, which is fairly long and plumed.

Weight: dogs 38 kg (84 lb); bitches 34 kg (75 lb). Height: dogs 63 cm (25 in); bitches 58 cm (23 in). Colour: all-white, all shades from light grey to black, with white mask, chest, underbody and legs.
Country of Origin: U.S.A.

Alaskan Malamute

Samoyed

The Samoyed owes its name to a tribe who roamed between the White Sea and the Yenisey River. It has been known since ancient times and is used as a sledge dog, a herder (of reindeer) and a guard against bears and wolves. Although not as swift as its fellow Spitz dogs, it is an exceptionally hardy animal. Intelligent, friendly, patient and good-natured, it is happy performing any kind of task, and also makes an excellent pet. Its build is both strong and elegant and is of handsome appearance with its thick, white coat of coarse, straight hair, which stands out from the body because of the unusually prolific, perfectly waterproof undercoat. The head is wedge-shaped, with very dark, almond-shaped eyes and small, triangular, pricked ears. The body is very muscular, the chest deep, the back and loins solid, and the legs strong and straight with fairly long, flat feet. The tail is very bushy and carried high.

Weight: dogs 20–30 kg (44–66 lb); bitches 17–25 kg (37½–55 lb). Height: dogs 50–55 cm (19½–21½ in); bitches 45–50 cm (17½–19½ in). Colour: pure white (preferable), cream, biscuit.
Country of Origin: Siberia.

70

Other Working Dogs

Breed: Cão Serra de Aires – *Origin*: Portugal – *Height*: dogs 42–48 cm (16½–19 in); bitches 40–46 cm (16–18 in) – *Weight*: 12–18 kg (26½–39½ lb) – *Colour*: fawn, grey, wolf grey, brown, yellow, black and tan – *Physical characteristics*: drop ears; long tail carried low; long coat (especially on the head), no undercoat.

Breed: Estrela Mountain Dog (Cão Serra da Estrela) – *Origin*: Portugal – *Height*: dogs 65–72 cm (25½–28 in); bitches 62–68 cm (24–26½ in) – *Weight*: dogs 40–50 kg (88–110 lb); bitches 30–40 kg (66–88 lb) – *Colour*: fawn, yellow, wolf grey (solid or flecked) – *Physical characteristics*: dark eyes; small, drop ears; thick tail carried scimitar-like; strong, thick coat.

Breed: Cão de Castro Laboreiro – *Origin*: Portugal – *Height*: dogs 56–60 cm (22–23½ in); bitches 52–57 cm (20½–22½ in) – *Weight*: dogs 30–40 kg (66–88 lb); bitches 20–30 kg (44–66 lb) – *Colour*: wolf grey (darkish) – *Physical characteristics*: drop ears with rounded tips; long, thick tail carried well; profuse coat approximately 5 cm (2 in) in length, no undercoat.

Breed: Gos d'Atura Cerdà – *Origin*: Spain – *Height*: dogs 50–60 cm (19½–23½ in); bitches 45–55 cm (18–21½ in) – *Weight*: dogs 18 kg (40 lb); bitches 16 kg (35 lb) – *Colour*: fawn, grey (various shades), grey-black with or without silver tan markings – *Physical characteristics*: little stop; black nose; dark eyes; short, straight ears; tail carried low, curved at the tip; strong, long, profuse coat (smooth on the head and not as long on the legs).

Breed: Catalonian Sheepdog (Perro de Pastor Catalan or Gos d'Atura) – *Origin*: Spain – *Height*: dogs 45–50 cm (18–20 in); bitches 43–48 cm (17–19 in) – *Weight*: 16–18 kg (35½–39½ lb) – *Colour*: greyish black with darkish tan markings on legs and feet, tricolour (white, black, cream) – *Physical characteristics*: dark eyes; drop ears covered in long hair, hanging close to the head (generally cropped); long or short tail (sometimes missing altogether) set low; two sets of dew claws on back legs; long, wavy coat.

Breed: Keeshond – *Origin*: Holland – *Height*: 45–46 cm (18 in) – *Weight*: 25–30 kg (55–66 lb) – *Colour*: wolf grey, silver grey with dark shading – *Physical characteristics*: small, erect, pointed ears; tail rolled over the back with white plume; harsh, thick coat with profuse, downy undercoat; feathering on elbows and thighs.

Breed: Hollandse Herdershond (Dutch Shepherd Dog) – *Origin*: Holland – *Height*: dogs 58–63 cm (23–25 in); bitches 55–62 cm (21½–24½ in) – *Weight*: approximately 30 kg (66 lb) – *Colour*: yellow, red, brown, streaked (gold or silver) – *Physical characteristics*: black nose; prick ears, long tail carried low; short, long or wiry coat (characterizing the three varieties).

Breed: Bouvier des Ardennes – *Origin*: Belgium – *Height*: 60–65 cm (23½–25½ in) – *Weight*: 60–65 kg (132½–143½ lb) – *Colour*: all colours allowed – *Physical characteristics*: dark eyes; prick ears; muzzle with moustache and beard; no dew claws; tail docked short or missing altogether; harsh, shaggy coat approximately 5 cm (2 in) in length (shorter on the head and legs), thick undercoat in winter.

Breed: Border Collie – *Origin*: Great Britain – *Height*: dogs 43–50 cm (17–20 in); bitches 40–45 cm (16–18 in) – *Weight*: 13–22 kg (28½–48½ lb) – *Colour*: white, black, brown, black and white – *Physical characteristics*: pointed muzzle; semi-drop ears; tail carried low and richly plumed; two types of coat: rough, 8 cm (3 in) long or smooth, 2.5 cm (1 in) long.

Breed: Entlebuch Sennenhund (Entlebuch Mountain Dog) – *Origin*: Switzerland – *Height*: 40–52 cm (16–20½ in) – *Weight*: 25–30 kg (55–66 lb) – *Colour*: black and tan (with symmetrical white markings) – *Physical characteristics*: brown eyes; not very large ears set high, hanging close to the head; short tail; short, hard coat.

Breed: Croatian Sheepdog (Hrvatški Ovčar) – *Origin*: Yugoslavia – *Height*: 40–50 cm (16–20 in) – *Weight*: not specified – *Colour*: black (white markings allowed on throat and chest) – *Physical characteristics*: erect, pointed ears; short tail (natural or docked), sometimes missing altogether; long coat with profuse undercoat.

Breed: Mudi – *Origin*: Hungary – *Height*: 35–47 cm (14–18½ in) – *Weight*: 8–13 kg (17½–28½ lb) – *Colour*: self-coloured white or black, spotted or flecked – *Physical characteristics*: long head; pointed nose; negligible stop; dark brown eyes; erect, pointed ears; tail carried low or docked; smooth coat (head and legs) from 5 to 7 cm (2–2½ in) in length and wavy in other parts (shaggy on the ears) with feathering on forelegs.

Breed: Polish Sheepdog (Polski Owczarek Nizinny or Lowlands Shepherd Dog) – *Origin*: Poland – *Height*: dogs 43–52 cm (17–20½ in); bitches 40–46 cm (16–18 in) – *Weight*: under 30 kg (66 lb) – *Colour*: extremely varied – *Physical characteristics*: drop ears; short tail (natural or docked); long, thick coat.

Breed: Polish Sheepdog (Owczarek Podlhalanski or Tatra Mountain Sheepdog) – *Origin*: Poland – *Height*: dogs over 65 cm (25½ in); bitches over 60 cm (23½ in) – *Weight*: around 35 kg (77 lb) – *Colour*: white, pale cream – *Physical characteristics*: ears hanging close to the head; tail carried low; profuse coat (slightly shorter on the head).

Estrela Mountain Dog

Cão Serra de Aires

Cão de Castro Laboreiro

Border Collie

Hollandse Herdershond

Bouvier des Ardennes

Croatian Sheepdog

Entlebuch Sennenhund

Keeshond

Polish Sheepdog
(Polski Owczarek Nizinny)

Mudi

Polish Sheepdog (Owczarek Podlhalanski)

Slovakian Kuvasz

Iceland Dog

Norwegian Buhund

Australian Cattle Dog

Lapphund

Greenland Dog

Canaan Dog

Australian Kelpie

Norrbottenspets

Lapponian Herder

Catahoula Leopard Dog

Australian Shepherd

Other Working Dogs

Breed: Slovakian Kuvasz (Slovensky Čuvač or Tsuvatch) – Origin: Czechoslovakia – Height: dogs 60–70 cm (23½–27½ in); bitches 55–65 cm (21½–25½ in) – Weight: 30–45 kg (66–99 lb) – Colour: white – Physical characteristics: drop ears; tail carried low; coat up to 10 cm (4 in) in length.

Breed: Lapphund (Lapland Spitz) – Origin: Sweden – Height: dogs 45–50 cm (18–20 in); bitches 40–45 cm (16–18 in) – Weight: not specified – Colour: black, dark brown, brown and white – Physical characteristics: black nose; small, erect, pointed ears; tail curled over the back (even missing or docked); long, thick coat (except on head and legs).

Breed: Norrbottenspets – Origin: Sweden – Height: approximately 40 cm (16 in) – Weight: not specified – Colour: very varied – Physical characteristics: erect ears with tips pricked forward;

muscular neck; tail curled over the back, carried towards the flank; fairly long, thick coat with profuse undercoat.

Breed: Iceland Dog – Origin: Iceland – Height: 30–40 cm (12–16 in) – Weight: 9–13 kg (20–28½ lb) – Colour: brown, fawn, grey, black, black and white, dirty white – Physical characteristics: dark nose; erect ears; tail curled over the back; coat of medium length with profuse undercoat.

Breed: Greenland Dog (Greenland Husky) – Origin: Northern countries – Height: over 60 cm (23½ in) (bitches not less than 55 cm [21½ in]) – Weight: not specified – Colour: very varied (excluding albinos) – Physical characteristics: erect ears; muscular neck; tail curled over the back; thick coat.

Breed: Lapponian Herder (Lapland Vallhund) – Origin: Finland – Height: dogs 49–55 cm (19½–21½ in); bitches 43–49 cm (17–19½ in) – Weight: 15–30 kg (33–66 lb) – Colour: black and tan (white markings allowed on throat, chest and legs), brown (various shades), white – Physical characteristics: pronounced stop; black, well-developed nose; dark eyes; short, erect, pointed ears; plumed tail curled over the back; long, hard, rough coat; profuse, woolly undercoat.

Breed; Norwegian Buhund (Norsk Buhund) – Origin: Norway – Height: 42–45 cm (16½–18 in) – Weight: approximately 25 kg (55 lb) – Colour: black, red, sandy, wolf-grey, biscuit – Physical characteristics: erect, pointed ears; short tail curved over the back; thick, rough coat.

Breed: Russian Owtscharka (Russian Sheepdog) – Origin: USSR – Height: 65–80 cm (25½–31½ in) – Weight: 45–50 kg (99–110 lb) – Colour: slate grey, fawn, white, black – Physical characteristics: dark eyes; not very long, rounded, drop ears, covered with thick hair; well-plumed tail (often docked); thick, woolly coat.

Breed: Canaan Dog – Origin: Israel – Height: 50–60 cm (19½–23½ in) – Weight: 18–25 kg (40–55 lb) – Colour: black and white, reddish brown, sandy, harlequin (large white markings allowed) – Physical characteristics: erect ears; tail curled over the back; rough, shaggy coat of medium length.

Breed: Anatolian Karabash (Anatolian Sheepdog or Turkish Shepherd Dog) – Origin: Turkey – Height: 66–98 cm (26–38½ in) – Weight: 41–68 kg (90½–150 lb) – Colour: white, chamois (often black mask and ears) – Physical characteristics: drop ears; thick, hard coat.

Breed: Catahoula Leopard Dog – Origin: United States – Height: 50–63 cm (20–25 in) – Weight: 22–36 kg (48½–79½ lb) – Colour: bluish grey with mottling or markings (black or fawn) – Physical characteristics: black nose; drop ears carried back; tail carried low and curved.

Breed: Australian Cattle Dog – Origin: Australia – Height: 40–48 cm (16–19 in) – Weight: 16–22 kg (35–48½ lb) – Colour: blue, blue with black or brown markings, fawn with black markings (on the head) – Physical characteristics: fairly large, erect ears; tail carried low; hard coat, not too short.

Breed: Australian Kelpie – Origin: Australia – Height: 50–60 cm (19½–23½ in) – Weight: approximately 25 kg (55 lb) – Colour: black, fawn, brown – Physical characteristics: dark, almond-shaped eyes; erect ears sometimes slightly pricked forward at the tip; tail carried low, slightly arched; coat of medium length and hard.

Breed: Australian Shepherd – Origin: Australia – Height: 43–58 cm (17–23 in) – Weight: 12–20 kg (26½–44 lb) – Colour: black, fawn, brown and white – Physical characteristics: usually blue eyes; drop ears; short, hard, profuse coat.

HUNTING BREEDS

Pointing Dogs

Pointing dogs belong to the vast group of sporting dogs classified as "scent hunters", so-called because they rely mainly on their sense of smell. They are generally of medium size, swift, light and streamlined, and of elegant appearance. The dominant feature which distinguishes this group of dogs is their ability to freeze into given positions (point or set) once the game has been discovered. Both Pointers and Setters hunt with head held high, being better able to pick up smells in the air rather than on the ground; they are therefore ideally suited to hunting wildfowl.

Pointer

The Pointer is a very well known, typically English hunting dog, which has been selectively bred in Great Britain since the middle of the seventeenth century. Its origins probably lie in the Spanish Pointer and the Portuguese Pointer, who were then crossed with the Foxhound, the Bloodhound and the Greyhound. According to the English classification, the Pointer is a member of the "sporting group", whose members differ from other hunting dogs in that they are used to point and retrieve game rather than to bring it down. The English consider this dog "difficult", not for the novice hunter because it is a pure sporting animal, suited to the hunter who is not interested in merely filling his game-bag, but also in long walks in the open air and close contact with nature. With its undeniable beauty, elegant build and

well-balanced movement, it rapidly gained popularity outside its homeland, even at times supplanting local breeds. The Pointer is known for its exceptional skill in tracking quarry, particularly feathered game, and its nose is so highly developed that not even fierce heat or other smells, no matter how powerful, can throw it off the scent. Its name stems from its habit of freezing into a characteristic position "pointing out" the quarry. Its point is so rigid, the muscles so taut, with head stretched out, one foreleg raised and tail extended, the muscular effort so intense and yet imperceptible, that the only signs of life are its breathing and the lively expression in its eyes. The Pointer is agile and very swift, able to sustain its pace and best suited to hunting on the flat, where it has no peer. But it is also very useful in woods and

74

marshes, since being a docile and highly intelligent animal it is exceptionally easy to train. The fundamental difference between it and other gundogs is the elongated Pointer head, characterized by the flat, moderately broad skull being on the same plane as the muzzle, and by the pronounced vertical stop. The upper lips are soft and well developed, with a clear labial join. The soft ears are set on high and are flat and pendulant, with pointing tips, hanging close to the cheek. The eyes are large, round, dark brown or hazel, bright and shining. The neck is long, arched, muscular but light. The brisket is full and well let down on a level with the elbows, and the back straight, falling slightly to the muscular croup with marked tuck-up of the belly. The tail is thick at the root, gradually tapering to the tip, of medium length and carried horizontal. The long, sinewy, sturdy legs give the Pointer a natural poise and lightness and a swift, smooth gait. The feet are oval, of medium size, with close arched toes and hard, elastic pads. The coat is smooth, very short and close to the body, light, fine but resistant, even all over the body and glossy, emphasizing the body outline and further adding to the graceful appearance of this magnificent animal.

Weight: 20–30 kg (44–66 lb). Height: dogs 63–69 cm (25–27 in); bitches 61–66 cm (24–26 in). Colour: usually white with black, brown, fawn, liver, orange or lemon markings. These colours may be solid. Country of Origin: Great Britain.

Gordon Setter

This beautiful dog owes its name and present form to the Duke of Gordon, who wanted to obtain a more solid and slightly bigger animal than the English Setter. All Setters, including the Gordon, were at one time trained to point the quarry and then, when the hunter arrived, to crouch or move aside while he threw a fowling-net over the bird or brood of partridges. Nowadays the Setter is trained not only to point but also to flush the game, as well as to retrieve mountain birds such as pheasants, quails, grouse and woodcock. A well-trained Setter never disturbs the point of another Setter. In addition to being more solid and marginally larger than the English Setter, the Gordon Setter also has a heavier head, with a slightly rounded skull and curved stop. The eyes are large and dark and the ears broad, soft and triangular, hanging close to the head. The neck is strong, of good length and the back level, with arched loins and sloping croup. The tail is set on high and carried almost horizontal. The legs are long and well let down, solid and muscular, with round, compact, sturdy feet. The coat is long, fine, silky and smooth, with feathering on the ears, tail, throat and chest, short hair on the skull and even shorter hair on the muzzle and cheeks. In winter it also has an undercoat. The Gordon has an affectionate, gentle, docile, noble, easy-going nature, and therefore makes a suitable family pet.

Weight: 26–30 kg (57–66 lb). Height: dogs 58–66 cm (23–26 in); bitches 56–62 cm (22–24½ in). Colour: black and tan.
Country of Origin: Great Britain.

Irish Setter
Red Setter

Of all the Setters, the Irish is the most spirited and fiery, needing exhaustive training before it can be used for hunting. Once trained, it is excellent over any ground, but excels on marshland, hunting snipe and all water game. Of the same basic stock as the English Setter, the Irish differs in the lighter, more tapering head, the gently sloping stop, the forward lean of the skull and muzzle and the more agile, spare build. Its long, sinewy legs and rather narrow chest give it a more streamlined shape. These characteristics combine to bestow an undeniable beauty on the Irish Setter, which is enhanced by the red mahogany colour of the coat. It has become so highly-prized and sought-after for its beauty that breeders have tried to produce even more long-limbed dogs by breeding it low. The result is greater elegance but also a reduction in muscle power, with the Setter not only losing the characteristics of the breed but often also undergoing a negative change of temperament. The Irish Setter is energetic and wilful, affectionate and faithful, but is subject to unexpected changes of mood, and sometimes takes a dislike to strangers. The coat is long, silky and smooth, with slight feathering on the throat and brisket and on the tail and backs of the legs.

Weight: dogs 20–25 kg (44–55 lb); bitches 18–22 kg (40–48½ lb). Height: dogs 52–62 cm (20½–24 in); bitches 50–60 cm (19½–23½ in). Colour: mahogany red.
Country of Origin: Ireland.

Gordon Setter

Irish Setter

English Setter

The name "setter" derives from the verb "to set", which means to stiffen, position and point. The name is therefore indicative of the role of the Setter as a pointing dog, although it adopts a different posture from the Pointer. It assumes a half-sitting position by flexing its hindquarters, keeping its tail at a slant and both forelegs as a rule firmly on the ground. The Setter hunts with its head held high in order not to miss the faintest scent of bird game. The most ancient setter breed is the English Setter, evolved from crosses between the Spanish Pointer and the Springer Spaniel. Known and used in England as a hunting dog for at least 400 years, it was first bred selectively by Sir Edward Laverack in the early nineteenth century and subsequently considerably modified by the breeder Llewellin, to whom credit is due for its present form. Now quite different from the Laverack variety, the breed is inaccurately referred to by some as the Laverack Setter. The English Setter is an excellent hunting dog, good on any terrain, be it flat land and marsh where its swimming abilities stand it in good stead, or woods and bush. In appearance it is elegant, well balanced and powerful without being heavy. It is clean in outline and slightly lower on the leg than the other setters. The head is long and light, with a well-defined stop half-way along. The skull and the muzzle are on parallel planes. The eyes are large, bright and dark and the ears, set low and well back, are long and hang close to the head. The coat is long, silky, fine and slightly wavy, short on the head, with abundant feathering.

Weight: 25–29 kg (55–64 lb). Height: dogs 65–68 cm (25½–27 in); bitches 61–65 cm (24–25½ in). Colour: black and white, orange and white, brown and white, tricolour, often with flecking which may be extensive.
Country of Origin: Great Britain.

French Pointer
Braque Français

The French Pointer, whose origins probably lie in the ancient Spanish Pointer which spread into south-west France via the Pyrenees, is the oldest of all the French pointers, and the progenitor of the different pointer breeds considered native to the regions in which they were developed by selective breeding. There are two varieties of the French Pointer, differeng only in size, the larger being the more typical and the more common. The small variety is also known by the name of Braque Français de Petite Taille. The French Pointer has a strong, sturdy frame and muscle structure and a rugged, powerful appearance. It is very resistant to fatigue and variations of climate, and a first-rate hunter on any type of terrain, be it mountain, wood or marsh. It has a natural and highly developed hunting instinct, but needs to be trained to obey and to curb its impulsive nature. The head is large but not heavy, with an oval, slightly domed skull and a level or slightly curved, broad muzzle with a well-developed nose. The ears, set low and back, are fine and hang in a slight fold; the eyes, brown or dark yellow in colour, have a patient, loving expression. The neck is fairly long, the chest broad and deep, and the back level, with gently sloping loins and croup. The legs are long and muscular, with broad, compact feet and strong, elastic pads. The coat is short, thick and coarse, softer on the head and ears.

Weight: large size 25–32 kg (55–70½ lb); small size 18–25 kg (40–55 lb). Height: large size 56–65 cm (22–25½ in); small size 47–56 cm (18½–22 in). Colour: white with brown or cinnamon markings, brown with white markings, with or without flecking. Flecked or speckled all over. The smaller variety may even be solid brown or cinnamon. Country of Origin: France.

Petite Taille

Auvergne Pointer
Braque d'Auvergne

The Auvergne Pointer is without doubt derived from the French Pointer, retaining the same hardiness but with a less heavy appearance. It is unquestionably the swiftest of all the pointers, making a remarkable hunter from a very early age and can also be trained to retrieve, on any terrain. Highly intelligent, docile, lively, sensitive and affectionate, it also adapts well to family life. The head is long, with an oval skull, broad forehead and faint stop. The foreface is level and long, and the heavy, pendulous lips give a square shape to the muzzle. The dark eyes are fairly deep-set and the ears, set well back at the level of the eye, are soft and hang in a slight fold. The neck is fairly long, with some dewlap. The chest is well let down to the level of the elbows and the belly shows slight tuck-up. The tail is carried horizontal and docked to about two-thirds of its length. The legs are powerful, muscular and long, with short, compact feet and tightly closed toes. The coat is short, fine, not too soft but never hard and dull.

Weight: 22–25 kg (48½–55 lb). Height: dogs 57–63 cm (22⅓–24½ in); bitches 55–60 cm (21½–23½ in). Colour: Light: white with large blue-black markings and flecking. Dark: charcoal or black overlay. Country of Origin: France.

80

Ariège Pointer
Braque de l'Ariège

Known also by the name of Toulouse Pointer, this dog is probably derived from crosses between the French Pointer and the Braque Saint-Germain, which, in turn, sprang from a union between a Pointer bitch and a French Pointer dog in about 1830. The Ariège Pointer was recognized as a separate breed around 1860. This dog has a solid, powerful build and yet an unspoilt natural elegance, largely due to its long legs which give it added height. It is a very intelligent animal with a natural hunting instinct, able to withstand fatigue and the rigours of climate. It is swift to search out the quarry and is also good at retrieving, but it is not very manageable and needs careful, patient training. Fairly independent, it tends to become snappy with age. The head is long and fairly narrow with a long, straight muzzle and sloping stop. The dark amber eyes have an intelligent, alert expression. The soft ears are set high and back, hanging close to the cheek. The neck is long with some dewlap, and the body is muscular. The tail is thick at the root, set low and docked fairly short. The coat is very short, fine, thick and glossy, with flecks of silver.

Weight: 25–30 kg (55–66 lb). Height: dogs 60–65 cm ($23\frac{1}{2}$–$25\frac{1}{2}$ in); bitches 56–62 cm (22–24 in). Colour: dull white with orange or brown markings and spots or just spots.
Country of Origin: France.

81

Brittany Spaniel

The Brittany Spaniel is a dog of medium size, developed by crossing the French Spaniel with the Setter to produce an excellent pointing dog, the most popular of the spaniel breeds. Officially recognized as a breed in 1938, it is very intelligent, with an instinct and passion for hunting. It has a fine nose, considerable stamina and a natural talent for pointing and retrieving, on any terrain. Of an affectionate and sensitive nature, it develops a close relationship with its owner, to whom it becomes very attached. Its general appearance is elegant despite its closely-knit structure. The head has a rounded skull and square muzzle, with a well-defined but gently sloping stop and short, triangular ears, set high and hanging close to the head. The eyes, the mucous membranes and tip of the nose should be very dark, if not black. The neck, of medium length, slopes elegantly down and is free from dewlap. The sturdy, muscular body rests on solid, straight legs. The Brittany Spaniel is often born without a tail, but if it should have one it is docked at no more than 10 cm (4 in) from the root. The coat is fairly fine, dense, flat and slightly wavy, thicker on the throat, belly and backs of the legs.

Weight: dogs 15 kg (33 lb); bitches 13 kg (28½ lb). Height: dogs 48–50 cm (19–19½ in); bitches 47–49 cm (18½–19 in). Colour: brown and white, orange and white, black and white.
Country of Origin: France.

French Spaniel

This dog is the parent of all the French spaniels. Its origins probably lie in the ancient "quail hound" which came to France and then Germany from Spain, giving rise to various native breeds. The French Spaniel is a long-haired pointing dog, medium to large in size, hardy and intelligent, a good swimmer and fine hunter, particularly on rough ground, less so on the flat, where its lack of speed means it compares unfavourably with other dogs. It has a sensitive nose and is patient and persevering in seeking out the quarry, and also makes a good retriever. Intelligent and faithful, it has an excellent temperament. The head is strong and massive but not unduly so, the stop well defined, the eyes large and dark amber in colour, and the ears set back at the level of the eye, hanging close to the head. The strong neck is of medium length, the chest well let down to the elbow, and the hindquarters well developed. The legs are sturdy, with oval, rather compact feet and resistant, elastic pads. The general appearance is of strength and elegance. The coat is long, soft and smooth, with slightly wavy hair feathering on the legs, ears, tail and neck.

Weight: 25–30 kg (55–66 lb). Height: dogs 55–65 cm (21½–25½ in); bitches 54–58 cm (21–22½ in). Colour: white with brown markings of various sizes (with or without flecking).
Country of Origin: France.

Picardy Spaniel

The Picardy Spaniel is another descendant of the French Spaniel, officially recognized as a breed in 1904. Some experts still tend to consider it a variety of the French, the only real differences being the smaller size and the colour of the coat. The Picardy is an excellent hunter, a good pointer and retriever over any ground. It has a good nose and is affectionate and demonstrative, obedient, cautious and patient, sensitive and easy to train. The characteristics described in the standard are practically identical to those of the French. There are two varieties of the Picardy, differentiated by the colour of the coat. The brown and white Picardy is of slightly heavier build, less swift, and suited to any terrain, whereas the Blue Picardy is lighter, swifter, and at its best on marshland. Both dogs are elegant and attractive in appearance, with a calm, steady expression, proud of bearing and solidly but not heavily built. The silky coat is fairly thick, slightly wavy, finer on the head and thicker in winter.

Weight: approximately 25 kg (55 lb). Height: 55–60 cm ($21\frac{1}{2}$–$23\frac{1}{2}$ in) (dogs up to 62 cm [24 in]). Colour: speckled grey with brown markings, head and legs often fawn. Blue Picardy: speckled black and grey.
Country of Origin: France.

Pont-Audemer Spaniel

The Pont-Audemer is a cross between the French and the Irish Water Spaniel, from which it has inherited its curly coat and the strange topknot on its head as well as the webbed feet typical of water dogs. Indeed the Pont-Audemer is a setting water spaniel, a skilful hunter on both marsh and woodland, but not so well suited to the flat because of its inferior scenting powers. Although rarely found outside Picardy and Normandy, it is a very intelligent and courageous dog, resistant to fatigue, cold and damp, patient and persevering. Furthermore it is faithful, affectionate and very attached to its owner, easily adapting to family life. This medium-sized spaniel has a hardy constitution, with a solid frame and well-developed limbs. The head is large but in proportion, with a round skull, slight stop, and a long muzzle with a roman nose. The eyes are small and dark and the ears long and pendant, set low and covered with curls which form a topknot on the skull. The neck is light but sturdy, free from dewlap, and the loins arched, with a powerful croup, the hallmark of a good galloper. The legs are strong, with round, broad, compact feet. The tail is set high, carried straight and docked to about a third of its original length. The coat is coarse, rough and glossy, with curls all over the body except on the muzzle, where it is short and fine. Because of the dog's association with water, the coat is naturally waterproof.

Weight: approximately 20 kg (44 lb). Height: 52–58 cm (20½–23 in). Colour: brown and roan, grey, brown and white, solid brown.
Country of Origin: France.

Korthals
Pointing Wire-haired Griffon

The Korthals owes its name to its creator, who developed it by crossing a woolly-haired dog with a short-haired one. The breeder, a Dutchman by birth who moved to the province of Hesse in Germany, used breeds from northern France rather than Germany as his basic stock so that, although the Korthals was actually developed in Germany, to all intents and purposes it is a French dog. It is of medium size, rugged in appearance, and a very fine retriever as well as pointer, on any terrain. Patient, persevering in the search for game, with a keen nose, intelligent and full of stamina, it also has a pleasant, affectionate nature, and shows great fondness for its owner. It should undergo firm, serious training from an early age to ensure an obedient, docile animal. The Korthals has a long, large head with a well-defined stop, long, straight, square muzzle, large brown eyes and medium-sized ears, set at eye level and hanging close to the head. The neck is rather long in spite of the dog's name (in Dutch korthals means short neck), and the body is sturdy, powerful and fairly long, with slight tuck-up of the belly. The legs are strong and solid, suited to prolonged running, with cat-like feet. The coat is thick, short, wiry and somewhat tousled or wavy, forming a long moustache and eyebrows on the head.

Weight: approximately 25 kg (55 lb). Height: dogs 55–60 cm (21½–23½ in); bitches 50–55 cm (19½–21½ in). Colour: steel grey with chestnut markings, chestnut, chestnut-roan. Brown and white and orange and white also allowed.
Country of Origin: France.

Boulet
Pointing Long-coated Griffon

The Boulet, also known as the *Griffon à poil laineaux*, owes its name to the breeder Emmanuel Boulet, who probably developed it from crossing poodles and sheepdogs. The pointing long-coated Griffon is a dog of medium size, solid and well built, rugged in appearance, very resistant to fatigue and extremes of weather. It is a good hunter endowed with a sensitive nose, able to cope with any terrain. Bred for pointing, it can also be trained to retrieve. The head is large and long, the length of the skull equal to its width, with straight foreface, large eyes beneath heavy brows, and medium-sized ears set at eye level and hanging close to the head. The Boulet has a moderately long neck, broad chest well let down to the level of the elbow, and a long body, with slightly arched loins, a powerful back and moderate belly tuck-up. The legs are muscular, have a solid bone structure, with long feet and toes well covered with hair. The tail hangs down, with a slight curve at the tip. The coat is soft, almost silky to the touch, not glossy, smooth or slightly wavy with feathering on the tail, chest, belly and backs of the legs.

Weight: approximately 25 kg (55 lb). Height: dogs 55–60 cm (21½–23½ in); bitches 50–55 cm (19½–21½ in). Colour: dead leaf brown.
Country of Origin: France.

Italian Spinone

The Spinone is a kind of pointing coarse-haired griffon, whose origins are closely linked to those of all European griffons. It is a medium to large dog, slightly bigger than its French and German cousins, a skilled swimmer even in deep, icy water, resistant to fatigue and all climates, with a rugged appearance which is not without a certain elegance. The Spinone has an excellent temperament, docile, obedient and friendly, adapting well to family life provided that it is often taken out and allowed to run about so that it does not put on weight. The head is long, with an oval skull, straight or slightly convex foreface, and a fairly well-defined but gently sloping stop. The eyes are large and wide open, with a sweet, friendly expression, and the triangular ears are set high and hang down. The neck is strong and muscular, with a suggestion of dewlap. The body is square in outline, sturdy and solid but not thick-set, with a broad, deep chest, wide back, slightly arched loins and very muscular rump. The tail, which is a continuation of the rump, is carried horizontal and docked at approximately 20 cm (8 in). The legs are muscular and sinewy with a solid bone structure. The feet are small, round, strongly knuckled up and covered with hair, with resistant pads. The coat is coarse, thick, wiry and fairly close, with a slight curl, approximately 4–6 cm ($1\frac{1}{2}$–$2\frac{1}{2}$ in) long, shorter on the nose, ears and head but with longer, coarser hair on the eyebrows, cheeks and lips.

Weight: dogs 32–37 kg ($70\frac{1}{2}$–$81\frac{1}{2}$ lb); bitches 28–32 kg (62–$70\frac{1}{2}$ lb). Height: dogs 60–70 cm ($23\frac{1}{2}$–$27\frac{1}{2}$ in); bitches 58–65 cm (23–$25\frac{1}{2}$ in). Colour: white, white with orange or chestnut markings or spots.
Country of Origin: Italy.

Bracco Italiano
Italian Gundog

The Italian Bracco is a typical pointer, held in high
esteem since ancient times as is evident from the
references to it in writings of the fourth and fifth
centuries B.C. Yet the breed is undoubtedly even
older and the remoteness of its origins gives scope
to a number of different theories. The most probable is that it sprang from a union between the
Molossus and the Egyptian Hound also known as
the Egyptian coursing hound. In temperament the
Bracco is docile, prudent, obedient, faithful and
attached to its owner. It is intelligent and responsive, and therefore easily trained. The general
conformation is well balanced and strong, its gait
agile and fairly swift, with a long, skimming stride.
The powerful musculature means it has great
stamina, but the dog cannot match the lighter and
more agile Pointer and Setter in speed. It has an
intelligent and sober face, with a pensive air,
particularly when the dog frowns and the skin falls
into its characteristic folds. The head is long and
angular, with fairly prominent orbital arches and a
straight or slightly convex foreface, its large nose
toning with the coat colour. The eyes are fairly
large, with a gentle, docile expression and their
colour also depends on that of the coat. The long,
soft ears are a characteristic feature, set low and
well back, and hang in a fold very close to the
cheek. The neck is strong and quite short, the
brisket wide and deep, the chest broad and the back
muscular, with sturdy croup and very slight tuck-
up of the belly. The tail is carried horizontal or
slightly lowered and is docked to 15–25 cm (6–10 in).
The legs are strong, with large, sturdy, rounded feet
and arched, tightly closed toes. The coat is short,
thick and glossy, shorter on the head, shoulders
and thighs.

Weight: 25–40 kg (55–88 lb). Height: 55–67 cm
(21½–26½ in). Colour: chestnut-roan, orange and
white, white, white speckled with brown, orange or
amber.
Country of Origin: Italy.

German Short-haired Pointer
Kurzhaar

The German Short-haired Pointer, like all its fellow pointers, is descended from the old Spanish Pointer. It was first crossed with the Bloodhound and then with the Pointer to produce its present form which is considerably lighter than the original. As a result, this dog has retained the muscular power of its progenitor, yet gained in grace and speed. Both an excellent setter and gundog, it is suited to any type of terrain and game, has a superb nose, and is intelligent, faithful and can be affectionate. However, it must be trained methodically and firmly from the start to make the most of its excellent qualities. The head is long and clean-cut, with a moderately defined stop, slight curve of foreface, and a slim muzzle with a pointed nose. The brown eyes have a lively expression and the ears are of medium length, set high and back, hanging close to the head and with rounded tips. The neck is long,

strong, elegant and free from dewlap. The body is muscular with a solid bone structure, well balanced on all points, and its movements are quick and agile. The back slopes gently down and the tuck-up at the loins is marked. The legs are lean, sturdy and sinewy, with strong, tight round feet and strong, hard pads. The coat is short and thick, hard and rough to the touch, shorter and softer on the head and ears. There is no excess of skin on the body, and no forming of wrinkles.

Weight: 25–30 kg (55–66 lb). Height: dogs 60–65 cm ($23\frac{1}{2}$–$25\frac{1}{2}$ in); bitches 58–60 cm (23–$23\frac{1}{2}$ in). Colour: liver, liver and white spotted or ticked, light or dark roan with brown head, white with brown mask, markings and flecks.
Country of Origin: Germany.

German Wire-haired Pointer
Drahthaar

The Drahthaar, whose name literally means "wire hair", was developed by German breeders specializing in creating rough-coated dogs, and is the result of crossing a woolly-haired dog (Poodle) with a short-haired dog (German Short-haired Pointer). Very similar to the Korthals Griffon, it differs mainly in that it is larger and the similarity with the pointer – particularly the prominence of the occipital bone – is more marked. The Drahthaar is a medium to large dog, fiery in temperament, excellent over any ground, whether pointing or retrieving, very courageous, resistant to cold, heat and damp, and has a remarkable nose. It is faithful and very attached to its owner, with whom it is docile and affectionate, whereas it is aloof and sometimes apprehensive, slow to make friends with strangers. It is intelligent and responsive, and therefore easy to train. It is slim and elegant in appearance, and the dog's movements are free and flowing, though not lacking in energy and vigour. The head is well proportioned, with a strong muzzle and moustache, a broad, domed skull, pronounced stop and curved foreface. The eyes are dark with a lively expression, and the high-set ears hang flat and forward. The muscular neck forms a graceful line with the body, which is of medium length with broad, deep brisket, slight belly tuck-up, and sturdy, lean, strong, straight legs, with almost oval feet, flatter than those of the Korthals. The coat is very harsh, wiry, thick and close-lying, without undercoat, short on the lower legs and feet, and forming a beard and eyebrows on the head.

Weight: 35–40 kg (77–88 lb). Height: dogs 60–67 cm (23½–26 in); bitches 56–62 cm (22–24 in). Colour: dark brown, brown, iron grey, brown roan.
Country of Origin: Germany.

89

German Long-haired Pointer
Langhaar

The Langhaar is a German pointer whose origins lie in spaniel stock. The breed is little known outside Germany, and so rare even in its homeland that it has come near to extinction several times. It is a dog of medium size, versatile in its work but fairly slow, with an unremarkable nose. Docile, affectionate, obedient and even-tempered, it makes a very good household pet. Its body structure is elegant, though powerful and muscular. The head is long, with a round skull and little stop, level foreface, brown eyes and broad, pendant, rounded ears. The neck is strong and lean and the body solid, set on sturdy limbs with long, narrow feet. The tail is curved at the tip and slightly docked. The coat is glossy, slightly waved, and approximately 5 cm (2 in) long, shorter on the head and forming feathering on the tail and backs of the legs.

Weight: approximately 30 kg (66 lb). Height: 60–66 cm ($23\frac{1}{2}$–$25\frac{1}{2}$ in). Colour: chestnut, brown and white spotted or flecked.
Country of Origin: Germany.

Weimaraner
Weimar Pointer

The Weimaraner is of German origin, but is also very well known and highly revered in America, and it undoubtedly stems from the German Short-haired Pointer, whom it closely resembles in appearance, ability and temperament. It was developed in the middle of the seventeenth century, either by, or a least under the guidance of, the dukes of Saxony and Weimar according to a breeding programme which, though not scientifically documented, led to a characteristic unique among hunting dogs – the solid silver grey colour of the coat – becoming part of the hereditary pattern. The Weimaraner is a sturdy, hardy dog, affectionate and docile, and very easily trained. It has a sensitive, refined nose, and adapts to any type of terrain and any game. It should present a picture of great elegance and distinction, a dog of perfect proportions on all points. The head is long, not very broad, with a moderate stop and straight or slightly convex foreface. The eyes are amber in colour (blue in puppies) and the ears broad and soft, set high and hanging down but not too close to the head. The neck is long, clean-cut and well arched; the body strong and muscular, but should never appear heavy. The tail is carried straight and docked to two or three joints shortly after birth. The legs are long, muscular and straight, with rather large, round, compact feet. The coat is normally soft and smooth, but there are short, hard, rough, or long-coated varieties, though these are more rare.

Weight: 23–28 kg (50½–61½ lb). Height: dogs 59–70 cm (23–27½ in); bitches 57–65 cm (22½–25½ in). Colour : silver grey, roe grey, mouse grey and intermediate shades.
Country of Origin: Germany.

Large and Small Munsterlander

The two Munsterlanders are named after the town of Münster in Westphalia, where they are still very popular. The first to appear was the small variety, which could be considered a German Brittany Spaniel, given the resemblance between the two dogs both in size and coat. It probably sprang from a union between the French Spaniel and the German Langhaar, and for a long time acted as a sheepdog and gundog for large game because of its considerable speed and great courage. Nowadays, however, it is mainly used to hunt fowl, particularly quail, and has earned the nickname of "quail dog". Very hardy, brave, intelligent, docile and friendly, it excels on any type of terrain, alone or in a pack. The Small Munsterlander is the smallest of all the German setters, and is not well known outside its country of origin. In general appearance it is a solid yet elegant dog, sturdy but light. The head is long with a slightly rounded skull, poorly defined stop and long, straight or marginally curved foreface. The eyes are light and the triangular ears are set high, hanging close to the head. The neck is muscular and not very long; the chest deep and broad; and the croup straight and well developed, with considerable tuck-up of the belly. The legs are solid, sturdy and straight, with compact, strongly knuckled-up feet. The coat is smooth and close-lying, slightly wavy on the ears and croup, but not curly, with feathering on the tail, belly and backs of the forelegs. The Large Munsterlander is ten years younger than its smaller brother, and its origins are somewhat unclear. It is very similar to the small variety both in physical appearance and in character and ability, and, like its smaller relation, is also a very versatile animal, a natural multi-purpose gundog, at home in pointing and retrieving, but also an excellent guard dog. Because of their equable temperaments, the two Munsterlanders are prized as pets and companions.

Weight: Small: 20 kg (44 lb); Large: no fixed weight. Height: Small: 48–52 cm (19–20½ in); Large: 55–65 cm (21½–25½ in). Colour. Small: all colours allowed, white roan with chestnut or ochre markings most common; Large: white with large black markings and black or blue flecking.
Country of Origin: Germany.

Large Munsterlander

Small Munsterlander

Spanish Pointer
Perdiguero de Burgos

The Spanish Pointer is a very ancient breed of dog, known and used in Spain from long ago, which, perhaps because of the high esteem in which it has always been held, has retained its purity to a much greater extent than other Spanish breeds. The Spanish Pointer has a similar background to that of kindred breeds. All pointers seem to derive from crosses between the Egyptian Hound and the Assyrian Mastiff. These crosses then spread throughout Europe, and their common characteristics gradually diversified either as a result of the action of the environment or the intervention of man, giving rise to the different breeds nowadays considered indigenous. The Spanish Pointer is not very well known outside Spain, not because it lacks ability but because local breeds are preferred elsewhere. In Spain it is the most popular gundog, esteemed for its sporting qualities and its temperament. It is very resistant to fatigue and variations of climate and works extremely well in all kinds of country and with all kinds of game, a natural pointer but also easily trained to retrieve. It has a very keen nose and is docile, patient and affectionate. It gives the impression of being a fairly heavy dog, mainly because of the large head and fairly short neck, which has a small amount of dewlap. The skull is slightly domed; it has a slight stop and a long, square muzzle. The body is fairly long, with slight tuck-up of the belly and solid, muscular legs. The tail should be docked by one-third of its length. The coat is short and thick.

Weight: 25–30 kg (55–66 lb). Height: approximately 70 cm (27½ in). Colour: white with patches and flecks of liver or vice versa. Country of Origin: Spain.

Ibizan Hound

The Ibizan Hound is a dog of the greyhound type, a native of the Balearic Islands, created by crossing the Sloughi with the Provençal Sheepdog. It belongs to a group of dogs of the Iberian peninsula which also includes the three varieties of Portuguese Warren Hound, the large, medium and small. They all specialize in the hunting of small game and are very agile and swift, cunning and of a lively, often aggressive and quarrelsome temperament, and therefore not very easy to train. The Ibizan Hound has a long, narrow head and body, and its excellent nose enables it to hunt by night. The eyes are small and slanting and the ears fairly large, broad at the base, erect and pricked forward. The neck is thin and arched, the rump sloping and the belly tucked up. The tail is set low and carried sickle-like in action. The coat can either be smooth and hard, or long and rough.

Weight: dogs 22 kg (48½ lb); bitches 19 kg (42 lb). Height: dogs 60–65 cm (23½–25½ in); bitches 57–63 cm (22½–24½ in). Colour: white marked with red or fawn, white, red, fawn.
Country of Origin: Spain.

Portuguese Pointer
Perdigueiro Português

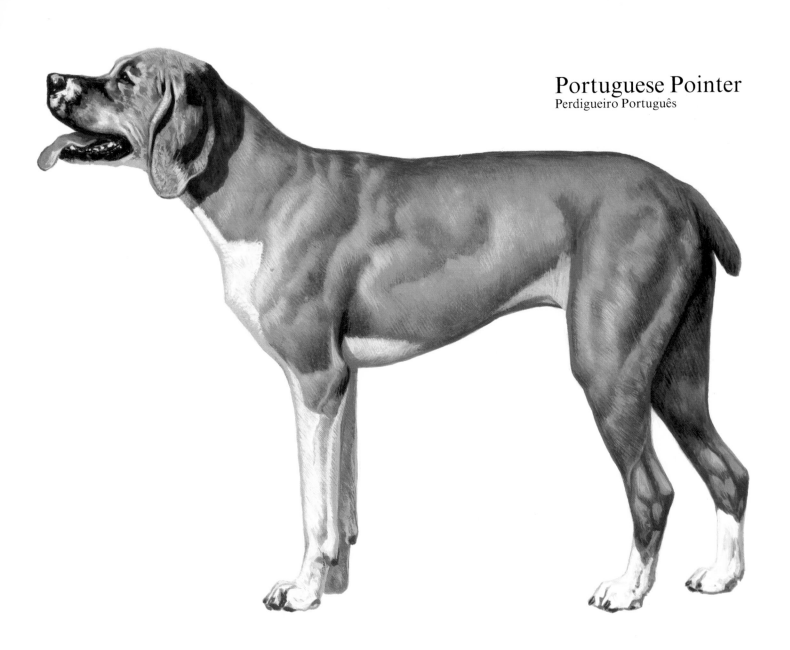

The Portuguese Pointer shares the origins of the other pointers, and resembles most closely the Italian Bracco, despite the inevitable diversification which has occurred during the evolutionary process. Like the Spanish Pointer, this dog has gained little recognition outside its own region and is almost unknown elsewhere. It has a natural hunting instinct, and works well on any type of terrain and with any kind of game. Its muscular build gives it considerable stamina but it is somewhat lacking in speed, although this is compensated for by its patience and perseverance in searching out the quarry, its superb nose and the perfect bond it establishes with its master, to whom it can become so exclusively attached that it resents the presence of other dogs. The Portuguese Pointer has a large but not disproportionate head, with a pronounced stop and level foreface. The eyes are chestnut, with an intelligent, thoughtful expression. The ears are soft, thin, set low and well back, and hang close to the head. The body is long, muscular with a sturdy frame, but the dog does not give an impression of coarseness or heaviness. The legs are sinewy but not very long, making this pointer slightly smaller than kindred breeds. The tail is straight, thick, set low and docked by two-thirds of its length. The coat is short, thick, even and soft on the head and ears.

Weight: 20–27 kg (44–59½ lb). Height: dogs 56 cm (22 in); bitches 52 cm (20½ in). Colour: yellow, brown, self-coloured or flecked.
Country of Origin: Portugal.

Hungarian Vizsla

The Hungarian Vizsla is a sporting dog which may be the result of interbreeding between different types of pointer imported from neighbouring regions. Its background and its origins are so obscure that the theories put forward border almost on legend. Certainly the German Short-haired Pointer, or more likely the Weimaraner whom it closely resembles, and the Pointer have assisted in its make-up. The Vizsla, though little known outside its own country, is a superb gundog, deserving greater appreciation and recognition. It is intelligent, quick to learn, obedient, affectionate, sensitive and easy to train provided that it is treated with kindness and an awareness of its sensitivity. It is suited to any type of game and any terrain, well able to retrieve as well as point. The Vizsla is a dog of medium size, with an elegant, well-proportioned build and a swift, light-footed gait. The head is gently domed, with a broad skull and only a slight drop to the muzzle which is long, straight and well squared. The eyes are dark, with a lively, intelligent expression and the ears, set quite high, are soft and hang close to the cheeks. The body is muscular, with a broad back, short, firm loins, long, broad croup and moderate belly tuck-up. The long legs have a light but solid bone structure to which the strong muscles are attached by very resistant tendons. The feet are round and well knit, with well-formed toes. The coat is short, close to the body, dense, smooth and glossy.

Weight: 22–28 kg (48½–61½ lb). Height: dogs 57–62 cm (22½–24½ in); bitches 53–58 cm (21–23 in). Colour: various shades of dark sandy yellow, without markings.
Country of Origin: Hungary.

Český Fousek

The Český Fousek is a hunting dog of the hound type, a native of Czechoslovakia, probably developed from local dogs crossed with the German Short-haired Pointer. Little known outside its country of origin, it has been in danger of extinction several times. The Český is a fairly intelligent dog, hardy and able to withstand fatigue and variations of climate, a good hunter over any type of terrain and with any game, a good swimmer, and skilled both at setting and retrieving, even in ponds and marshes. It is elegant though rugged in appearance, agile and quick to react. It has both an affectionate nature and an impulsive and independent streak, which means that it should be trained with great firmness in order to bring out its excellent qualities. The head is long and lean, with a flat skull, slightly curved foreface and fairly pronounced stop. The eyes are dark and gentle, the ears set back and dropped, of good length and with rounded tips. The neck is strong and of medium length, the back arched and the loins straight. The croup is muscular, the chest broad and deep and the underline fairly well tucked up. The legs are long, lean, sound and straight, with compact, rounded feet and resistant pads. The tail is docked at three-fifths of its length. The coat consists of a very short, thick undercoat, no more than 1.5 cm ($\frac{1}{2}$ in) in length, and a dense, rough outer coat approximately 3–4 cm (1–1$\frac{1}{2}$ in) in length, with tufts of hair up to 7 cm (2$\frac{3}{4}$ in) in length. There are none of these tufts on the head and ears, although the muzzle has a long, thick beard.

Weight: dogs 28–34 kg (61$\frac{1}{2}$–75 lb); bitches 22–28 kg (48$\frac{1}{2}$–61$\frac{1}{2}$ lb).
Height: dogs 60–66 cm (23$\frac{1}{2}$–26 in); bitches 58–62 cm (23–24$\frac{1}{2}$ in).
Colour: white base with brown patches and flecks, brown without any markings.
Country of Origin: Czechoslovakia.

97

HUNTING BREEDS

Gundogs

This group covers those dogs which all possess a sharp nose and, more important, have a natural tendency to retrieve game which has been shot down, whether on land or often in very cold, deep water. Apart from this, their characteristics and origins are very varied: it is not an homogenous group like that of the hound or pointer. These gundogs are resistant to fatigue and extremes of weather, and are tenacious, hardy, intelligent and easy to train. Their coat is always thick, never short, and has a waterproof undercoat.

Labrador Retriever

The Labrador Retriever is classed as a member of the "Sporting Dogs" group in England. The breed is native to the island of Newfoundland and later moved to Labrador, but it was in England, where the natural retrieving ability of this dog was highly prized, that it underwent rigorous selection. A powerful swimmer, it is especially suited to retrieving small and medium-sized feathered game in marshy country but is also capable of distinguishing itself on other terrain, being easy to train from an early age. It is very resistant to fatigue and extremes of weather, and is patient, docile, obedient, attached to its owner and faithful, as well as highly intelligent and responsive. The body is strongly and solidly built; it has a broad, square head, well-defined stop, dark eyes and triangular ears with pointed tips, hanging close to the head. The neck is powerful, strong and muscular like the rest of the body, so that the dog appears massive and yet retains a certain elegance. The legs are solid and well developed with round, compact feet, arched toes and well-developed pads. The characteristic tail is strong, free from feathering, thick at the root and tapering gradually towards the tip, and covered with thick, close-lying hair, hence its name of "otter tail". The coat is flat, short, close, dense, quite hard and straight, with a weather-resistant undercoat which gives the dog complete protection from the water.

Weight: 25–32 kg (55–70½ lb). Height: dogs 55–60 cm (21½–23½ in); bitches 54–56 cm (21–22 in). Colour: black, liver, yellow, cream. Country of Origin: Great Britain.

Flat-coated Retriever

Curly-coated Retriever

The Flat-coated and Curly-coated Retrievers are gundogs which are classed as separate breeds but actually have such similar standards that some experts still consider them to be varieties of the same breed. The only obvious differences lie in their coat and in the Flat-coated's lighter build. Theories about their origins are, as usual, complicated and sometimes conflicting. One of their ancestors was possibly the Newfoundland, which was brought to England towards the middle of the nineteenth century, where it was then crossed with Irish Setters, Irish Water Spaniels and Poodles. As their names suggest, these two dogs make first-class retrievers over any ground, particularly of feathered game. English breeders carefully selected their stock to develop the sort of dog which would work together with their famous pointing dogs, the Pointer and the Setter, since the English hunter prefers to use specialized rather than all-purpose dogs. Both retrievers are medium to large in size, hardy and impervious to fatigue and the worst weather, easy to train, intelligent and responsive, lively, affectionate, faithful and attached to their owners, and adapt to family life provided that they are allowed plenty of space to move about freely. These two very beautiful dogs have a solid but well-proportioned frame perfectly combined with strong, powerful muscles, giving an overall effect of balance, elegance and agility. In both retrievers the head is large but nicely in proportion with the rest of the body, long and well chiselled, with a moderately broad, domed skull, straight or sometimes slightly convex foreface and fairly pronounced, though not too steep, drop from forehead to muzzle. The medium-sized eyes are generally dark with a keen, intelligent expression, and the ears rather small, lying close to the head. The neck is fairly long, sturdy and free from dewlap; the chest wide and deep. The body is long and relatively low. This in no way detracts from the overall balance, and is positive from a functional viewpoint in that it allows the dog a more rapid gait and longer stride. The strong croup and muscular thighs enable the retriever to keep up its stride even over long and uneven stretches. The feet are large and broad, perfectly adapted to swimming (at which both retrievers excel), with arched toes and hard, elastic pads. The coat is the characteristic feature which differentiates the two types. The Flat-coated Retriever has flat, dry, glossy, medium-length hair, with ample feathering on the chest, belly, tail and backs of the forelegs; whereas the Curly-coated Retriever has a short, thick, curly coat, strongly reminiscent of astrakhan. The coat of both dogs is waterproof, enabling them to remain in the water for long periods, even when it is deep and cold.

Weight: Flat-coated 32 kg (70½ lb); Curly-coated 32–36 kg (70½–79½ lb). Height: Flat-coated maximum 65 cm (25½ in) (adult dog); Curly-coated 50–66 cm (19½–26 in). Colour: black or liver in both.
Country of Origin: Great Britain.

Golden Retriever

The Golden Retriever is a very popular English dog, whose origins are still the subject of some controversy. The most probable theory is that it developed from the Russian Retrievers, native to the Caucasus, crossed with the Bloodhound. It seems unlikely that it is related to the Labrador Retriever, despite sharing the latter's superb swimming ability and love of water. The Golden Retriever is of elegant appearance, though a powerfully built dog. The body is long and does not stand very high in the leg, making it rectangular in profile. The head is well proportioned, with a broad, arched skull and strong muzzle, very well-defined stop, dark, gentle eyes and medium-sized ears set high and hanging flat against the head. The neck is moderately long, clean and muscular, and the long body has a straight back, with slight tuck-up of the belly. The legs are solid, with rounded, cat-like feet. Because of its body structure, the Golden Retriever is a very hardy dog, splendid in marshy country but also easy to train on other types of ground. Docile, affectionate and patient, it makes an ideal child's playmate. The coat is of medium length and flat or slightly wavy, short on the head and ears, with feathering on the tail, chest, backs of the forelegs and under the belly. The undercoat is thick and abundant.

Weight: dogs 29–32 kg (64–70½ lb); bitches 25–27 kg (55–59½ lb). Height: dogs 56–61 cm (22–24 in); bitches 51–56 cm (20–22 in). Colour: any shade of gold or cream.
Country of Origin: Great Britain.

Chesapeake Bay Retriever

The Chesapeake Bay Retriever is named after the wide stretch of the North Atlantic Ocean along the eastern coast of Maryland and Virginia in the United States of America. The breed is native to America, and was developed by clever crossbreeding between the Flat-coated and Curly-coated Retrievers; the Newfoundland is one of its more remote ancestors. The Chesapeake Bay Retriever is a medium to large dog, very resistant to fatigue and adverse weather conditions, courageous, tenacious and an excellent swimmer, which makes it best suited to marsh hunting. Intelligent, alert, faithful and good-natured, it makes an excellent companion. It is a powerful, heavy-set animal, with a broad head and slightly domed skull, steep stop and straight or slightly curved foreface. The eyes are small with a gentle expression, and the ears comparatively small and triangular, with rounded tips. The neck is slim and free from dewlap; the body is sturdy and long, set on strong legs with large, webbed feet. The coat is thick, short and slightly curly on the back; and the undercoat dense, oily to the touch and completely waterproof, enabling the dog to remain even in icy water for long periods.

Weight: 25–34 kg (55–75 lb). Height: dogs 58–66 cm (23–26 in); bitches 53–61 cm (21–24 in). Colour: dark chestnut, light fawn, straw colour.
Country of Origin: U.S.A.

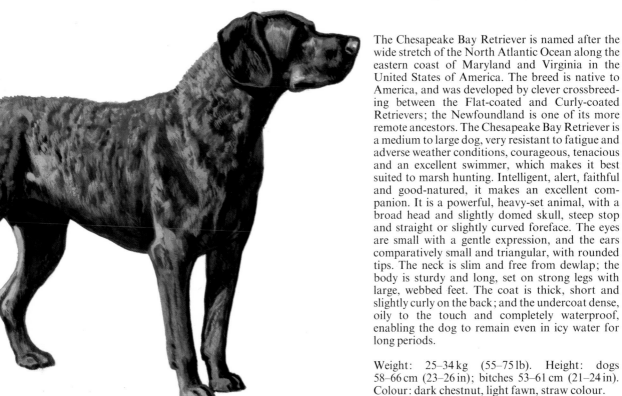

English Cocker Spaniel

The nationality, origins and special abilities of the English Cocker Spaniel are all summed up in its name. Developed in England from the large hunting spaniels crossed with small King Charles and Blenheims (toy spaniels), it belongs to the group of "land spaniels" rather than "water spaniels". The English Cocker Spaniel was established as a separate breed towards the end of the last century (1893), and until then had formed part of a large group which included the present Springer, Sussex and Field Spaniels. The attribute of "cocker" arises from its particular aptitude for hunting woodcock. Its hunting abilities show to their best advantage in the undergrowth, which it is small enough to penetrate with ease in order to flush out the game sheltering there, whereas its inability to build up any great speed makes it

unsuited for work on open ground. It is also an excellent swimmer and well able to retrieve game from water, no matter how deep. The English Cocker Spaniel is a highly intelligent, lively dog, very affectionate, faithful and attached to its owner, and should be treated and trained with great kindness and firmness from a very early age if it is not to become disobedient or nervous. Its outstanding ability and unquestionable beauty have made the Cocker a great favourite all over the world not only as a gundog but also as a pet and companion, and it has become one of the best known breeds outside specialist circles. The Cocker, though small, is sturdily built, with strong muscles, rendering it very agile and hardy. The head reveals its spaniel ancestry, with the broad, arched, evenly developed skull and long, straight muzzle like

that of the setter. The eyes are large and dark with a very gentle expression, and the long pendant ears, set low (but not lower than the line of the nose), are soft and fine. The neck is of moderate length, sturdy and slightly arched, the chest deep and wide, and the loins powerful, with muscular croup. The strong, straight forelegs and hind legs with their long, muscular thighs are short in relation to the length of the body, but without creating a low-bodied effect. The Cocker should present an overall picture of balance and elegance. The feet are compact, rounded and not too big, with arched, strongly knuckled-up toes. The tail is set low and docked to two-fifths of its original length a few days after birth; its constant wagging is a characteristic feature. The Cocker's coat is one of its main attractions; silky and smooth, or slightly wavy, it is of medium length all over the body except on the head, forming abundant feathering on the long ears, chest, backs of the legs and underneath the belly.

Weight: 13–14 kg (28½–31 lb). Height: dogs approximately 40 cm (16 in); bitches 38–39 cm (15–15½ in). Colour: self-coloured (all shades of black, red, fawn, gold, cream), black or brown and tan, tricolour, flecked.
Country of Origin: Great Britain.

American Cocker Spaniel

The American Cocker Spaniel is one of the smallest "hunting spaniels", and though it possesses the hunting ability typical of this group of dogs, it is nowadays more of a pet. A direct descendant of the English Cocker, it has retained so many of the latter's general characteristics that it might pass for its smaller brother. As in the case of the Collie and the Shetland, the two official standards are so similar that the only sure way of telling them apart is the size, which should never exceed the prescribed limits. The American Cocker is a dog of great beauty, intelligent, lively, affectionate, friendly and cheerful, quite noisy, and easy to train provided it is treated firmly and with kindness. Apart from size, it differs from the English Cocker in the more cleanly chiselled head, the slightly shorter muzzle, and the greater compactness of body structure. The eyes are large and the ears very long, which can create problems in that they attract foreign bodies and parasites. The coat is particularly attractive, more luxuriant and longer than the Cocker's, fine and silky to the touch, smooth or slightly wavy, short on the head, with profuse feathering on the ears, brisket, abdomen and backs of the legs. But the coat is never so long that it hides the lines and movements of the body, which is elegant and well balanced. The thick undercoat protects the dog from the cold and damp.

Weight: approximately 12 kg (26½ lb). Height: dogs 38 cm (15 in); bitches: 35 cm (14 in). Colour: black, black and tan, buff, fawn, cream, silver, black and white, orange and white.
Country of Origin: U.S.A.

English Springer Spaniel

The English Springer Spaniel belongs to the group of English "land dogs" and owes its name to the fact that it is trained to "spring" the birds from their hiding-places. The breed was developed in England and officially recognized in 1902. Its more remote ancestors are also those of the Cocker and the Setter, and it is undoubtedly related to Spanish dogs loosely defined as spaniels. The Springer is a dog of elegant, sturdy but not heavy build, very well known both in its homeland and elsewhere. Strong and hardy, excellent in undergrowth and marshland, a good retriever on land and in water, swifter than the Cocker and with a superb nose, it also has an excellent temperament, which makes it a popular pet. The Springer is the largest of the land spaniels, and is well proportioned and nicely balanced. The head is long with a fairly broad, slightly egg-shaped skull, an indefinite stop and a long, square muzzle. The eyes are dark hazel with a gentle expression, and the ears long, pendant and well covered with hair. The neck is strong and free from dewlap, the body well coupled, and the legs solid with rounded feet. The tail is set low and docked. The coat is long, thick, smooth or slightly wavy, and waterproof.

Weight: 22–25 kg (48½–55 lb). Height: approximately 50 cm (19½ in). Colour: liver, black, roan, brown (all with obligatory white markings), black or white with tan markings, black and white, liver and white (preferable).
Country of Origin: Great Britain.

Welsh Springer Spaniel

The Welsh Springer Spaniel is a breed of very ancient origin, undoubtedly related to the English Springer, from which it differs mainly in that it is smaller; indeed it is still considered by some to be a variety of the English breed. The two Springers were divided into separate breeds in 1902, when their respective standards were drawn up. The characteristics of the Welsh variety are practically identical to those of the English Springer. It is intelligent, lively, good in scrub and marshland, a fine retriever, full of stamina, with an excellent nose, active and fairly swift. It has a splendid temperament, affectionate, docile and loyal, which also makes it a much cherished pet. The Welsh Springer gives an impression of symmetry and elegance despite its solid, muscular frame. The head is long with an egg-shaped skull, little stop, and a straight, somewhat square muzzle. The eyes are dark and of medium size, the ears long and pendant. The neck is of medium length and free from dewlap; the body is long and solid, set on strong, fairly short legs, with compact, rounded feet. The coat is thick, flat, silky and close-lying, with feathering on the chest, belly and backs of the legs.

Weight: 18–22 kg (39½–48½ lb). Height: 45–48 cm (18–19 in). Colour: white with large red or orange markings.
Country of Origin: Great Britain.

Sussex Spaniel

Clumber Spaniel

This unmistakable spaniel is named after Clumber Castle in Nottinghamshire, where it was probably developed from crossing large spaniels with St Hubert Hounds and Basset Hounds. The Clumber Spaniel enjoyed a period of celebrity in England in the first decades of the nineteenth century, mainly thanks to the favour it found with the English monarchs. Nowadays, however, it is not common even in England and is little known elsewhere, with the result that the breed's numbers tend to fluctuate. The Clumber is an intelligent, hardy animal, resistant to fatigue and bad weather, suited to hunting in woods or marshes, but less good on the flat because of its lack of speed. Silent and tenacious, with an excellent nose, it usually works close to the hunter (about twenty yards away). It is friendly, calm and particularly suited for use in a pack, where it assumes the role of beater; its great patience also makes it eminently suitable for family life. It is a massive dog, powerful despite its modest size, its short legs making it longer than it is tall. The head is large, massive and square, broad between the ears and slightly domed, with a distinct, almost vertical stop, a roman nose, and heavy muzzle with well-developed but not pendulous flews. The eyes are dark amber in colour and slightly sunken, and the ears large, pendant and set low. The neck is muscular and free from dewlap, continuing gracefully into the long, solid body, which has powerful, slightly arched loins and muscular croup. The tail is set low and not very long; the feet large and rounded. The coat is thick, flat, silky, smooth or slightly wavy, with profuse feathering.

Weight: dogs 25–31 kg (55–68½ lb); bitches 20–27 kg (44–59½ lb). Height: 30–35 cm (12–14 in). Colour: pure white with lemon speckling on head and muzzle.
Country of Origin: Great Britain.

The Sussex Spaniel is another small, English "land dog", whose origins remain controversial. Very well known in its place of birth, some consider it a lighter offshoot of the Clumber Spaniel, and when first shown officially it was classified in the same category; it was only in the first years of the present century that it received recognition as a separate breed. Other experts have suggested that it may be descended from crosses between spaniels and hunting dogs of the hound type; it might well have inherited the colour of its coat and its characteristic way of barking from the latter. Of a lively and active disposition, the Sussex Spaniel is an intelligent, affectionate and faithful animal, not very easy to train, and its rather unfriendly attitude towards other dogs makes it unsuitable for hunting in a pack. It is rarely found outside England, being outshone by the Cocker which is a more versatile and useful dog. The Sussex Spaniel is attractive in appearance, elegant and well balanced in spite of its low-slung body. The head is well chiselled, with a broad, flat skull which has an indentation in the centre, a pronounced, straight stop, and fairly long muzzle. The large, hazel eyes have a kindly expression, and the thick, lobate ears are set low at eye level and hang close to the head. The neck is strong and slightly arched, with a hint of dewlap, the body long and the back straight with moderate tuck-up of the belly. The tail is set low and docked to a length of 20 cm (8 in). The legs are short and sturdy, with broad, round feet. The coat is thick, smooth or slightly wavy and of medium length, with abundant feathering.

Weight: 18 kg (39½ lb). Height: 25–32 cm (10–12½ in). Colour: golden liver (shaded on the legs).
Country of Origin: Great Britain.

Irish Water Spaniel

The Irish Water Spaniel, like the American Water Spaniel, is one of the "water dogs", related to the other spaniels but quite different in appearance. The Irish variety is of very ancient origin, and was selectively bred in England probably using dogs brought from Ireland. Its ancestors include the Barbet, the Irish Setter and perhaps even the Curly-coated Retriever, as well as spaniel root stock; it was shown for the first time in 1862, and the breed was officially recognized shortly after this. The Irish Water Spaniel is a dog of medium size, with great stamina and endurance, second to none in hunting and retrieving from water no matter how deep and icy, which it is capable of withstanding for long periods, being protected by a completely water-resistant coat. It is very intelligent, obedient and eager to learn, loyal and friendly, making a much-loved child's playmate. The Irish Water Spaniel is strongly and compactly built, sturdy but not heavy, and its unusual appearance is not without a certain elegance. The head is long with a high, domed skull and long, strong muzzle. The eyes are small and dark and the ears long, flat, rounded and set low. The neck is long, arched and free from dewlap, and the body sturdy and well ribbed-up, with a wide, deep brisket and powerful hindquarters. The legs are straight, solid and muscular, with broad, round, webbed feet. The tail is short, thick at the root and tapering to a point. The coat is dense, with thick tight curls covering the whole of the body, including the feet; a topknot of curls grows on the top of the head. Only the tail is covered in short hair. The undercoat is also oily and waterproof.

Weight: 22–26 kg (48½–57½ lb). Height: dogs 53–58 cm (21–23 in); bitches 51–56 cm (20–22 in). Colour: dark liver, verging on mahogany. Country of Origin: Great Britain.

HUNTING BREEDS

Tracking Dogs

Hounds are a fairly homogenous group of dogs of medium size, hardy and resistant, generally quite swift, endowed with an excellent nose and powerful bark. They are characteristic "scent hunters" whose long, broad ears help guide the smells from the ground to the nose. Some of them are capable of sniffing out trails several days old and smelling game a considerable distance away. Found practically all over the world, they are highly valued for their innate hunting abilities, their natural cleanliness and their generally docile, affectionate character. They are dignified and unobtrusive dogs of pleasing appearance.

Foxhound

The development of this breed arose, as its name implies, out of the need to create a dog suited to fox-hunting, a sport which replaced stag-hunting towards the fifteenth century, for which the Staghound had been used. A long, careful breeding programme was initiated to develop the present-day Foxhound from the Staghound, crossed with the Greyhound, terriers and possibly even the Bulldog. But this is only a theory, no matter how plausible, because no reliable documentation exists of the methods used to select the stock. Nowadays there are two varieties of Foxhound: the original English breed and its offshoot, the American Foxhound. The Foxhound is a very swift dog, second only to greyhounds in speed. It is not suited to hunting stag or roe-deer, but has proved to be particularly adept at hunting wild boar and is used for this to some extent in France. The Foxhound is an even-tempered, gregarious dog, particularly suited to hunting in a pack, where it shows great enthusiasm, individual effort and zeal, as well as demonstrating a strong team spirit when it is time for the pack to attack even the most ferocious of boar. This extraordinary hound, which bears a certain resemblance to the mastiff, has a solid, bony body structure, which emanates strength and stamina and gives it a swift, untiring gait. The head of the Foxhound is large but not disproportionately so, long and sturdy, with a broad skull, which is flat between the ears, and a straight muzzle. The lips are thick and droop slightly; the eyes large and dark with a gentle expression; the ears are set high, flat and thick, and hang close to the cheek. The neck is long, strong and clean, the chest quite deep, and the back long, broad and muscular, with powerful croup. The legs have a solid bone structure with heavy muscles, attached by strong, elastic tendons. The feet are round and cat-like. The tail is thick at the root tapering to a point, with a fine fringe of coarse hair and resembles a sabre. The coat is dense, short, coarse in texture and close-lying.

Weight: 35 kg (77 lb). Height: dogs 56–65 cm (22–25½ in); bitches 53–62 cm (21–24½ in). Colour: any colour allowed; most common: lemon and white, black and white, white and badger pied, tricolour with or without cape.
Country of Origin: Great Britain.

English Foxhound

American Foxhound

Beagle

The Beagle is the smallest English hound, and specializes in hare-hunting, either alone or in a pack. A dog of ancient origin, it won the favour of Queen Elizabeth I, who particularly liked the very small Beagles. This led to a variety below 30 cm (12 in), the Elizabeth Beagle, being established. Its bark has a characteristic bell-like tone and the sound made by a pack of these small dogs – so swift in relation to their size – is quite melodious. The Beagle is an intelligent, docile, good-natured and even-tempered dog which also makes a very popular pet. The Beagle has a large but not massive head, with a broad skull, flat on top, well-defined stop and relatively short but not flattened muzzle. The eyes are large and round, dark and expressive, and the ears rounded at the tip, broad, flat and set fairly high. The neck is very strong, and the body longer than it is high, solid and muscular, set on very sturdy, substantial legs. The coat is flat and dense, smooth or hard depending on the variety.

Weight: 17 kg (37½ lb); small size: 14 kg (31 lb). Height: 37–42 cm (14–16 in); small size: 30–36 cm (12–14 in). Colour: any colour allowed; most common: lemon and white, black and white, white and badger pied, tricolour with or without cape. Country of Origin: Great Britain.

Harrier

The Harrier is a small English hound bred to hunt hare, and also used to hunt fox in a pack. Fairly close to the Foxhound in general conformation, it also bears a strong resemblance to the Beagle, some of whose origins it shares. The modern Harrier is of fairly recent development, whereas the West Country Harrier, which is slightly larger and more like the French tracking dogs, is a very ancient breed to which many others may be traced. The Harrier is a very swift animal, best suited to even ground, and has an excellent nose. It is tenacious and persevering, intelligent and easy to train, and is also of equable temperament. It has a strong yet light body structure. The head is expressive, with a slightly domed skull, not very pronounced occiput, well-defined stop and level muzzle, equal in length to the skull. The eyes are small, the ears flat and V-shaped. The neck and body are strong and muscular; the legs sturdy, with the toes thick and close. The coat is smooth, not too short, close and even.

Weight: approximately 25 kg (55 lb). Height: 48–55 cm (19–21½ in). Colour: any colour allowed; most common: lemon and white, black and white, white and badger pied, tricolour with or without cape.
Country of Origin: Great Britain.

Otterhound

The Otterhound is of British nationality and very ancient origin, probably developed from crossing Bloodhounds, rough-haired Terriers, Harriers and possibly Griffons. A medium to large dog, with a massive, powerful structure, it is a good and fast swimmer, capable of pursuing otters for a long time, even in deep, icy water, and very adept at avoiding their sharp teeth. It has an exceptionally good nose which enables it to sniff out the otter in its underwater den and distinguish its smell even if mingled with other scents. Courageous, hardy, patient and affectionate, it also makes a good child's playmate. The influence of the Bloodhound is clearly visible in the Otterhound, particularly in the shape of the head, which is large, well formed and quite narrow, with a domed skull, well-defined stop, wide foreface and black nose. The flews are well developed and pendulous, and have thick whiskers. The eyes are fairly dark, with a drooping lower lid revealing the haw; the ears long, pendulous and set fairly low. The neck is strong, of medium length and with abundant dewlap; the body has a solid, muscular frame, with a wide, deep chest, very strong back, well-developed hindquarters and slight tuck-up of the belly. The tail reaches down to the hocks and is carried well up and in a curve, but not curled. The legs are straight, sturdy and muscular, with rounded, compact feet and resistant pads. The coat is of medium length, hard, rough and bushy, even all over the body, and covers a dense, woolly undercoat, which is oily to the touch and completely waterproof.

Weight: 30–35 kg (66–77 lb). Height: 60–65 cm ($23\frac{1}{2}$–$25\frac{1}{2}$ in). Colour: grizzle, white with grizzle or black, reddish, black and tan.
Country of Origin: Great Britain.

Grand Gascon Saintongeois or Virelade

This beautiful dog is a native of France and was developed in the second half of the last century by the Baron de Virelade, after whom it was named. The Grand Gascon Saintongeois originated from crosses between the Grand Bleu de Gascogne and the Saintongeois, and is therefore also a descendant of the black St Hubert Hound. It is a large dog with a fine nose, and its considerable speed makes it admirably suited to hunt with the horse, be it deer, hare or roebuck. Of a friendly and non-aggressive nature, it can also be used in a pack. It is very faithful to its owner, towards whom it can display great affection. Its light, graceful bearing gives it an air of nobility and pride. The head is long and dry, with an oval, not very broad skull, slight stop and pronounced occiput. The eyes are chestnut with a mild expression, and the ears are thin and slightly curled, set low but not as low as in the Grand Bleu. The neck is sturdy without being heavy and is moderately long. The body is long but more compact than that of the Grand Bleu, with a rounded back and more solid croup. The tail reaches down to the hocks and tapers to a point. The legs have strong bones and are muscular, with oval feet. The coat is thick and short, without undercoat.

Weight: approximately 35 kg (77 lb). Height: dogs 63–70 cm (24½–27½ in); bitches 60–65 cm (23½–25½ in). Colour: white with black spots and irregular markings.
Country of Origin: France.

Billy

The Billy is another French hound particularly adept at hunting large game such as deer and wild boar. It is a fairly recent breed, dating back no more than fifty years, and is named after the place where it was developed by Hublot du Rivault. The Billy was the result of crosses made between a number of breeds of dog which are now extinct, such as the orange and white Chien de Ceris, a hare-hunter; the Montain-boeuf, also orange and white, a hunter of wolf and wild boar; and the Larrye, an excellent hound with a reddish coat. The Billy is a good-sized dog, swift and agile, suited both to the flat and the thickest undergrowth, and, combining as it does all the characteristics of its ancestors, it excels at hunting deer, roebuck, hare and even wolf. It has an excellent nose and is courageous and aggressive, but lacks the physical strength necessary for hunting boar. The Billy has a quarrelsome streak, and does not therefore make a good pet. It has a slim, fairly fine head, with a flat skull and pronounced occiput, gently sloping stop, straight foreface, dark, medium-sized eyes, and long, broad, flat ears, set at eye-level and hanging close to the head. The neck is long, muscular and well arched. The long body has a sturdy frame, set on strong legs; the toes are slightly spread and have strong pads. The tail is long and thin. The coat is very short and coarse, thick and even.

Weight: approximately 35 kg (77 lb). Height: dogs 61–66 cm (24–26 in); bitches 58–62 cm (23–24½ in). Colour: orange and white, lemon and white, beige and white, always with markings and shading.
Country of Origin: France.

Ariégeois

Ariégeois

The Ariégeois is a versatile French tracking dog, which can be used for hunting both large and small game. It is a smaller version of the black and white Chien Français, and was created by crossing the local *briquets* (gundogs) with the Grand Bleu de Gascogne and the Saintongeois. Officially recognized in 1912, nowadays there are only a few remaining, although some specialized breeders are trying to prevent the breed becoming extinct. Because of its many good qualities, this dog is often used to give new life to other breeds and improve their nose and voice, as well as contributing to Anglo-French crosses much admired by hunters. Indeed the Ariégeois is an excellent animal, the best French dog for hunting hare, with a powerful sense of smell, great stamina for work on any type of terrain, perfect balance and considerable initiative. It is also docile, easy to train, devoted to its owner, and therefore also makes a good pet. It is light and elegant in build, with a swift, flowing gait. The head is long and lean, with a narrow skull and little stop, pronounced occiput and straight foreface. The eyes are dark, of medium size, with close lids; the ears are large, fine and folded, not too long and set rather low. The neck is long, light and free from dewlap, and the body long, with good tuck-up of the belly. The tail is thin and carried like a sickle. The legs are sturdy and lean, with long feet. The coat is thick and fine, short and even.

Weight: 28–30 kg (62–66 lb). Height: dogs 55–60 cm (21½–23½ in); bitches 53–58 cm (21–23 in). Colour: black and white with tan markings on the muzzle and edges of the ear.
Country of Origin: France.

Chien Français

Three different dogs are classed under the name Chien Français; all belong to the group of French hounds for larger game and all have very similar origins and standards, the most marked difference lying in the colour of the coat. The origins of the Chiens Français can be traced back to the Grand Bleu de Gascogne and the Grand Gascon Saintongeois, probably crossed with the Foxhound. The Chiens Français, officially recognized in 1957, are fairly large dogs, elegant and slender, yet well built and muscular, swift and courageous, sometimes showing a streak of ferociousness during the hunt. However, they are generally affectionate and obedient with their owner, silent and unobtrusive, and can adapt to family life, though not when cooped up in a flat. The head is long, with a slightly domed skull, gently sloping stop and slim muzzle. The neck is muscular and the body long in outline, solid and compact, set on strong legs with sturdy, lean feet. The coat is short, dense, flat, smooth and close to the body.

Weight: approximately 35 kg (77 lb). Height: 65–72 cm (25½–28 in). Colour: tricolour, black and white, orange and white.
Country of Origin: France.

Grand Bleu de Gascogne and Petit Bleu de Gascogne

Petit Bleu de Gascogne

The Grand Bleu de Gascogne is the largest of all the hounds. A very ancient breed, it was admired and used in France by the aristocracy and enjoyed successive periods of great favour until the English hounds – smaller but considerably swifter – began to gain preference over it. The Grand Bleu therefore went into decline, partly because the breed became contaminated by unprofessional crossing with dogs which were not always suitable, until, in the last century, a number of French breeders salvaged what remained of the breed and restored it to its former glory. The Grand Bleu is a native of France and, of all the hounds, bears the closest resemblance to the black St Hubert Hound, which is now extinct. It is a dog for large game, bred as a brave and tenacious hunter of wolves and used to hunt fox and hare with the horse. It has an exceptional nose, an iron constitution, and is courageous and persevering, never abandoning the trail without finding the quarry. Its great handicap is its lack of speed, but because of

its superb tracking ability it is very often used by breeders both to create and instil new life into other breeds, such as the black and white Chien Français and the Virelade. The Grand Bleu de Gascogne is an intelligent dog, but not always very quick and alert, and is ill-suited to family life because of its size and a tendency to bite, not to mention its noisiness, given its frequent loud and sonorous bark. The head is strong and long, with a relatively narrow, egg-shaped skull, slight stop and·curved foreface. The eyes are hooded and the hair is dark, as are the nose, lips, palate and pads of the feet. The ears, set very low, are thin, long and hang in folds. The neck is strong and of medium length, continuing gracefully into the long body; the forequarters are sturdier than the hindquarters. The tail is thick, fairly long and carried like a sickle when the dog is in action. The legs are long and sturdy, with oval, wolf-like feet. The coat is coarse, short but not excessively so, fairly thin and close-lying. The Petit Bleu de Gascogne has the same origins

114

as its larger brother, and was developed to combine the excellent qualities of the Grand Bleu with greater speed in order to create a dog better suited to hunting small game. The Petit Bleu is a very intelligent dog with a fine nose, and its bark is similar to that of the Grand Bleu. The standard is also very similar, the main differences being its slightly finer head and flatter ears; its neck is longer with slight dewlap; the body structure is more compact and the coat thicker.

Weight: Grand Bleu: 35–40 kg (77–88 lb). Petit Bleu: 25–30 kg (55–66 lb). Height: Grand Bleu: 65–72 cm ($25\frac{1}{2}$–$28\frac{1}{2}$ in) dogs; 62–68 cm ($24\frac{1}{2}$–$26\frac{1}{2}$ in) bitches. Petit Bleu: 48–56 cm (19–22 in). Colour: white mottled with slate blue; white with large slate blue patches and mottling. The Petit Bleu may also be completely slate blue (the most desirable).

Country of Origin: France.

Grand Bleu de Gascogne

115

Poitevin

This large hound was developed in France for hunting large game, and is unquestionably one of the most beautiful hunting dogs, though unfortunately its numbers are nowadays diminishing because of the gradual disappearance of large packs. It is a first-class hunter both of large game, such as wolf and deer, and "difficult" game like hare and roebuck. The Poitevin officially came into being in the second half of the nineteenth century, as a result of skilful crossing of the Larrye, the Ceris, the Greyhound and the old Faublas (French coursing dog). It is a highly intelligent, lively hound, very keen in searching out game, with an acute sense of smell and a loud, sonorous voice. Able and very resistant to fatigue, it is suited to hunting on any type of terrain, including marshland; it is swift and fearless in flushing and pursuing the quarry and is not easily discouraged. The body structure of the Poitevin is elegant and light, though it has a solid frame and powerful muscles. The head is long and lean, with a slightly domed skull and long, slightly curved muzzle. The eyes are large and dark, and the ears fine, folded, not too long and set low. The neck is long and fine and completely free from dewlap; the body is elongated, with moderate tuck-up of the belly. The legs are long, sturdy and lean, with long, compact feet and closely-set toes. The coat is short and sleek, even and close to the body.

Weight: approximately 35 kg (77 lb). Height: 60–70 cm (23½–27½ in). Colour: tricolour: white with large red-brown markings and black saddle. Country of Origin: France.

Griffon Nivernais

The Griffon Nivernais is a very versatile, medium-sized, long-haired tracking dog, equally good at hunting with the horse or on foot, and suited to both large and small game. Its many qualities include courage, stamina, resistance to bad weather and an ability to adapt to any terrain. It is not outstandingly swift, but makes up for this by its great staying power, its excellent nose and loud, piercing bark. The Griffon Nivernais is a dog of very ancient origin, probably an offshoot of the Grey Dog of St Luigi, nowadays extinct, which was in turn derived from crossing Arab greyhounds with French hounds (Gascon and Vendée dogs). This excellent hunter is nowadays fairly rare, though its considerable ability, its initiative and hardiness make it an ideal companion for the occasional or amateur hunter. A possible handicap is its somewhat stubborn temperament, for which reason it must be trained with skill and firmness from an early age. The head is lean and clean cut, with a flat skull, moderate stop and straight muzzle. The orbital arches are prominent and emphasized by thick, bushy eyebrows which partly hide its dark, lively eyes. The soft ears, set at eye level, are of medium length and slightly folded. The neck is lean and free from dewlap, and the body long, with deep brisket and solid, slightly sloping croup. The legs are long and slim, with long, compact feet. The coat is rough, fairly long and shaggy, but not woolly. The skin and the mucous membranes have black pigmentation.

Weight: approximately 28 kg (61½ lb). Height: 50–60 cm (19½–23½ in). Colour: wolf grey, blue grey, wild boar grey, grey with black rump and tan markings.
Country of Origin: France.

Basset Bleu de Gascogne

The Basset Bleu de Gascogne is the short-legged variety of the Grand Bleu de Gascogne, developed by establishing a chance malformation of the legs as part of the hereditary pattern. This was achieved through very careful breeding aimed at creating a dog able to penetrate the thickest undergrowth and even enter lairs, yet which retained the characteristics of the large hounds. Its short legs obviously limit its speed, and it works best in conjunction with the Grand Bleu: together they make an excellent team. This small dog has a powerful bark and an excellent sense of smell; it is tenacious and hardy, intelligent, friendly, easy to train and affectionate, which also makes it a good candidate for the home. The Basset Bleu de Gascogne is of leaner, lighter build than the Artésien-Normand. It has a long head with the pointed skull typical of the Gascony dogs, a slight stop and long muzzle. It also has the long, folded ears of its progenitor, set below the level of the eyes, which are dark and sometimes reveal the haw. The neck is long and arched, with a fair amount of dewlap; the body is solid, sturdy and very long, with a broad, deep chest and muscular shoulders. The legs are short and sturdy, the forelegs either straight, half-crooked or wholly crooked; the feet are large, strong like those of a large dog, with black nails and pads. The coat is thick, short and very close to the body.

Weight: approximately 15 kg (33 lb). Height: 30–38 cm (12–15 in). Colour: white mottled with slate blue; white with large slate blue patches and mottling.
Country of Origin: France.

Basset Artésien-Normand

This small French dog, an excellent hunter of hare and rabbit, but also of other small wild animals, developed from a cross between the Artesian and Norman Bassets, and resembles the latter in appearance. The Artésien-Normand may also be thought of as the short-legged variety of the Artesian Hound, whose influence can most clearly be seen in the shape of the head. This dog also therefore belongs to the large family whose common ancestor is the black St Hubert Hound. The Artésien-Normand shows great ability as a hunting dog, is sure and agile in searching out the quarry, enterprising and intelligent, limited only by its modest speed. Like all bassets, it can penetrate lairs and is particularly suited to hunting in the thickest undergrowth. Because of its gentle, affectionate character and its strong, hardy constitution it is becoming increasingly popular as a pet. The head is large but not massive, with a dome-shaped, not too broad skull, well-defined stop and straight foreface. The skin forms wrinkles on the cheeks, and the upper lips are soft and pendulous. The eyes are large and dark, with a melancholy expression, and the ears fine, soft, very long, folded and set low. The strong neck is of good length, with slight dewlap; the body solid and muscular, resting on short, thick legs, the forelegs crooked or half-crooked, with large, sturdy feet and toes spread slightly apart. The body length should be approximately double the height, yet the overall appearance is attractive. The coat is short, thick, of medium texture and close to the body.

Height: approximately 15 kg (33 lb). Height: 26–36 cm (10–14 in). Colour: tricolour (orange, fawn and white); two-coloured (orange and white).
Country of Origin: France.

Basset Fauve de Bretagne

This Basset is also the result of a mutation which occurred not long ago in a breed which is now extinct, the Grand Griffon Fauve, and which was later consolidated through crosses with the Basset Vendéen. The Fauve de Bretagne is a small, intelligent dog, very agile and lively, swift for its size and suited to any type of game, but particularly adept at driving out small animals from the most inaccessible refuges and the thickest covert. Docile and affectionate, it also makes a very popular pet, but is not well known outside Brittany. The head is slim, lean and well chiselled, with a round skull, flat on top, well-defined stop and long, straight foreface. The eyes are dark and lively, and the ears, of medium length, are set no higher than eye level, are pointed at the tip and slightly folded. The neck is strong and short and the body long, with muscular croup and strong thighs, characteristics which make the Basset Fauve the swiftest of all the bassets. The legs are short, sturdy and generally straight. The coat is thick, fairly hard, short but not excessively so, with eyebrows and beard of longer hair, and smooth ears.

Weight: approximately 15 kg (33 lb). Height: 32–36 cm (12½–14 in). Colour: various shades of fawn.
Country of Origin: France.

Basset Griffon Vendéen

This French Basset is the largest of its kind, and is derived from the Grand Griffon Vendéen, crossed with the white St Hubert Hound and perhaps with the Italian Bracco. There is also a smaller variety of this Basset but it is not very popular, as it has no special attribute, whereas the larger variety has the advantage of combining greater speed with the usual basset qualities. The Basset Griffon Vendéen is an intelligent, hardy, courageous dog with a good nose, suited to both small and large game. The head is large and long, with a domed, relatively narrow skull, long, square muzzle and well-defined stop and occiput. The eyes are large and dark, protected by bushy eyebrows, and the ears are long, fine, soft, folded and set low. The neck is long, strong and free from dewlap; the body sturdy and muscular, not as long as in other bassets. The forelegs are straight, with large, strong, compact feet. The coat is hard, of medium length, coarse, not woolly, with slight feathering and thick whiskers.

Weight: not specified. Height: 38–42 cm (15–16½ in) (large size); 34–38 cm (13½–15 in) (small size). Colour: two-coloured (white with black, grey, fawn or hare); tricolour (white and fawn with black, grey or hare grizzle).
Country of Origin: France.

Sicilian Hound
Cirneco dell'Etna

The Sicilian Hound is a beautiful, elegant and slender animal of very ancient lineage, though it has only recently become well known. It is probably descended from the Arab greyhounds brought over to Sicily by Phoenician merchants, which then evolved as a result of differences in terrain and climate, and through crosses with local breeds. The Cirneco is not therefore a true greyhound, not being as thin or tall, or having the latter's long legs. It is small to medium in size, with a light, active build. It has an excellent nose and great stamina, and is swift, tenacious and unsurpassed at hunting rabbit on rough ground. It is intelligent, dignified, even-tempered, faithful and obedient. All these qualities, combined with its unquestionable elegance, are making it increasingly popular as a pet. The head is long and slim, with a flat, pointed skull, straight, tapering muzzle and slight stop approximately midway along the total length. The light eyes are ochre or grey, wide and slightly slanting; the ears are large, triangular and pointed, set high and close together, erect and pricked forward. The neck is long and very arched, strong and free from dewlap, and the body long, sturdy and lean, well balanced and elegant. The legs are sinewy, straight and with a fine bone structure with round, compact front feet and oval hind ones, all of which have a hard sole with pigmentation ranging from pink to brown according to coat colour,. The tail is thick, set low and carried like a sabre when the dog is in repose. The coat is of medium length, glossy and close, shorter on the head, ears and legs.

Weight: dogs 10–12 kg (22–26½ lb); bitches 8–10 kg (17½–22 lb).
Height: dogs 46–50 cm (18–19½ in); bitches 42–46 cm (16½–18 in).
Colour: all shades of fawn, fawn and white.
Country of Origin: Italy.

Italian Hound

The Italian Hound, both the rough-haired and the smooth-haired, is undoubtedly the only breed of hound to have remained practically unchanged since ancient times. Like all continental hounds, it is descended from the Egyptian coursing dogs who were brought over to Europe by Phoenician merchants and then spread far and wide, mating with native dogs to give rise to the various different breeds of hound. In the past the Italian Hound held the status of escort to the rich and noble. It later spread throughout the peninsula, though it is not uncommon to come across impure specimens which have been crossed with other breeds. This bodes ill for the conservation of the breed, especially since the dog's hunting ability is directly related to its purity. The Italian Hound is a very versatile dog, one might say an "all purpose" dog, excellent at following a trail, at finding, flushing and pursuing the quarry, and at leading its master to it. It is particularly suited to hunting hare, but proves admirable with any kind of game, even large game such as wild boar. It is a good worker either alone or in small groups or packs, on any type of terrain. The Italian Hound is an intelligent dog, endowed with an excellent nose; it is swift, agile and cunning, with great tenacity and endurance, and capable of acting on its own initiative. All these qualities make it a dog of great value to even the most inexperienced of hunters. Undemonstrative by nature, it remains aloof and dignified, self-contained and unobtrusive. It adapts to family life, but needs its own private space, and would not suit anybody who expects more than loyalty and sincere devotion from a pet. The two varieties of the Italian Hound – the rough-haired and the smooth-haired – have practically identical standards, the coat being the basic difference between them. The dog's loud and melodious bark is a characteristic feature. This hound has a long head, with a flat, relatively narrow skull, pronounced occiput and very little stop. The muzzle is sloping, with fine, soft lips drooping just below the jaw. The dark ochre-coloured eyes are large and expressive, and the ears are fine, triangular, broad and long, hanging close to the head and should be set at, or below, the level of the cheek-bones. The neck is long and lean, with no trace of dewlap. The body is solidly built, with strong, clean-cut muscles and no excess fat. In order to stop the dog gaining weight, which would slow it down, when it is not out hunting it should be taken out for frequent walks and allowed to run about freely. The back is convex, with the croup level and the belly fairly well tucked up. The tail, which is set high and reaches down to the hocks, is thin and carried like a sabre when the dog is in action. The legs are long, sturdy and lean, with compact, oval-shaped feet, arched toes and strong pads. The two types of coat are markedly different: in the smooth-haired it is dense and shiny, fine, even, smooth and close, with a glossy sheen; in the rough-haired it is up to 5 cm (2 in) in length, coarse and not close to the body, forming shaggy eyebrows and whiskers on the muzzle.

Smooth-haired Italian Hound

Rough-haired Italian Hound

Weight: 18–20 kg (39½–44 lb). Height: dogs 52–58 cm (20½–23 in); bitches 48–56 cm (19–22 in). Colour: all shades of fawn; black with tan markings on the muzzle, eyebrows, chest, legs and perineum. Country of Origin: Italy.

Bernese Hound

The Bernese Hound belongs to a group of medium-sized hounds known and held in high esteem in Switzerland since ancient times. Because the origins of this breed are so remote, its ancestors are difficult to identify. Some would say that it comes from the same stock as the Italian Hound and is therefore descended from Phoenician coursing dogs, while others prefer to trace its lineage back to the white St Hubert Hound which is now extinct. Like the other Swiss hounds, however, the Bernese appears in the course of time to have become very closely related to the large French tracking dogs. There is a clear resemblance to the Grand Gascon Saintongeois, from which the Bernese has inherited its physical characteristics and its good, loud, strident voice and keen nose. It is very resistant to fatigue and tenacious in its work, lively and intelligent, easy to train and suited to hunting over any ground. It is a first-rate hunter of hare but also proves good with other types of game. Its shape is streamlined, with elegant lines, although the dog does not stand very high in the leg. The head is long, dry and fairly narrow, with a slightly domed skull, well-defined stop and long, slim, straight or slightly curved muzzle. The eyes are generally dark and the ears very long, set low and back, narrow at the base and wider in the centre, soft, fine and often folded. The neck is sturdy, and the body long and compact, with a tucked-up belly. The legs are strong and lean, with rounded feet. The coat is thick and smooth, with a fine, dense undercoat. There is also a variety with hard, wiry hair.

Weight: 27–30 kg (59½–66 lb). Height: minimum 40–42 cm (16–16½ in). Colour: tricolour (black and white with tan markings). Country of Origin: Switzerland.

Lucernese Hound

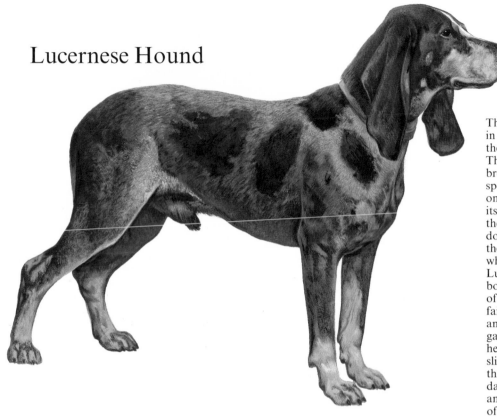

The Lucernese Hound is very similar to the Bernese in size, physical appearance and temperament, and therefore the same theories are held as to its origins. The prime aim of the Swiss who developed the breed was to create a dog which, though lacking the speed of the French hounds, would carry on alone once the trail had been found, capable of acting on its own initiative without the continual guidance of the hunter. A strong resemblance to the Gascony dogs, mainly the Petit Bleu de Gascogne, reveals the inevitable crossbreeding with French hounds which has again occurred in this animal. The Lucernese is of medium size, hardy and untiring, born with a passion for the hunt, suited to any type of terrain and game, intelligent and easy to train, faithful and affectionate. It has a streamlined shape and well-balanced structure, with a light, speedy gait, superb nose and a good, resounding bark. The head is long, clean and fairly narrow, with a flat or slightly domed skull, well-defined stop and long, thin, more or less straight muzzle. The eyes are dark, and the ears soft, fine and pendant, set low and back, long and broad but not as large as those of the Bernese. The neck and body are very similar to those of its Bernese cousin. The coat is smooth and even, thick and glossy, and when it is wet the white disappears and the colour turns darker, becoming blue or slate.

Weight: 27–30 kg (59½–66 lb). Height: minimum 42 cm (16½ in). Colour: white with grey or blue mottling and large patches of slate blue or black. Tan markings all over the body.
Country of Origin: Switzerland.

Bruno de Jura

This Swiss hound, similar in many respects to the Bernese and the Lucernese Hounds, differs from them in its slightly heavier build and a greater resemblance to the St Hubert Hound. This resemblance was once so marked that it was often confused with the Bruno de Jura of the St Hubert type, but the breed has subsequently been made considerably lighter through crosses with French hounds. A first-rate hunter of roe-deer and fox, it is equally good with hare and rabbit. It has a keen nose and a very loud, howling voice, which only develops after the dog's third year. It is a tenacious and courageous animal, hardy and untiring, a sure, independent worker, faithful and intelligent. The Bruno de Jura is of medium size, and has a long, clean, narrow head with a broad, domed skull, pronounced stop, long muzzle and strong jaws. The eyes are large, dark and expressive and the ears broad and long, with rounded tips, set low and back, falling in graceful folds. The neck is very strong and of medium length; the body is long, muscular with a solid bone structure and moderate tuck-up of the belly. The legs are sturdy and lean, not very long, with round, compact feet and hard pads. The coat is short and smooth, thick and even. Like the French hounds, there is also a basset-like variety of the Swiss hound differentiated solely by the fact that it has short legs. These are the Small Bernese, Lucernese and Bruno de Jura Hounds.

Weight: approximately 30 kg (66 lb). Height: approximately 45 cm (17½ in). Colour: dark yellow or dark red with or without black saddle; black and tan.
Country of Origin: Switzerland.

Bloodhound

The Bloodhound is one of the most ancient hounds, selectively bred for centuries by the monks of the monastery of St Hubert in the Ardennes. It was then taken to England where, much admired for its superb hunting ability, it has been so well preserved and carefully bred that it is nowadays considered an English dog. Most of the French and Swiss hunting dogs are descended from it, and it has often been used in crosses to improve the characteristics of other breeds. Very hardy and sturdy, suited to any terrain, it has an exceptional nose and great intelligence. Its only drawback is its modest speed, which means it is mainly used as a tracker, capable of uncovering trails possibly days old; it is therefore of great assistance in searching for people who are lost or buried beneath debris. It is an affectionate and obedient animal, provided that it is treated with kindness, but is capable of turning aggressive and vicious if treated badly. The Bloodhound is a massive dog, with a powerful, majestic gait. Its most outstanding feature is its very large head, which is long and narrow with a domed skull and prominent occipital peak. The muzzle is long and deep, with a curved foreface. The eyes are generally light, the lower lid droops, revealing the haw. The ears are very long, narrow and soft, and set low. There is a super-abundance of skin on the forehead and cheeks, hanging in deep, characteristic folds. The neck is long with plenty of dewlap, and the body long and heavy, very strong, and covered in extremely loose skin. The coat is short and fine; the hair on the body is hard and soft on the head.

Weight: 40–48 kg (88–106 lb). Height: dogs 65–70 cm ($25\frac{1}{2}$–$27\frac{1}{2}$ in); bitches 60 cm ($23\frac{1}{2}$ in). Colour: self-coloured red; black and tan. Country of Origin: France.

Styrian Mountain Hound

The Styrian Hound is one of the few dogs known to have originated in Austria. It was created fairly recently by crossing the Hanoverian Schweisshund with the rough-haired Istrian Hound with the aim of developing a well-built, muscular though not heavy dog, suited to uneven, mountainous ground and capable of working at high altitudes where the temperature is often very low. It is therefore a typical mountain hound, admired beyond its country of origin, for instance in Germany and Switzerland wherever the mountainous terrain requires a dog with special aptitudes. The Styrian Hound is a dog of medium size, alert, courageous and persevering, suited predominantly to hunting small game, which it seeks out with its keen nose. Its head is strongly reminiscent of the Istrian Hound, being fairly long, with a slightly domed, wrinkle-free forehead. The muzzle is also fairly long, broad at the base and tapering to the black nose. The stop is not pronounced. The eyes are oval and light or dark depending on the coat, with a sweet, intelligent expression. The ears are set high and are broad at the base and narrow at the tip, soft, folded and pendant. The neck is long, strong and lean and the body long, with slanting, fairly long croup. The legs are strong and lean with rounded, compact feet. The coat is coarse, rough and shaggy, neither too short nor close.

Weight: unspecified. Height: 40–50 cm (16–20 in).
Colour: yellowish red.
Country of Origin: Austria.

Tyrolean Hound
Tyroler Bracke

The Tyrolean Hound is a hunting dog of Austrian origin, similar in many respects, but particularly in the shape of the head, to the Styrian Mountain Hound. Developed in the Tyrol as an all-purpose dog, suited to searching out and pursuing the quarry and also to pointing and retrieving it, it is a sturdy and very hardy animal, undaunted by both the rigours of the mountainous terrain and climate. Courageous, intelligent, tenacious and lively, it is perfectly suited to someone who is an occasional hunter, because of its versatility and modest size. The Tyrolean Hound has a sturdy build. The head is long, with a slightly domed forehead free of wrinkles, a straight or slightly curved muzzle, broad at the base and tapering to a point. The soft lips extend very slightly below the lower jaw. The eyes are large, dark and lively; the ears fine and soft, broad but not too long, set high and hanging close to the head. The body is long, with a broad, deep chest, extended croup and little belly tuck-up. The forelegs are always straight. The coat is thick, dense, short and fairly rough, longer on the throat and chest and smooth on the head and ears.

Weight: 15–22 kg (33–48½ lb). Height: 40–48 cm (16–19 in) (small specimens under 40 cm [16 in] and down to 30 cm [12 in]). Colour: self-coloured black, yellow, red. Also tricolour.
Country of Origin: Austria.

127

Hanoverian Schweisshund

The Hanoverian Schweisshund belongs to a group of German tracking dogs, smaller on the whole than the French ones, whose origins lie in the black St Hubert Hound. Developed in Hanover in Saxony in the last century, this German hound is of medium size, but of very strong, rather massive build, not very high in the leg. It is a sturdy, very hardy dog, with a good sense of smell and tenacious in its search for and pursuit of the quarry; once found, it attracts the hunter's attention with its characteristic way of barking. It is intelligent and obedient, easy to train, faithful and affectionate, which makes it a good family dog. It is a good hunter whether alone or in small groups or packs. The head is of medium size with a slightly domed skull, prominent brows and straight or slightly convex muzzle. The skin on the head is very abundant, forming wrinkles on the forehead, which gives the dog a somewhat melancholy expression. The eyes are fairly deep-set, light or dark in colour depending on the coat, and the ears are long and wide, rounded at the tip and set high. The neck is long, sturdy and free from dewlap, the chest broad and deep, and the back slightly convex, with sloping croup. The legs are powerful and muscular with round, solid feet and strong pads. The tail is long and set low, thick at the root and tapering to a point. The coat is thick, smooth, soft, glossy and fairly short.

Weight: 25–35 kg (55–77 lb). Height: 50–57 cm (19½–22½ in). Colour: grey-brown, reddish brown, reddish yellow, yellow ochre, dark grey, fawn and tan, blackish-brown.
Country of Origin: Germany.

Westphalian Dachsbracke

The Westphalian Dachsbracke owes its name to the region where it originated and its basset-like appearance, its legs being short in relation to the length of the body. This dog belongs to the group of German hounds known for their skill in hunting fox, deer, roe, hare and, in packs, even wild boar. It is intelligent and agile, tenaciously tracking down its quarry. It excels over difficult mountainous terrain and in undergrowth, but is less efficient over open ground due to its lack of speed. Its excellent nose enables it to sniff out game some considerable distance away. The Westphalian Dachsbracke has a larger brother, differing predominantly in size with a slight variation in coat colour. The Westphalian Dachsbracke has a long head, with a slightly domed skull, a gently sloping, not very pronounced stop and a straight muzzle with fine lips hanging just below the jaw. The eyes can be light or dark depending on coat colour, and the ears are long, broad, fine and set high, hanging close to the head. The neck is long, strong and well arched, and the body long with a broad, deep chest and slight tuck-up of the belly. The legs are strong and sturdy with large, compact feet and arched toes. The coat is short, dense and close to the body.

Dachsbracke

Weight: 15–18 kg (33–39½ lb). Height: 30–35 cm (12–14 in) (small size); 35–40 cm (12–16 in) (large size). Colour: black and tan, brown with pale stripes, reddish, red with black overlay.
Country of Origin: Germany.

Wachtelhund

German Spaniel

Although officially classified as a hound for small game, the Wachtelhund is also, as its name suggests, an able pointing dog and can be trained to make an admirable gundog. It is therefore very versatile, a fine sporting companion for the person who can only have one dog. Its creator, the breeder F. Roberth, developed it at the beginning of this century, but it is not known which dogs were used as the basic stock and its origins remain a mystery. There is unquestionably some spaniel influence in its background, as is evident both from its appearance and abilities. Hardy, courageous, efficient over any ground, it has a good nose and is intelligent, lively and easy to train. Impetuous by nature, it is affectionate and obedient with its owner, but does not easily take to strangers. It is attractive in appearance and not lacking in elegance. The head is well proportioned, with a well-defined stop and long, tapering muzzle. The medium-sized eyes are oval and hazel in colour. The ears are broad, long and pendant. The neck is strong and the body long, with sturdy croup and moderate belly tuck-up. The coat is long, even, thick and wavy, not silky.

Weight: unspecified. Height: 40–50 cm (16–20 in). Colour: black and tan, brown, stag-red. Country of Origin: Germany.

Hamilton Hound

Hamiltonstövare

The Hamilton Hound is named after its creator, who developed it by crossing the Hanover Hound and the Foxhound, to produce the most attractive of the Swedish hounds, a dog of superior quality incorporating the characteristics of its forebears. It is sturdy and hardy like the Hanover, and it is swift and has almost as fine a nose as the Foxhound. It excels over any ground, even the most difficult. Although able to deal with all types of game, it has a special affinity for large game, such as reindeer, roe and wild boar. Intelligent and courageous, with a strongly aggressive streak, it has very strong jaws and sharp teeth, suited to its favoured game. It has a solid, sturdy, well-balanced and elegant build, with a flat or slightly domed skull, straight muzzle and well-defined stop. The eyes are dark and oval, and the ears are set high and are not too long, hanging close to the head. The neck is long, lean and arched, and the body solid and slim with moderate belly tuck-up. The legs are long and sinewy. The coat is short, dense, close and shiny, with a thick, soft undercoat in winter.

Weight: unspecified. Height: dogs 50–60 cm (20–23½ in); bitches 46–57 cm (18–22½ in). Colour: tricolour (white, brown, black). Country of Origin: Sweden.

Drever

The Drever, together with the Hamilton, Schiller and Smalands Hounds, belongs to a small group of native Swedish hounds closely related to the continental, particularly German, hounds. The Drever is undoubtedly a very ancient breed whose origins are obscure, which did not receive official recognition until 1947 despite being well known and highly esteemed in its own country since long ago. This small hound with its basset-like appearance excels at hunting hare and fox, and is so fearless that it will even tackle wild boar. Tenacious, strong and very hardy, it has an excellent nose and a natural hunting ability, which makes it quick and easy to train. It is docile, obedient and faithful, and possessed of a powerful bark which belies its small size. The head is large and long with a slightly domed skull, shallow stop and straight, tapering muzzle. The eyes are large and dark, and the ears are set at medium height, broad at the base with pointed tips, and hang close to the head. The neck is long and strong; the body almost cylindrical, resting on short, thick but not bandy legs, with well-developed feet like those of a large dog. The coat is thick, strong, close and short, with slight feathering on the neck and tail.

Weight: approximately 16 kg (35 lb). Height: dogs 32–40 cm (12½–16 in); bitches 30–38 cm (12–15 in). Colour: any colour allowed, but always combined with white.
Country of Origin: Sweden.

Finnish Spitz
Suomenpystykorva

The Finnish Spitz is a descendant of the northern wolf, and is a very ancient native breed of Finland used by the Laplanders for hunting birds, particularly wood grouse, summoning the hunter with its unmistakable bark. It has a highly developed nose and very sharp vision, enabling it to flush out the bird and follow its flight without losing track of it. It is small to medium in size, courageous, fearless, faithful, tenacious and hardy. Very popular in its own country where it is considered the national dog, it has gained popularity further afield, being admired for its beauty, natural cleanliness, friendly nature and obedience. The adult dog is very hardy, but young puppies require a certain amount of care. The Finnish Spitz has a solid but light build. The head is clean cut with a rounded skull and pronounced stop, the muzzle tapering to a sharp point. The eyes are dark and lively and the ears triangular and very mobile, set high and carried erect. The neck is strong and muscular, the body short and compact. The legs are strong and straight, with round feet. The tail is long, set high and curled over the back. The coat is long, dense and stands out from the body, with an undercoat and more abundant hair on the neck forming a ruff, and on the backs of the thighs and tail.

Weight: unspecified. Height: dogs 44–50 cm (17½–19½ in); bitches 39–45 cm (15½–18 in). Colour: reddish brown with paler shading, red gold.
Country of Origin: Finland.

Karelian Bear Dog

This Finnish dog, like the Elkhound, belongs to the group of Nordic dogs classified as hounds for larger game but which are still used as draught dogs. Its origins are somewhat obscure. Some it has in common with the Spitz, one of its ancestors being the Arctic wolf. This was the progenitor of all northern dogs, some of which were bred selectively as draught dogs (Samoyed, Husky, Malamute), while others, though not abandoning this activity, were bred more for hunting and developed their sense of smell and speed. The Russian Bear Dog seems to be an offshoot of the Karelian Bear Dog through crossbreeding with local sheepdogs. The Karelian Bear Dog is very sturdy and hardy, courageous, aggressive and vicious, its powerful jaws and sharp teeth making its bite particularly formidable. Obedient and loyal to its owner, it is not suited to family life. The head is long and clean-cut with a relatively narrow skull, not very pronounced stop and wedge-shaped muzzle with a straight topline. The neck is long, strong and lean; the body long and powerful with little tuck-up of the belly, set on strong, fairly long legs which are, however, short in comparison with the length of the torso. It gives an overall impression of elegance, and its gait is swift and easy. The feet are strong and compact. The tail is set on high and carried curled over the back. The coat is thick, stiff and long on the throat and chest, with feathering on the underside of the tail and on the thighs and belly. The undercoat is thick and waterproof.

Weight: approximately 28 kg (62 lb). Height: dogs 54–60 cm (21–23½ in); bitches 48–53 cm (19–21 in). Colour: black with white markings on the throat, chest, muzzle, tip of the tail and legs.
Country of Origin: Finland.

Finnish Hound
Suomenajokoira

There are not many breeds native to Finland, and the most well known of these is the Finnish Spitz, but this beautiful, medium-sized hound, popular in its homeland for centuries but uncommon elsewhere, also deserves a place of honour. Its origins are probably interwoven with those of the continental, particularly the German, hounds. It has a good nose and great hunting prowess, although it only has an opportunity to hunt hare and fox during the long days of the short Nordic summers. Its tenacity, courage, hardiness and the patience with which it flushes out and pursues the quarry is admirable. The Finnish Hound has a solid but not heavy appearance, sturdy yet light in build; the body longer than it is high but not with basset proportions; it has a swift, easy gait. The head is long and clean cut, with a flat or slightly domed skull, gently sloping stop and straight muzzle. The oval eyes have a gentle, intelligent expression, and the ears, set rather high for a hound, are broad, soft and pendant, standing out slightly from the cheek. The neck is of medium length and free from dewlap; the body elongated and strong, with straight, sound legs. The coat is thick, coarse and rough.

Weight: approximately 26 kg (57 lb). Height: dogs 55–61 cm (21½–24 in); bitches 52–58 cm (20½–23 in). Colour: characteristic tricolour markings (black, red, white).
Country of Origin: Finland.

Elkhound and Swedish Elkhound

Norsk Elghund and Jämthund

The name Elkhound covers a number of very similar dogs, whose ancient origins have been revealed by excavations carried out in Scandinavia. Elkhounds are unmistakably dogs of the Spitz type, a common ancestor being the northern wolf. The Norwegian breeds are the grey and black Norwegian Elkhounds, and the Swedish ones are the Jämthund or larger grey elkhound and the Grähund or smaller grey elkhound. The differences are not major and are predominantly of colour and size. The Elkhound is a dog of medium size; an excellent hunter of elk and bear, it barks noisily to summon the hunter and is capable of varying the sound according to the stage of the struggle to signal the right moment for human intervention. It can also be used for other kinds of game, and is sometimes used to kill vermin such as beech-martens, rats and moles. It has an outstanding sense of smell and resistance to fatigue and cold, fearing neither rain nor snow. It is very strong and tenacious and can be used as a sledge and rescue dog, sheepdog and guard – an indication of its intelligence as well as its versatility. In addition it has an equable disposition and is affectionate and sensitive, making a good household pet, and is often adopted as such in England and America. Its other attractive qualities are a natural cleanliness and a lack of doggy odour. It has a long, dry head, large but in proportion, with a slightly arched skull, clearly defined stop and wedge-shaped muzzle of medium length. The jaws are very strong, with scissor bite. The eyes are small, dark and oval in shape; the ears pointed, not very large, set high and carried erect. The neck is of medium length, thick, strong and free from dewlap. The body is short and compact, light in build with a deep brisket, straight croup and slight belly tuck-up. The legs are long, straight and firm, with sturdy, compact, wolf-like feet. The tail is set high and tightly curved over the back. The general impression is one of pride and dignity, with a certain elegance and harmony. The coat is long and coarse in texture, longer on neck and chest, underneath the tail and on the back of the thighs, and shorter on the head and legs. A thick, soft, woolly undercoat protects the dog from damp and all severe weather conditions.

Weight: Elkhound: dogs 24 kg (53 lb); bitches 21 kg (46 lb). Jämthund: dogs 30 kg (66 lb); bitches 27 kg (59½ lb). Height: Elkhound: dogs 45–50 cm (18–20 in); bitches 42–48 cm (16½–19 in) (the grey: dogs approximately 52 cm [20½ in]; bitches approximately 49 cm [19½ in]). Jämthund: dogs 58–63 cm (23–25 in); bitches 53–58 cm (21–23 in). Colour: Elkhound: black or grey, solid or shaded. Jämthund: light or dark grey, with or without shading.
Countries of Origin: Norway and Sweden.

Posavaski Goniči

This hound – together with others of its kind native to different regions – belongs to a group of excellent Yugoslav hunting dogs which, despite the inevitable differences arising from methods of selective breeding, share many of the same physical characteristics and abilities. This hound is also a fine hunter of hare and roe over montainous and very uneven terrain. With its excellent nose and resistance to fatigue and the rigours of climate, it is capable of uncovering even the faintest trail and then pursuing the quarry until it is found. In appearance it is solid and sturdy, dignified and not without a certain elegance. Intelligent, lively and obedient, it is also very affectionate and makes a good family pet. The head is large and long but not out of proportion, and bears an overall resemblance to the other Yugoslav hounds. The neck is strong, long and arched, and the body long and compact with a sloping croup and slight tuck-up of the underline. The legs are sturdy and slightly short in relation to the length of the body. The coat is no more than 4 cm (1½ in) in length, thick, hard and close.

Weight: approximately 18 kg (40 lb). Height: 40–58 cm (16–23 in). Colour: shades of yellow ranging to fawn.
Country of Origin: Yugoslavia.

Istrian Hound

Little is known of the origins of this ancient hound, very popular and much admired in the Istrian region. It probably shares a common background with its cousins, which it resembles to a considerable degree. It is a dog of slim, elegant build with a well-knit frame and powerful, streamlined muscles. It has a keen sense of smell and an alert, lively nature; it is very resistant to fatigue and severe weather conditions and suited to hunting over rough, mountainous ground, alone or in a pack. It specializes in hunting hare and deer as well as fox. It is of equable temperament, friendly, docile and affectionate, which also makes it a cherished pet and companion. The head is long and slim, with a slightly domed skull, gently sloping stop and straight, tapering muzzle. The skin of the head is taut and fine, without wrinkles on the forehead or pendulous lips. The oval eyes are very dark, and the ears are fine, narrow at the tip and broad at the base, set high and hang close to the cheek. The neck is long, slim, lean and arched; the long body is set on sturdy legs, with compact feet and strong nails. The coat is dense, very short, fine and glossy. There is also a rough-haired variety.

Weight: approximately 18 kg (40 lb). Height: dogs 50 cm (20 in); bitches 48 cm (19 in). Colour: snow white with orange markings, all white.
Country of Origin: Yugoslavia.

Podengo Pequeño
Small Portuguese Warren Hound

The Podengo Pequeño belongs to the same family as the Podengo Grande and the Podengo Medio. All three are greyhound-like dogs, descendants of the Greyhound of the Balearic Islands, but whereas this relationship is clearly visible in the large and medium-sized varieties, it is far from obvious in the small one. The three dogs also possess different skills, the Grande being used for larger game, the Medio being a hunter and guard dog, and the Pequeño only a hunter, excelling at searching out hare and rabbit in ravines and over rough ground. It is intelligent, lively and fearless, tenacious and persevering, and relatively fast for its small size. The Small Portuguese Warren Hound can be considered the basset variety of the two larger dogs, which it closely resembles in the shape of the head, which is similar to that of the greyhound and also to that of the Sicilian Hound. The Podengo Pequeño has a long, lean head with a flat or slightly rounded skull, not very pronounced stop and straight, pointed muzzle with thin, fine, taut lips. The slanting eyes are not very large, and are dark or light depending on the colour of the coat. The ears, set fairly high, are erect, pointed and very mobile. The neck is long, lean and arched; the body longer than it is high, set on short but not thick legs. The forelegs are generally straight, sometimes slightly crooked. There is little tuck-up of the belly. The tail reaches down to the hocks and is carried low at rest and horizontal in action. The coat is short and smooth.

Weight: 4–5 kg (9–11 lb). Height: 20–30 cm (8–12 in). Colour: self-coloured (yellow, fawn, grey-black); markings in these colours.
Country of Origin: Portugal.

Basenji

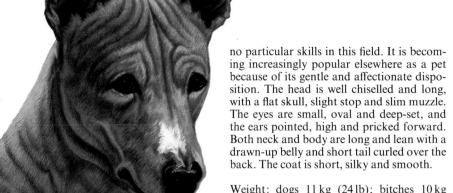

The Basenji is a small, very ancient hunting dog, bred in northern and central Africa, particularly in the Sudan and the Congo. It is probably an offshoot of the Congo Terrier, greatly modified through crossbreeding and environmental selection. Officially recognized in England in 1939, it is little known in other countries, though it has gained a foothold in America. This dog has some unusual characteristics: first, it does not bark, but has a soft cry which is a mixture of a chortle and a yodel; secondly, it trots like a horse; and finally, it assumes a characteristic expression when attentive or alert: when it pricks up its ears its forehead is covered in wrinkles. The Basenji is used locally as a hunting dog for small game, although it has no particular skills in this field. It is becoming increasingly popular elsewhere as a pet because of its gentle and affectionate disposition. The head is well chiselled and long, with a flat skull, slight stop and slim muzzle. The eyes are small, oval and deep-set, and the ears pointed, high and pricked forward. Both neck and body are long and lean with a drawn-up belly and short tail curled over the back. The coat is short, silky and smooth.

Weight: dogs 11 kg (24 lb); bitches 10 kg (22 lb). Height: dogs 42 cm (16½ in); bitches 40 cm (16 in). Colour: black and white; fawn and white; black, white and tan; chestnut speckled with white.
Country of Origin: Central Africa.

Rhodesian Ridgeback

This very unusual dog lives in South Africa, where it is considered a native breed, and is little known elsewhere. Its origins are rather obscure, and its standard was drawn up in Rhodesia in 1922, after the Ridgeback was brought to public attention by Cornelius van Rooyen, who admired the virtues of this dog. The characteristic feature of this unique animal is its ridge, formed by a strip of hair growing in the opposite direction to the rest of the coat. This ridge is very distinctive and narrow, running down the spine from immediately behind the shoulders to the haunches, and must contain two identical crowns opposite each other and behind the shoulders. The Ridgeback is commonly considered a dog for small game, but is so courageous and fearless that it will not retreat even in the face of ferocious animals such as lions and pumas, which it pursues by swerving rapidly to avoid being bitten. It is solidly built with powerful muscles, able to withstand fatigue and the great extremes of temperature between night and day, resistant to insect bites, and able to go without food and water if necessary. The head is strong and well proportioned, the skull flat and broad between the ears, with a well-defined stop and long, powerful muzzle. The teeth are particularly well developed, with long, sharp canines. The colour of the eyes depends on that of the coat, and the ears, very wide at the base and not very long, are set high and hang close to the head. The neck is thick, strong and lean; the body long, powerful and muscular without any excess fat; there is some tuck-up of the belly. The legs are sturdy with round, compact feet. The coat is dense, short, sleek and glossy.

Weight: dogs 34 kg (75 lb); bitches 29 kg (64 lb). Height: dogs 63–68 cm (24½–26½ in); bitches 61–66 cm (24–26 in). Colour: all shades from wheaten to fawn.
Country of Origin: South Africa.

HUNTING BREEDS

Earth Dogs

This group consists of small to medium-sized dogs, characterized by their long bodies and short legs. The forelegs are particularly sturdy and equipped with strong nails for digging. Robust and hardy in spite of their modest size, they have good noses and are relentless in their pursuit of the quarry, following it to its lair and into the thickest undergrowth. They generally have long muzzles and powerful jaws, with which they capture and kill their prey. They are natural enemies and destroyers of vermin.

Basset Hound

The Basset Hound is considered an American dog, but the breed actually owes its existence to the French and the English. Its ancestors can be traced back to the Basset Artésien-Normand. It was then transformed and developed selectively by the British, who introduced some physical characteristics of the Bloodhound (shape of the skull, ears, substance of body, eyes, slack skin), and improved its scenting powers to an exceptional degree. The stock was selected largely by Sir John Everett Millais. Towards the end of the last century, breeders from America discovered the dog, imported it and were so enamoured with it that they developed an American variety, more massive and heavy than the English; it then became known worldwide. The Basset Hound, descended as it is from the French bassets, has the general characteristics of tracking dogs and will ably follow the tracks of hare, rabbit, fox and deer. It is particularly suited to tracking down wounded game; thanks to its size it is able to follow it through the most tangled undergrowth right into its lair. However, although the Basset Hound undoubtedly possesses a good nose, a good voice and reasonable speeed considering its short legs, it has primarily been kept as a pet rather than a sporting dog, with the result that its true ability is not so marked as in other sporting dogs. By nature it is gentle and dignified, unobtrusive, calm and affable. It does, however, have a stubborn streak and is sometimes a little slow to learn, requiring firm but sympathetic handling, which will make it into an ideal children's friend and playmate. Its appearance is characterized by the short, thick legs and an exceptionally heavy frame in relation to its stature. The head is large, with a domed skull, well-developed occipital bone and some stop. The muzzle is deep, fairly narrow and slightly convex, with a large nose. The eyes are dark and relatively deep-set, with the lower lid drooping to reveal the haw. The ears, set low and back, are long, velvety and hang in loose folds. The head is covered with loose skin which forms wrinkles on the forehead. The neck is powerful, with pronounced dewlap. The body is long and strong, with a broad chest and prominent breastbone, slight tuck-up of the belly and very powerful hindquarters. The legs are short and thick, with the elbows of the forelegs very close together. The feet are massive. The tail is long and tapering. The coat is hard, smooth and thick.

Weight: 20–23 kg (44–50½ lb). Height: maximum 38 cm (15 in). Colour: any hound colour allowed. The distribution of markings is of no importance.
Country of Origin: France.

Dachshund
Teckel

The Dachshund is an excellent earth dog, although its modest size and sweet appearance have made it a popular pet. It is probably the basset variety of some large hound, perhaps the St Hubert type, Bruno de Jura or the Ardennes Hound, and is an ancient breed, accurately described in thirteenth-century documents. Its German name Dachshund (Badger Hound) indicates its ability to flush out small game such as hare, rabbit, pheasant, partridge and fox, as it is capable of penetrating the narrowest burrows and thickest covert. It is highly versatile in that it can uncover trails, provided that they are fairly warm, and even "point" game. It is also a useful destroyer of vermin, such as rats and moles. It is very intelligent, alert and resourceful, with a self-willed and independent streak. It is affectionate with its owner but does not like to be bothered, and so is not always good with children. Its attitude will reflect the way in which it is reared and it should be handled kindly yet firmly. There are three varieties of Dachshund; all share a common standard, differing only in the coat, which may be smooth, wiry or long. The smooth-haired Dachshund is the oldest and the most common in France. Its coat is hard, dense, smooth, glossy and close-lying. The Wire-haired, created in the eighteenth century by crossing the smooth-haired variety first with a Griffon and then with the Dandie Dinmont Terrier, has a coat of shortish, rough, close hair, and a bushy beard and eyebrows. The long-haired variety, dating back to the sixteenth century, is the result of crossing the Smooth-haired with spaniels, and its characteristic feature is its long, wavy, sleek, silky coat, with feathering on the chest, belly, tail and backs of the legs. The Dachshund is a long-bodied dog, with a strong, sturdy build and very short legs, but it never looks ungainly or heavy, nor should it look ridiculous; it should have great dignity and a certain elegance. The head is long, clean cut and well chiselled, with little stop and slightly arched skull and muzzle. The eyes are oval, dark and of medium size, with a lively expression. The ears are set high and well back, broad at the base, triangular, not too long, flat and mobile. The neck is of medium length, clean, muscular and well arched. The body is characterized by its length, with a broad, deep chest and prominent breastbone, moderate belly tuck-up and strong, muscular hindquarters. The legs are short, with arched, compact feet, slightly turned outwards. The tail is in line with the back and carried straight. There are two sizes of Dachshund, differing in weight and height.

Weight: standard: dogs 9–11 kg (20–25 lb); bitches 8–10 kg (18–23 lb); miniature: 4.5 kg (10 lb). Colour. Self-coloured: red, fawn, solid or speckled with black. Two-coloured: black, grey or white with rust or yellowy tan markings. Other colours: brindled, dappled, with brown, grey, white underground, with irregular markings in the other colours mentioned.
Country of Origin: Germany.

Wire-haired Dachshund

140

Smooth-haired Dachshund

Long-haired Dachshund

141

German Hunt Terrier
Deutscher Jagdterrier

The German Hunt Terrier belongs to a group of dogs native to the British Isles, which then spread to other countries and developed along different lines. Because of their small size, German terriers have been kept as pets, but as a result they have lost some of their instinct and the typical fearlessness of earth dogs, becoming less and less suited to hunting. But the Jagdterrier is an exception, being one of the few terriers to have retained its original characteristics. It is a first-class hunter, tenacious, hardy and courageous, unafraid of even large game like the wild boar. Small in size, it has a long head, with a flat skull, slight stop and straight, tapering muzzle, with a black or brown nose depending on the colour of the coat. The eyes are small, oval and dark, and the ears V-shaped, set high and folded forward. The jaws are very powerful, with strong teeth. The neck is well arched and reasonably long; the body sturdy, compact and well-knit but not short, with moderate tuck-up of the belly. The legs are lean, straight with sturdy feet (the forefeet are sometimes longer than the hind ones. The tail is fairly short and carried straight. The coat may either be short and harsh or short and smooth.

Weight: dogs 9–10 kg (20–22 lb); bitches 7.5–8.5 kg (16–18 lb). Height: maximum 40 cm (16 in). Colour: black, black and tan, black and grey, dark brown with lighter tints of brown, brown with tan markings.
Country of Origin: Germany.

Fox Terrier

Wire-haired Fox Terrier

There are two varieties of Fox Terrier: smooth and wire-haired. Although this dog is universally known and considered essentially English, its origins are still obscure, with conflicting but unsubstantiated theories. Bred for foxhunting, it has demonstrated a considerable talent for hunting wild boar, which has earned it a large following in France. It is also a fine hunter of vermin and makes a good pet, although the breed is often nervous and independent with an aversion to authority. It is a sturdy, hardy dog which can cover considerable distances at some speed without tiring, and is courageous and aggressive with its quarry, often excessively so. The body is very slightly longer than it is high, with a strong but not heavy frame. The head is long and sturdy, with little stop, a flat skull, straight, tapering muzzle and pointed nose. The eyes are large, dark and almond-shaped, and the ears small and V-shaped, set high and folded forward. The neck is long and muscular, gradually widening towards the shoulders, and the body compact, with a level back and drawn-up belly. The tail is set high and carried upright. The coat of the smooth-haired variety is dense, hard, flat and of medium length, whereas that of the wire-haired variety is hard and wiry, and should be kept in shape by trimming.

Weight: dogs 8–9 kg (17½–20 lb); bitches 7.5–8.5 kg (16–18 lb). Height: 36–38 cm (14–15 in). Colour: white with patches of black or tan.
Country of Origin: Great Britain.

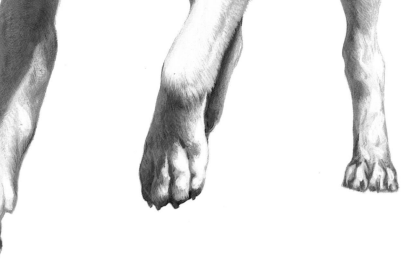

Smooth-haired Fox Terrier

Irish Terrier

The Irish Terrier is an ancient, Irish breed. It has a lively, impulsive, belligerent character and a tendency to pick fights with other dogs. Very courageous and devoted to its owner, it makes him a fine watch-dog, unafraid to tackle other animals even if they are larger than itself. It is loyal, faithful, proud and dignified, unable to bear a slight, and only if it is treated with kindness and affection will it make an excellent pet. It has a keen nose, is adept at going to ground, and is a fine swimmer. It is strong, hardy and swift, suited to any type of terrain, and a born ratter. It has a slim, lithe build. The head is long, with a flat skull, barely perceptible stop and level foreface. The eyes are small, dark, not prominent and full of life; the ears are V-shaped, set high and drop forward. The neck is of medium length and free of throatiness, and the body compact and square in outline. The legs are long, sinewy and straight and the feet small and round. The tail is docked and carried upright. The coat is hard, not too short, and wiry, with a fine, soft undercoat.

Weight: 10–12 kg (22–26½ lb). Height: 40–45 cm (16–18 in). Colour: various shades of red. Country of Origin: Ireland.

Welsh Terrier

This Welsh Terrier closely resembles the wire-haired Fox Terrier, differing in its slightly smaller size and in the colour and length of its coat, which gives it a particularly attractive appearance. Its temperament has also been strongly influenced by selective breeding and, though retaining the typical terrier characteristics of gameness and independence, it is also gay and affectionate, and easily adapts to home life provided that it gets sufficient exercise. Bred as a hunting dog, it is courageous, resistant to fatigue and robust. It has an attractive, slim build, is well balanced and agile. The head is long (less so than in the Fox Terrier), with a flat, wide skull, not very pronounced stop and long, clean-cut muzzle. The eyes are small, dark and expressive, and the ears small, V-shaped and set high and forward. The neck is strong, lean and of medium length, the body compact and square. The legs are sturdy and sinewy, with small, cat-like feet. The tail is docked and carried upright. The coat is long, wiry, abundant, thick and wavy.

Weight: approximately 8–9 kg (17½–20 lb). Height: approximately 38 cm (15 in). Colour: black and tan, grizzle and tan.
Country of Origin: Great Britain.

Lakeland Terrier

This terrier, native to the Lake District in the north of England (Cumbria), is, in many respects, similar to the Welsh Terrier; indeed the resemblance is so strong that the two breeds are sometimes mistaken for each other. Apart from being slightly smaller, the Lakeland differs in the colour of its coat, which reveals the influence of the Bedlington Terrier; in the eyes, which have a characteristic gentle, yet keen expression; in its elegant yet rugged appearance; and the docile, affectionate, but also gay and playful nature, which makes this terrier a first-class family pet. Nevertheless it is well able to command respect when necessary and, despite its modest size, makes a fine house guard, signalling the presence of intruders with its insistent, piercing bark. The Lakeland is not often found outside its native country and has achieved recognition only fairly recently, its standard being established in 1925. The

head is strong and long, but not like that of the other terriers. The stop is barely perceptible and the skull flat. The eyes are dark, of medium size and slightly sunken, and the ears V-shaped and small, set high and forward. The neck is strong, long and elegant, and the body strong and square with a sturdy brisket and powerful rump. The legs are sturdy and straight, with round, compact feet. The tail is set high, docked and carried upright. The coat is of medium length, dense, hard and water-resistant, with a thick undercoat.

Weight: dogs 8 kg (17½ lb); bitches 6.5 kg (14½ lb). Height: maximum 37 cm (14½ in). Colour: blue and tan, black and tan, blue, black, liver, red grizzle, wheaten.
Country of Origin: Great Britain.

Kerry Blue Terrier

Scottish Terrier

Scottish Terrier

Kerry Blue Terrier

The Scottish Terrier, a native of the Highlands, has the same origins as its fellow terriers, with the addition of some individual characteristics obtained by selective breeding. Its stately gait, proudly held, high, pointed ears and powerful build are in sharp contrast to its low-slung structure and small appearance. The Scottish Terrier is nevertheless an excellent earth dog, hardy, courageous and tenacious. Devoted to its owner, it is wary of and sometimes snappy with strangers and nervous of children. It is a low-bodied terrier, rectangular in outline, with a large head and small, erect, triangular ears set high and close together. The skull is flat, with a slight stop and long muzzle trimmed with whiskers and beard. The brows are prominent and bushy, partially hiding the dark, almond-shaped, deep-set eyes. The neck is muscular and fairly short, gradually widening towards the shoulders, and the body well ribbed up, with level topline and moderate belly tuck-up. The legs are strong and very short; the feet fairly large with arched, close toes. The tail is at the most 17 cm (7 in) long, set high and carried erect or with a slight curve, thick at the base and tapering to the tip. The coat is very dense, approximately 5 cm (2 in) long, hard and wiry with a short, thick, soft undercoat.

Weight: 7–9 kg (15½–20 lb). Height: 25–28 cm (10–11 in) maximum 30 cm (12 in). Colour: grey, black, wheaten, brindle of various shades. Country of Origin: Great Britain.

This Irish Terrier has ancient origins, although it was only officially recognized in 1920. Its ancestors include the Bedlington Terrier, the Dandie Dinmont, the Irish Terrier and perhaps even the Bull Terrier. Very common in Ireland, where it is used as an earth dog, it is increasing in popularity abroad as a pet. It is a sturdily built, well-proportioned dog, hardy, courageous and agile. A fine working terrier, intelligent, it is also a good tracking dog and may be trained to retrieve and is suited to all kinds of terrain, even marshland. The head is long and strong, with very slight stop, flat skull and square muzzle. The eyes are small and dark and the ears V-shaped and carried close to the cheek. The neck is strong and muscular and the body compact and well knit, with tuck-up at the loins, set on strong, muscular legs (forelegs perfectly straight), with small, round feet. The tail is docked at two-thirds of its length, set high and carried erect. The coat is soft, silky and sometimes wavy. The characteristic appearance derives from the way the coat is trimmed, which tends to make the dog look even shorter. The skull and neck are trimmed to make the thick eyebrows, whiskers and beard stand out.

Weight: 15–17 kg (33–37½ lb). Height: dogs 45–50 cm (18–20 in); bitches 43–48 cm (17–19 in). Colour: all shades of blue. Country of Origin: Ireland.

Sealyham Terrier

West Highland White Terrier

Sealyham Terrier

West Highland White Terrier

This breed developed at Sealyham in Pembrokeshire, Wales, by crossing different terriers such as the Bull, Dandie Dinmont, West Highland and Wire-haired Fox Terriers, with a contribution from the Flanders Basset Hound. In appearance it is more of the basset type than terrier, which makes it particularly suited to going to earth. It was deliberately bred to have a light-coloured coat so that the other dogs would not mistake it for the quarry when it emerged from the underground lair. Less common outside Britain, it is now mainly kept as a pet because of its size and its cheerful, friendly, lovable character. It is courageous and sturdy, very active and agile, and also makes a good guard dog. It has the large, rectangular head characteristic of the terrier, with stop not very clearly defined, slightly domed skull and square muzzle with powerful jaws. The eyes are dark and round and the medium-sized ears are set high and fall forward. The neck is strong and muscular and the body substantial and powerful, with back slightly arched. The legs are short, thick and very straight, with cat-like feet. The tail is docked and carried high and erect. The coat is long, dense and wiry, not curly, with a soft undercoat.

Weight: dogs 9 kg (20 lb); bitches 8 kg (17½ lb). Height: maximum 30 cm (12 in). Colour: white with lemon or brown markings on head and ears.
Country of Origin: Great Britain.

This small terrier bears some similarity to the Scottish, but differs in colour and the shape of the head, which is shorter and less powerful. It also has a shorter back, and smaller ears. Initially considered a variety of the Scottish, it was subjected to a strict breeding programme in order to establish its distinctive characteristics, and was granted its own official standard at the start of the century. Bred to hunt small animals and often used for vermin, the West Highland is a game, hardy, courageous dog, intelligent and very willing, docile and affectionate with its owner and wary of strangers. Nowadays it is kept mainly as a pet. The head is strong, with a slightly domed skull, well-defined stop and straight, relatively short muzzle, with powerful jaws. The eyes are dark, widely placed and slightly sunken and the ears small, pointed, triangular, erect and set wide apart. The neck is fairly long and strong; the body compact, cobby and very sturdy, set on short, powerful legs. The forefeet are broader than the hind ones. The tail (13–15 cm [5–6 in]) is not docked and is carried high and erect.

Weight: 7–8.5 kg (15–18 lb). Height: 25–27 cm (10–11 in). Colour: pure white.
Country of Origin: Great Britain.

Dandie Dinmont Terrier

Cairn Terrier

Dandie Dinmont Terrier

This small terrier, which owes its name to a character in one of Walter Scott's novels, has the same origins as the rest of the terrier family and excels at hunting rabbit and killing vermin. It has an excellent nose and is keen at searching out game, being plucky, hardy and tenacious, with a disproportionately loud bark for its size, which makes it a good guard dog. Little known outside the British Isles, it is now kept mainly as a pet because of its cheerful, friendly nature, although it is slow to trust a stranger. The head is large, with a broad skull, rounded forehead and relatively short muzzle. The eyes are large and dark hazel in colour, shielded by the hair hanging down from the head; the ears are broad at the base and set low, hanging close to the cheek,. The neck is strong and well developed and the body sturdy and long like that of a basset, set on very short but strong legs (the hind legs are slightly longer than the forelegs). The tail is 20–25 cm (8–10 in) in length and carried curved like a scimitar. The feet are compact and sometimes turned outwards, a typical feature of low-bodied dogs. The coat is a mixture of hard and soft hair, silky on the head.

Weight: ideally 8 kg (17½ lb). Height: 20–25 cm (8–10 in). Colour: Pepper type: black, blue, light grey. Mustard type: pale fawn or reddish brown with creamy head.
Country of Origin: Great Britain.

Cairn Terrier

Some experts consider this small dog to be the oldest representative of the group and therefore the forerunner of all Scottish terriers. Its name derives from the stony, rocky terrain which is its special hunting ground; it is also an expert killer of vermin. Nowadays it is kept mainly as a pet, because of its size and its gay, friendly, affectionate and loyal disposition. It also makes a willing guard dog. The general appearance is of a shaggy, rugged, sturdy and compact, somewhat low-bodied dog. The head is in proportion to the body and triangular in shape, with a broad skull, well-defined stop and long, strong muzzle. The eyes are small and dark, rather sunken and set wide apart, and the ears are small and triangular, set far apart and carried erect. The neck and body are sturdy and well proportioned. The legs are short and strong, with the feet turned slightly outwards (as in a basset type). The tail is of medium length and carried erect. The coat is long, profuse and hard, neither wavy nor curly, covering a thick, soft undercoat.

Weight: 5–7.5 kg (11–16½ lb). Height: maximum 25 cm (10 in). Colour: red, grey, pepper and salt (light or nearly black).
Country of Origin: Great Britain.

Norwich Terrier

Skye Terrier

Norwich Terrier

This small terrier, named after the town of Norwich, has rather obscure origins and was only recognized as a breed in 1932. It is possibly a descendant of the Irish Terrier, whose influence is evident in the dog's character – independent, very lively, sometimes stubborn – and its colour, which tends to be reddish. It differs from the other terriers in the fox-like head and the close general resemblance to the Dachshund. Courageous, tenacious and hardy, it makes a fine hunter of badger and fox and an excellent killer of vermin, though its main role nowadays is that of pet. Its characteristic shaggy appearance is due to the straight, hard, close coat, longer and rougher on the shoulders and neck, where it forms a ruff. The head is strong, with a broad skull, well-defined stop and pointed muzzle. The eyes are large and dark, the ears triangular, set high and held erect. The neck is of medium length, lean and free from dewlap, the body compact, cobby and moderately short, set on short, sound legs. The tail should be docked to about half its original length.

Weight: 8–9 kg (17½–20 lb). Height: approximately 25 cm (10 in). Colour: all shades of red, also wheaten, grizzle, black and tan. Country of Origin: Great Britain.

Skye Terrier

This small, well-known terrier is named after the Isle of Skye in the Hebrides. It is a very ancient breed, which has retained its present form for at least 250 years and, together with the Cairn, contributed to the genetic pattern inherited by all other Scottish terriers. Its distinctive feature is the length of its body, which is considerable in comparison with its height, measuring up to 105 cm (41 in) from nose to tail, and emphasized by the long coat which falls to the ground, completely hiding the legs and feet. The length of the coat, developed for decorative purposes, means that the dog is no longer suited to its original role of earth dog and it has become a pet, prized for its affectionate nature, liveliness and intelligence, and its natural guarding instinct. The head is long, with a slight stop and substantial muzzle. The eyes are dark and close together, and the ears may either be large and hang close to the head (drop ears) or small, erect, parallel and feathered (prick ears). The neck and body are long and sturdy and the legs short and muscular (the hind ones slightly longer), with large feet which stand square. The coat is up to 14 cm (5½ in) long, hard, flat and always smooth, shorter on the head.

Weight: 7–9 kg (15½–20 lb). Height: maximum 24–25 cm (9½–10 in). Colour: blue grey (dark or light), fawn, russet, cream. Country of Origin: Great Britain.

Soft-coated Wheaten Terrier

Manchester Terrier

Manchester Terrier or Black and Tan Terrier

The Manchester terrier, once very popular in England, differs from the other varieties in its large, slender shape, as a result of being crossed with Whippet bitches. It is a courageous, swift dog, excellent for hunting fox and badger to earth and very valuable for killing vermin. Originally its ears were cropped so that they were erect and pointed, but nowadays, as a result of the banning of ear-cropping of dogs in England, the large ears are folded forward, set high and close together. It has a reputation for being snappy and does not make a good pet, though it is devoted to its owner and affectionate. The Manchester Terrier is a dog of graceful and elegant appearance, but is solidly built. It has a long, wedge-shaped head, with a flat skull, moderate stop and tapering muzzle. The round eyes are not prominent. The neck is lean, free from throatiness and of moderate length; the body is sturdy and slim, with pronounced tuck-up of the belly. The legs are slim, straight and sinewy, with rounded feet. The tail is not docked, is of medium length and set low. The coat is thick, short, smooth and glossy.

Weight: 4–10 kg (9–22 lb). Height: dogs 35–38 cm (14–15 in); bitches 30–35 cm (12–14 in). Colour: black with characteristic well-defined tan markings.
Country of Origin: Great Britain.

Soft-coated Wheaten Terrier

This English terrier is a very young breed, which first appeared in public around 1930. In general appearance it bears a slight resemblance to the Kerry Blue, differing mainly in colour and its smaller size. Little known and rarely found even in England in spite of its many qualities, it is potentially a fine earth dog, an excellent guard and sheepdog, and also makes a delightful pet. Solidly built, active and courageous, it has a certain grace and suppleness of movement which also makes it aesthetically pleasing. The head is well proportioned, not too long or flat, with a well-defined stop and muzzle equal in length to the skull. The dark eyes are often covered by the long coat, and the ears are small and thin, set forward and covered in long hair which mingles with the hair on the head. The neck is solid and not too long; the body compact with relatively short coupling, a sturdy rump and very little belly tuck-up. The tail is short, and the legs are solid and muscular with small feet. The coat is abundant, long, soft and silky, wavy and evenly distributed.

Weight: approximately 16 kg (35 lb). Height: approximately 46–49 cm (18–19½ in). Colour: only wheaten.
Country of Origin: Great Britain.

Border Terrier

Norfolk Terrier

Norfolk Terrier

The Norfolk is very similar to the Norwich, both in origin, Norwich being the main town in Norfolk, and in general appearance. Practically unknown outside England, it is not common even there, where its original role of earth dog has been replaced by that of pet. Its singular characteristics lend it an attractive appearance. This is due partly to the ears which drop forward close to the cheeks, the alert, keen expression, the submissive, easy-going nature, and partly to the slightly longer coat with feathering on chest and legs. It is a fairly sturdily built dog. The head is in proportion to the rest of the body, with a pronounced stop, and straight muzzle with powerful jaws. The eyes are dark and bright. The neck is strong and muscular and the body long and compact, with moderate tuck-up of the belly. The legs are short, straight and strong. The tail should be docked to half its original length. The coat is hard, wiry and straight.

Weight: 8–9 kg (17½–20 lb). Height: maximum 25 cm (10 in). Colour: all shades of red, also wheaten, black and tan, grizzle.
Country of Origin: Great Britain.

Border Terrier

This breed is a native of Northumberland, hence its name refers to the Anglo-Scottish border. The breed was officially recognized in 1920, but very little is known of the history of its development, and the standard is still fairly imprecise. It is an excellent hunter, courageous, hardy and indomitable, with a good nose, very capable over difficult ground and swifter than the other terriers, able to keep pace with a horse. Because of all these qualities, it is also used to improve or develop other breeds. The head differs from those of other terriers: it is narrower and not as long, with a pronounced stop. The forehead is flat and the muzzle short and strong. The eyes are dark and the ears small, V-shaped and set high, hanging close to the cheek. The neck is fairly long and the body short and sturdy, resting on lean, strong, relatively long legs with cat-like feet. The tail, thick at the base and tapering to the tip, is set high and should not be docked. The coat is short, harsh and wiry, with a dense, completely waterproof undercoat.

Weight: 6–7 kg (13–15½ lb). Height: not specified by the standard. Usually between 28 and 37 cm (11 and 14½ in). Colour: red, wheaten. Less common: grizzle and tan, black and tan, blue and tan.
Country of Origin: Great Britain.

Bull Terrier

Staffordshire Bull Terrier

Staffordshire Bull Terrier

This terrier is the direct ancestor of the Bull Terrier and is derived from crossing the Bulldog with the smooth-haired Fox Terrier. Evolved for the purpose of bull-baiting, the breed underwent a rapid decline when such cruel sports were outlawed in 1835, but was kept alive by a number of breeders who refined its appearance by crossing it with the Manchester Terrier. Nowadays it has all the attributes of a fine guard dog and watch dog. Hostile and menacing towards strangers, it is a courageous and intelligent animal, which will make its owner an affectionate companion and fearsome guard. It is strong and powerful in build, yet does not lack elegance. The head is of the mastiff type, fairly short, with a flat, broad skull, distinct stop and short foreface with strong, powerful jaws. The eyes are dark and almond-shaped, and the ears rose or half pricked, never drop. The neck is muscular and rather short and the body compact and sturdy, with a broad, deep chest and powerful hindquarters. The legs are straight and the forelegs in particular are set rather wide apart; the feet are round and cat-like. The coat is short, smooth, glossy, soft and close.

Weight: approximately 18 kg (39½ lb). Height: 35–40 cm (14–16 in). Colour: solid red, beige, black, white, blue, parti-coloured, brindle. Country of Origin: Great Britain.

Bull Terrier

The Bull Terrier is an offshoot of the Staffordshire. In this animal the characteristics of the Bulldog have been modified by the contribution of Dalmatian, Greyhound and Whippet blood, so that not only has the physical body been refined but the aggressiveness and ferocity which made it into a fighting dog have now been eliminated from its character. In its present form, established in 1860, it has found increasing popularity as a pet, though its great strength and boisterous behaviour make it difficult to control unless carefully disciplined. Courageous and often reckless in character, Bull Terriers are aggressive and vicious towards strangers, but touchingly loyal, rising to their owner's defence without a thought for their own safety. The manner in which they are reared and trained will determine whether they will be a satisfactory family pet. If treated brutally, they become extremely dangerous. The general conformation is solid and powerful. The head is characteristically egg-shaped. The eyes are dark and obliquely placed and the ears set high, erect and pointed. The powerful, muscular neck and the solid, sturdy body clearly reflect the influence of the Bulldog. The coat is short, flat, harsh, glossy and close to the body.

Weight: 18–22 kg (39½–48½ lb). Height: 30–45 cm (12–18 in). Colour: pure white (preferable) or brindle on white. Other colours possible. Country of Origin: Great Britain.

152

Bedlington Terrier

Australian Terrier

Bedlington Terrier

This unusual terrier, known in its present form for at least 200 years, but undoubtedly older, emerged from the judicious crossing of Dandie Dinmonts, Bull Terriers and Otterhounds, with a contribution of Whippet blood. Despite its mild, lamb-like appearance, this terrier was bred by the Northumberland miners in order to catch mice down the pits. Nowadays it is mainly valued as a pet because of its lithe, elegant outline, but it still retains the plucky, independent character typical of the terrier family. It is intelligent, courageous, affectionate and silent, hardly ever barking. The head is long and narrow, not as rounded as the customary trimming makes it seem, with a narrow skull and no real stop. The eyes are small and sunken, the colour depending on that of the coat, and the ears are set back and hang flat to the cheek. The neck is lean, arched and long, and the body is light and long, with a roached back, sloping croup and greyhound-like belly. The tail is gracefully curved. The coat consists of a thick, woolly, curly undercoat and a longer outer coat trimmed to give the Bedlington its distinctive appearance.

Weight: 9–11 kg (20–24 lb). Height: 37–40 cm (14½–16 in). Colour: dark blue, liver, sandy (solid or with tan markings).
Country of Origin: Great Britain.

Australian Terrier

This small dog was selectively bred in Australia from Yorkshire, Dandie Dinmont, Cairn and Scottish Terriers. Although it has been classified as a separate breed, it bears such a close resemblance to its forebears that it is not always easily distinguishable. It is a low-set terrier which, though an excellent worker, intelligent, courageous and hardy, has always been popular as a pet because of its gay, affectionate, friendly disposition and its "toy dog" appearance. It has a long head, with a flat skull, definite stop and strong, straight muzzle. The eyes are small, dark and full of life, and the ears small, set high and carried erect or semi-erect. The neck is quite long and the body is long in proportion to the dog's height. The legs are short, strong and straight, with small, rounded feet and closely-knit toes. The tail is docked very short. The coat is long, harsh on the body and silky on the head.

Weight: 4–5 kg (9–11 lb). Height: 25 cm (10 in) on average. Colour: blue, grey, red, sandy. Silver hue (as in the Yorkshire) to be avoided.
Country of Origin: Australia.

Silky Terrier

The Silky Terrier is very closely related to the Australian Terrier, having the same country of origin and, for the most part, the same origins. It is linked not only to the Australian, but also to the Skye, the Cairn and the Yorkshire Terrier. It has a very recent official standard (1962), which was revised in 1967 and is still not clearly defined, the differences with its ancestors being at times so minor that it is difficult to identify. In the opinion of some dog experts both the Silky and the Australian would be better considered local varieties rather than separate breeds. Although the Silky makes a fairly capable earth dog and is strong and hardy in spite of its small size, the process of selection, aimed at increasing the length of the coat, has gradually diminished its potential as a hunter and increased its attraction as a pet and companion. The characteristics laid down by the standard do not differ greatly from those of its Áustralian cousin. The head – strong and wedge-shaped, carried proudly and with dignity – immediately identifies it as a member of the terrier family. The eyes are dark and round, with a lively expression, and the ears are V-shaped, set high and carried erect. Neither neck nor body are as long as the Australian's. The tail is docked short and carried erect. The short legs are almost completely hidden by the long, silky coat which may be 12–16 cm (4½–6 in) in length and is parted along the back.

Weight: 4–5 kg (9–11 lb). Height: approximately 22 cm (9 in). Colour: blue and tan, steel grey and tan.
Country of Origin: Australia.

HUNTING BREEDS

Greyhounds

Because they rely on their eyesight when hunting due to a poorly developed sense of smell, greyhounds are classified as "sight hunters". They are generally dogs of a good size, light and very swift, with long, slender bodies and long, sinewy limbs. Strong and hardy in spite of a sometimes fragile and delicate appearance, they are actually solidly built with long, lean muscles attached by powerful tendons. They are suited to hunting in open spaces, for either small or large game.

Afghan Hound

This dog, with its unmistakable appearance, is descended from Arab greyhounds and is an ancient breed, depicted in carvings that date from 2000 BC. However, it was only towards the end of the nineteenth century that this magnificent animal arrived in Europe, or rather England, and from there it began to spread further afield. Bred to hunt wild goat and gazelle, and even leopard in packs, it is a naturally hardy and agile animal, swift and full of stamina, as befits a dog used to living on rough, mountainous ground with a harsh climate, against which it is protected by its thick coat. Its method of hunting is based on speed and very sharp vision, whereas its sense of smell is very poorly developed. It still has a solid, powerful build, despite having been refined by the English who have turned it into a pet with a certain prestige. It is courageous, very proud and dignified, but loves to be petted and often reveals quite a lazy streak. It cannot stand ill-treatment and will bear a grudge for a long time. The Afghan's gallop is smooth and springy, and there is always a certain majesty and elegance about its movements. The head has a long skull, not too narrow, with a topknot of long, thick hair, and a slight stop. The eyes are dark and slanting, with an intelligent, thoughtful expression, and the ears are set low, flat, and covered in long hair. The neck is of good length and strong, and the body long and lean, with a level back and arched loins and croup. The legs are long and well boned with fine, dry feet. The coat is very abundant, fine, silky and very long, shorter on the back and short and smooth on the tail.

Weight: dogs 28 kg (61½ lb); bitches 25 kg (55 lb). Height: dogs 69–74 cm (27–29 in); bitches 62–68 cm (24–26½ in). Colour: any colour allowed. Gold, red, black and tan preferred.
Country of Origin: Afghanistan.

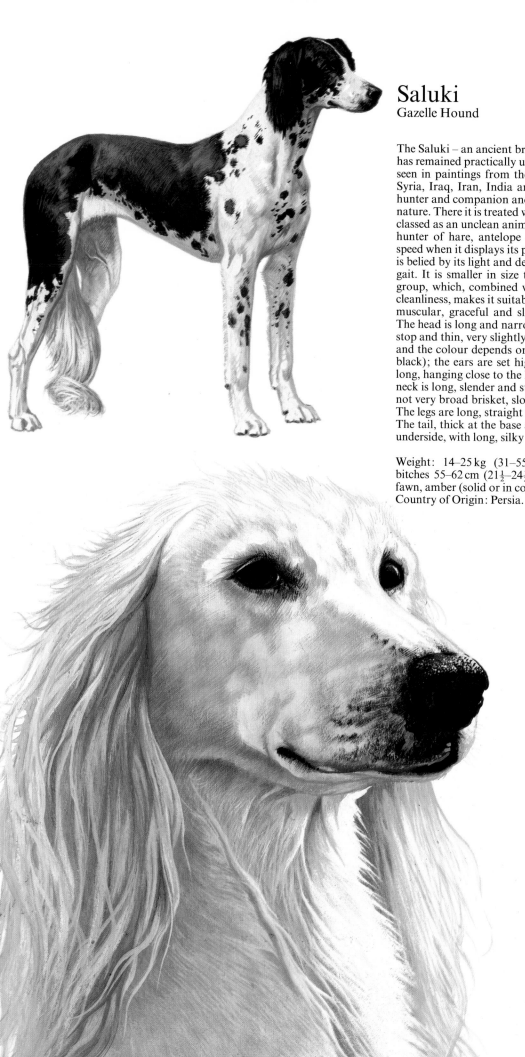

Saluki
Gazelle Hound

The Saluki – an ancient breed descended from the Arab greyhounds – has remained practically unchanged for thousands of years, as may be seen in paintings from the fifteenth century BC. It is widespread in Syria, Iraq, Iran, India and Egypt, where it is highly esteemed as a hunter and companion and for its intelligence and gentle, affectionate nature. There it is treated with love and respect, even though the dog is classed as an unclean animal in the Islamic religion. It is an instinctive hunter of hare, antelope and gazelle, pursuing the quarry at great speed when it displays its powerful, well-balanced musculature, which is belied by its light and delicate appearance. It has a smooth, springy gait. It is smaller in size than the other members of the greyhound group, which, combined with its excellent temperament and love of cleanliness, makes it suitable for town life. The dog's build is solid and muscular, graceful and slender, supple and perfectly proportioned. The head is long and narrow, with a flat or slightly domed skull, little stop and thin, very slightly arched muzzle. The eyes are large and oval and the colour depends on that of the coat (amber, sky-blue, brown, black); the ears are set high, are broad and up to 10–15 cm (4–6 in) long, hanging close to the head and covered with long, silky hair. The neck is long, slender and supple, and the body very long, with a deep, not very broad brisket, sloping croup and considerable belly tuck-up. The legs are long, straight and sinewy, with long feet and arched toes. The tail, thick at the base and tapering to a point, is feathered on the underside, with long, silky hair. The coat is short and smooth.

Weight: 14–25 kg (31–55 lb). Height: dogs 61–68 cm (24–27 in); bitches 55–62 cm (21½–24½ in). Colour: white, grizzle, black, cream, fawn, amber (solid or in combination).
Country of Origin: Persia.

Borzoi

The history of the Borzoi is linked to the historical events which took place in its homeland. Originally both a hunting dog and fashionable pet, it was used to hunt wolf in the steppes, and was the national dog of Russia until the October Revolution, when some of the splendid Perchino strain of the Grand Duke Nicholas was destroyed and the rest scattered throughout Europe, which allowed the breed to continue. The English have greatly modified the original model with the intention of turning it into more of a companion dog than a hunting animal. The English Borzois are therefore less magnificent, lacking the nobility of appearance and thickness of coat of the original Borzoi, but splendid authentic specimens can still be found in Holland and Germany. A majestic animal, with a splendidly silky, wavy coat and profuse feathering and frill round the neck, the Borzoi is unquestionably the most beautiful of the greyhound family. Its grace and elegance, its proud and noble bearing, made the Borzoi the favourite of high society. It was considered a symbol of status and power, and therefore ceased to be used for its original purpose of hunting large game (wolf, wild boar, deer and even bear), a role in which it displayed great courage and ability. It is affectionate and obedient with its owner, but aloof and distrustful, sometimes to the point of being vicious with strangers. It has a long, narrow head which is clean-cut and well chiselled, a flat skull, slight stop and very long, tapering muzzle. The eyes are large, oblong and set quite close together; the ears are small, fine and narrow, set high and back, of the rose type. The neck is long and clean, and the body long with belly well drawn up. The legs are long, strong and sinewy, with oval, almost hare-shaped feet.

Weight: 35–45 kg (77–99 lb). Height: dogs 75 cm (29½ in) and over (up to 82 cm [32 in]); bitches 71 cm (28 in) and over. Colour: all white or marked with yellow, orange, grey, brown.
Country of Origin: Russia.

Deerhound
Scottish Deerhound

The Deerhound, like the other greyhounds, is a dog of ancient origin depicted in engravings dating back more than 1000 years. The favourite hunting dog of the Scottish, it was considered a prized possession, the escort of the rich and powerful for whom it was a status symbol. With the gradual decline in the numbers of deer and the consequent curtailment of hunting, the dog's numbers dwindled and it is now fairly rare. In the last few years the breed has shown some signs of increasing in popularity on both sides of the Atlantic. The Deerhound is good-natured, affectionate, calm, thoughtful and patient with children, which makes it a suitable pet. The general conformation is that of a large, sturdy dog, of powerful bone (more so than the Greyhound), graceful though rugged in appearance, agile and swift, intelligent and responsive. The head is long, broad between the ears, with an almost flat skull, little stop and very long muzzle tapering

to the nose, with a moustache and beard. The eyes are dark and protected by thick, shaggy eyebrows; the ears are small and set high, covered with short hair and folded back like the Greyhound's. The neck is long, but shorter than the Greyhound's, strong and muscular. The body is long, with a deep chest, slightly arched back and belly well drawn up. The tail, set very low, reaches to the ground and is straight or slightly curved at the tip. The legs are powerful, with close, compact feet. The coat is rough, wiry and harsh, up to 8–10 cm (3–4 in) long, thick and not woolly.

Weight: dogs 38–47 kg (84–103½ lb); bitches 29–36 kg (64–79½ lb).
Height: dogs minimum 76 cm (30 in); bitches minimum 71 cm (28 in).
Colour: grey (light, dark, brindle), blue, orange, fawn. Never white.
Country of Origin: Great Britain.

Irish Wolfhound

In its present form the Irish Wolfhound is a fairly recent breed, although it has existed for centuries, as is shown by the accurate descriptions of it found in writings of the tenth and eleventh centuries. The present-day Irish Wolfhound was developed by crossing the old Irish Wolfhound, the Deerhound and the Great Dane: this programme was begun in 1862 by Captain Graham. The Irish Wolfhound was excellent at hunting wolves, because of its intelligence, courage, strength and physical stamina. Unlike other greyhounds, it also possesses a good sense of smell. Nowadays it is kept mainly as a guard and watch dog, a role in which it excels because of the great attachment it has for its owner, which makes it fearsome with intruders. In the U.S.A. it is still used to hunt wolf and coyote. In appearance it is not as massive or heavy as the Great Dane, but more so than the Deerhound; its build and bearing is graceful despite its great size. The head is long, with the frontal bones on the forehead very slightly raised, a moderately broad skull, very little stop and a long, moderately pointed muzzle. The eyes are dark and the ears small and greyhound-like in carriage. The neck is long, strong and muscular, without dewlap. The body is long and very sturdy, with back arched and belly well drawn up, set on long, muscular legs, with round, moderately large feet. The tail is long and slightly curved, the coat hard and rough, forming shaggy eyebrows, whiskers and beard on the muzzle.

Weight: 40–54 kg (88–119 lb) dogs minimum 50 kg (110 lb), bitches minimum 40 kg (89 lb)). Height: dogs 81–86 cm (32–34 in) minimum 79 cm (31 in); bitches minimum 71 cm (28 in). Colour: grey, red, black, fawn, white, brindle.
Country of Origin: Ireland.

161

Greyhound

The Greyhound is the best-known of its family, and is descended from the Arab greyhounds. Careful breeding by the English, aimed at developing its muscle power and build to obtain the maximum speed, has made it the fleetest of all dogs, capable of reaching 70 km (45 miles) per hour. Bred for hunting (deer, wolf and bear) and endowed with little sense of smell but very keen eyesight, it was the dog of the nobility, a symbol of elegance and distinction. Indeed it was worth so much that it was even used instead of money for the payment of taxes and duties. With the decline of large game hunting, it was used in crosses to develop the Foxhound, which is smaller but still very swift. Nowadays the Greyhound is kept exclusively as a racing dog and pet, although it is unhappy living in cramped quarters, nor does it like to be disturbed and is not very good with children. It is built for speed, with its sloping shoulders, deep chest, arched loins, well drawn-up belly, powerful hindquarters and long, sturdy thighs. It has a smooth gait, with a long, springing stride, enabling it to cover a long distance with each bound. This kind of movement uses so much energy that the dog can only maintain its rhythm for short periods (distances of 350 to 600 metres). The head is long, with a flat skull, slight stop and tapering muzzle. The eyes vary in colour and are shiny and bright, the ears small and fine, folded over and back. The neck is very long and arched; the body is slender and powerful, with smooth, fine, thick hair.

Weight: 23–35 kg (51–77 lb). Height: dogs 71–76 cm (28–30 in); bitches 68–71 cm (27–28 in). Colour: black, red, brown, fawn, blue grey (solid or striped), white.
Country of Origin: Great Britain.

Italian Greyhound

Whippet

Italian Greyhound

The Whippet is a small member of the greyhound family created by crossing the Greyhound, the Fox Terrier and the Bull Terrier. Developed about one hundred years ago by miners and working men of the north, it has since gained popularity as a pet. Extremely swift and agile, the Whippet owes its nickname of snap-dog to its ability to change direction with incredible speed. It can move at over 50 km (30 miles) per hour, an extraordinary feat for a dog of its size. Being a recent breed, the Whippet has never been a hunting dog, and its present characteristics are those for which it was originally created. It bears a strong resemblance to the Greyhound in appearance, although it has much in common with the Italian Greyhound, possessing the same grace and gentleness, combined with the muscle power of the Greyhound and the fearlessness inherited from the Terrier. The head is long and lean, wide between the eyes, with a sharply tapering muzzle. The eyes are lively and bright, and the ears small, fine and rose-shaped. The neck is long and arched; the body is long with a curved back, arched loins and croup. The brisket is deep and the belly well tucked up. The coat is short, fine, thick and close.

Weight: dogs 9–10 kg (20–22 lb); bitches 7–8 kg (15½–17½ lb). Height: dogs 46–49 cm (18–19½ in); bitches 45–48 cm (17½–19 in). Colour: black, red, white, fawn, blue (all one colour or mixed).
Country of Origin: Great Britain.

This small, graceful animal, like a miniature Greyhound, is an ancient breed. Imported to ancient Rome possibly from Egypt, it then spread to France and the rest of Europe. The Italian Greyhound makes a fine hunter of small game, as a result of its agility and speed. Despite its fragile and delicate appearance, it is a strong, hardy dog. It is also intelligent and lively, with a sweet nature, docile and affectionate, making an ideal pet. It has a similar build to the Greyhound, but more slender in all proportions. The head is very long, with a flat skull, slight stop, and muzzle equal in length to the skull. The eyes are very large, dark, round and full of expression, and the ears are small, set low and rose-shaped. The neck is long, light, lean, arched and very mobile, and the length of the body corresponds approximately to the height at the withers, but never exceeds it. The back is arched with the loins sloping down in a long curve to the croup. The chest is narrow and the belly well drawn up. The legs are long and fine, with long, narrow feet and thin toes. The tail is low, long and fine. The coat is very short, smooth, glossy and even.

Weight: approximately 3 kg (7 lb). Height: optimum 33 cm (13 in); maximum 36 cm (14 in). Colour: black, slate, fawn, isabella.
Country of Origin: Italy.

163

Pharaoh Hound

The Pharaoh Hound – so called because about 3000 years ago the Egyptians depicted Anubis, God of the Dead, with the head of this animal – probably sprang from crosses between different Arab greyhounds and is sometimes confused with the Ibizan Hound. Swift and hardy, it is a keen hunter of small game, even over difficult terrain, and unlike the other greyhounds it possesses a good nose. However, it is quite difficult to train and slow to learn, nor does it have an ideal temperament, as it is often snappy and headstrong, and is not therefore to be recommended as a pet. It is more massive in build than the other greyhounds and lacks some of their grace and harmony. The head is long, narrow and wedge-shaped, with a flat skull, prominent occiput and slight stop. The eyes are small, light and obliquely set, and the ears, unique among the greyhound breeds, are broad at the base, set high, carried erect and pricked forward. The neck is long, clean and muscular with only a slight curve. The body is long and sturdy, with a narrow, deep chest and prominent breast-bone. The belly is drawn up, though less so than in the other greyhounds. The tail is thick and set low, long and whip-like, carried high and curved when the dog is in action, never curled. The legs are long and straight, strong and sturdy. The coat may either be smooth, hard and short, or long, rough and thick, shorter on the head and ears.

Weight: dogs 22.5 kg (49 lb); bitches 19 kg (42 lb). Height: dogs 60–65 cm (23–25 in); bitches 57–63 cm (22–25 in). Colour: white, red, fawn (all one colour or marked in these colours).
Country of Origin: various.

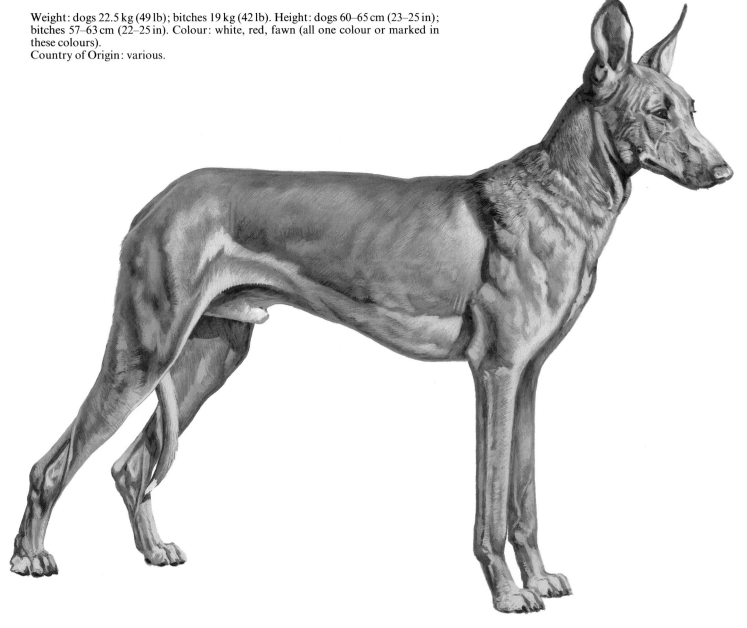

Spanish Greyhound
Galgo Español

The Galgo, also descended from the Arab Greyhound, now looks fairly like the Greyhound as a result of frequent crossbreeding over the last fifty years. Its original characteristics have therefore been slowly modified and the main differences between it and the Greyhound now consist of the brisket, which is not so well let down, the tail, which is longer and thicker, sometimes curled like a corkscrew but never like a hook, and the overall build, which is sturdier and not as elegant. Some consider the Galgo an Anglo-Spanish breed, which explains why an official standard has yet to be drawn up for this greyhound. Very sturdy and swift (but not as fast as the Greyhound), hardy and intelligent, with little sense of smell like almost all greyhounds, the Galgo is nowadays mainly a racing dog, whereas until the last century it was widely used to hunt hare. It has a long head with a narrow skull, very slight stop and strong jaws. The eyes are large, dark and lustrous; the ears fine, soft, set high and back and carried semi-dropped. The neck is of good length, strong and straight; the body muscular and long, with a strongly arched back, rounded croup, marked belly tuck-up, and lean flanks. The legs are slender, straight and muscular, with compact, rounded (but not cat-like) feet; the toes are well-arched with solid pads. The coat is short, fine, even, thick, glossy and close.

Weight: dogs 25–30 kg (55–66 lb); bitches 20–25 kg (44–55 lb). Height: dogs approximately 65 cm (25½ in); bitches approximately 60 cm (23½ in). Colour: white, red, chestnut, black (either one colour or speckled or striped in these colours). Country of Origin: Spain.

Braque Dupuy

Braque du Bourbonnais

Braque Saint-Germain

German Rough-haired Pointer

Poodle Pointer

Drentse Partridge Dog

Wetterhoun

Stabyhoun

Barbet

Other Pointing Dogs

Breed: Braque Dupuy – *Origin*: France – *Height*: 65–68 cm (25½–26½ in) – *Weight*: approximately 22 kg (48½ lb) – *Colour*: white base with dark brown markings – *Physical characteristics*: dark brown nose; long ears hanging in folds and carried back; tail carried low reaching down to the hocks and slightly curved towards the tip; smooth, fine hair on the head, coat smooth and fairly short elsewhere.

Breed: Braque du Bourbonnais – *Origin*: France – *Height*: 53–58 cm (21–23 in) – *Weight*: approximately 30 kg (66 lb) – *Colour*: white with light brown or fawn flecking – *Physical characteristics*: negligible stop; ears not too broad, falling in slight folds; no tail or short tail (no longer than 8 cm [3 in]); thick, fine, short coat.

Breed: Braque Saint-Germain – *Origin*: France – *Height*: dogs 56–62 cm (22–24 in); bitches 54–59 cm (21–23 in) – *Weight*: 20–25 kg (44–55 lb) – *Colour*: white with orange markings – *Physical characteristics*: not very well defined stop; pink nose; yellow eyes; ears of medium length hanging away from the head; tail carried horizontally; short, reasonably hard coat.

Breed: Drentse Partridge Dog (Drentse Patrijshond) – *Origin*: Holland – *Height*: approximately 65 cm (25½ in) – *Weight*: not specified – *Colour*: white with orange or brown markings – *Physical characteristics*: well-developed, brown nose; well-feathered, pendulous ears; long tail carried horizontally (in action); coat of medium length.

Breed: German Rough-haired Pointer (Stichelhaar) – *Origin*: Germany – *Height*: 60–66 cm (23½–26 in) – *Weight*: approximately 30 kg (66 lb) – *Colour*: brown and white, grey and brown (mixed or with large brown markings) – *Physical characteristics*: brown eyes; ears hanging close to the head; tail of medium length; coarse coat, 4 cm (1½ in) long.

Breed: Poodle Pointer (Pudelpointer) – *Origin*: Germany – *Height*: 60–65 cm (23½–25½ in) – *Weight*: 25–30 kg (55–66 lb) – *Colour*: brown – *Physical characteristics*: medium-sized ears hanging close to the head; horizontal tail (docked); harsh, thick coat of medium length.

Breed: Wetterhoun (Dutch Water Spaniel) – *Origin*: Holland – *Height*: dogs 57–62 cm (22½–24½ in); bitches 53–58 cm (21–23 in) – *Weight*: 22–28 kg (48½–61½ lb) – *Colour*: black, brown and white, blue and white – *Physical characteristics*: brown eyes; spiral tail; curly coat (except on the head).

Breed: Stabyhoun – *Origin*: Holland – *Height*: approximately 50 cm (19½ in) – *Weight*: not specified – *Colour*: black, orange, brown (all with white) – *Physical characteristics*: dark eyes; ears hanging close to the head; tail hanging down with a slight upward curve towards the tip; long, smooth coat.

Breed: Barbet – *Origin*: France – *Height*: 45–55 cm (18–21½ in) – *Weight*: 20–25 kg (44–55 lb) – *Colour*: black, grey, brown, dirty white, brown and white, black and white – *Physical characteristics*: eyes with long, thick eyelashes; long ears hanging close to the head, richly covered with long hair; tail set low and carried with a slight upward curve; long, woolly, curly or wavy coat.

Old Danish Pointer

Drotszoruvizsla

American Water Spaniel

Field Spaniel

Redtick Coonhound

Bluetick Coonhound

Breed: Drotszoruvizsla (Rough-haired Hungarian Vizsla) – *Origin*: Hungary – *Height*: dogs 57–64 cm (22½–25 in); bitches 53–60 cm (21–23½ in) – *Weight*: 22–30 kg (48½–66 lb) – *Colour*: dark yellow all over – *Physical characteristics*: well-developed nose; dark eyes (not black); long, pendulous ears; tail set quite low and docked to two-thirds of its length; hard, rough coat.

Breed: Old Danish Pointer (Gammmel Dansk Honsehund) – *Origin*: Denmark – *Height*: dogs 52–58 cm (20½–23 in); bitches 48–54 cm (19–21 in) – *Weight*: not specified – *Colour*: white with liver markings – *Physical characteristics*: hazel eyes; pendulous ears; tail thick at the root tapering to the tip; short, thick coat.

Other Tracking dogs

Breed: Redtick Coonhound – *Origin*: United States – *Height*: 50–68 cm (19½–26½ in) – *Weight*: 20–36 kg (44–79½ lb) – *Colour*: reddish brown flecked with white – *Physical characteristics*: pendulous ears; long tail; smooth coat.

Breed: Bluetick Coonhound – *Origin*: United States – *Height*: 50–68 cm (19½–26½ in) – *Weight*: 20–36 kg (44–79½ lb) – *Colour*: white with blue ticking and black markings on head and body – *Physical characteristics*: pendulous ears; tail carried horizontally; short, soft coat.

Breed: West Country Harrier – *Origin*: Great Britain – *Height*: approximately 55 cm (21½ in) – *Weight*: not specified – *Colour*: white, lemon and white, grey and white, fawn and white, white and light tan – *Physical characteristics*: black nose; straight foreface; negligible stop; brown or dark hazel eyes; drooping ears of medium length; slightly spiked tail; thick but flat coat.

Breed: Dunker (Norwegian Hound) – *Origin*: Norway – *Height*: 47–55 cm (18½–21½ in) – *Weight*: not specified – *Colour*: black or blue mottled (harlequin) with fawn and white markings – *Physical characteristics*: dark eyes; ears hanging close to the head; tail carried slightly curved; coat slightly rough to the touch.

Other Gundogs

Breed: American Water Spaniel – *Origin*: United States – *Height*: 38–45 cm (15–18 in) – *Weight*: 12–20 kg (26½–44 lb) – *Colour*: dark brown, liver – *Physical characteristics*: dark eyes; long, pendulous ears covered with curls; slightly curved, feathered tail; curly, waterproof coat.

Breed: Field Spaniel – *Origin*: Great Britain – *Height*: around 40 cm (16 in) – *Weight*: 15–25 kg (33–55 lb) – *Colour*: black, mahogany red, liver, black and white, orange – *Physical characteristics*: dark eyes; pendulous, well-feathered ears; tail carried low; flat or slightly wavy coat.

West Country Harrier

Dunker

Halden Hound

Hygen Hound

Lundehund

Schiller Hound

Smalands Hound

Grähund

Grand Griffon Vendéen

Porcelaine

Grand Anglo-français

Other Tracking dogs

Breed: Halden Hound (Haldenstövare) – *Origin*: Norway – *Height*: 47–55 cm (18½–21½ in) – *Weight*: not specified – *Colour*: black and white (brown shading on head and legs) – *Physical characteristics*: dark eyes; drooping ears; tail reaching down to the hocks; short, thick coat.

Breed: Hygen Hound (Hygenhund) – *Origin*: Norway – *Height*: 47–55 cm (18½–21½ in) (dogs even up to 60 cm [23½ in]) – *Weight*: not specified – *Colour*: brown and reddish yellow (with or without black shading), black and tan, tricolour (with white) – *Physical characteristics*: black nose; dark or hazel eyes; broad, fairly short, drooping ears; long tail but not reaching past the hocks; dense, straight coat.

Breed: Lundehund (Puffin Dog) – *Origin*: Norway – *Height*: 32–36 cm (12½–14 in) – *Weight*: 6–7 kg (13–15½ lb) – *Colour*: black, grey, brown (with white shading) – *Physical characteristics*: brown eyes; erect ears; short tail with thick hair but no feathering; long, harsh coat.

Breed: Schiller Hound (Schillerstövare) – *Origin*: Sweden – *Height*: dogs 50–60 cm (19½–23½ in); bitches 46–57 cm (18–22½ in) – *Weight*: not specified – *Colour*: black and tan – *Physical characteristics*: well-developed, black nose; brown eyes; pendulous ears; tail carried straight or slightly sabre-like; smooth coat with profuse undercoat.

Breed: Smalands Hound (Smalandsstövare) – *Origin*: Sweden – *Height*: dogs 45–54 cm (18–21½ in); bitches 42–50 cm (16½–19½ in) – *Weight*: not specified – *Colour*: black and tan – *Physical characteristics*: dark eyes; ears hanging, not in folds; tail carried sabre-like or docked at birth; thick, smooth, not fine coat.

Breed: Grähund (Swedish Grey Dog) – *Origin*: Sweden – *Height*: 49–52 cm (19½–20½ in) – *Weight*: approximately 30 kg (66 lb) – *Colour*: shaded grey on legs and darker grey on muzzle and ears – *Physical characteristics*: brown eyes; erect, pointed ears; short tail carried curled over the back; coat of medium length, smooth and strong (short on the head and fronts of the legs).

Breed: Grand Griffon Vendéen – *Origin*: France – *Height*: 60–65 cm (23½–25½ in) – *Weight*: not specified – *Colour*: fawn, orange and white, grey, grey and white, hare (with or without white), tricolour – *Physical characteristics*: dark eyes; long, drooping ears; tail carried sabre-like tapering to the tip; long, rough, sometimes shaggy coat.

Breed: Porcelaine – *Origin*: France – *Height*: dogs 55–58 cm (21½–23 in); bitches 53–56 cm (21–22 in) – *Weight*: 25–30 kg (55–66 lb) – *Colour*: pure white, with orange shading on the ears and sometimes round orange spots – *Physical characteristics*: black nose; dark eyes; soft ears falling in folds and reaching the tip of the nose at full length; tail of medium length, thick at the root and tapering to the tip, carried low with a slight curve; very short, thick, glossy coat with a porcelain hue (hence the name).

Breed: Grand Anglo-français (Grand Bâtard) – *Origin*: France – *Height*: 60–70 cm (23½–27½ in) – *Weight*: approximately 35 kg (77 lb) – *Colour*: black and white, orange and white, tricolour (black, white, orange) – *Physical characteristics*: somewhat thin muzzle; brown eyes, not very long, pendulous ears; thin, slightly curved tail, carried well; short coat.

Anglo-français

Petit Anglo-français

Griffon Fauve de Bretagne

Steinbracke

Polish Hound

Hungarian Hound

Slovakian Hound

Jugoslavenski Planinski Gonič

Jugoslavenski Drobojni Gonič

Basanski Ostrodlaki Gonič-Barak

Breed: Anglo-français (Bâtard) – *Origin*: France – *Height*: 51–60 cm (20–23½ in) – *Weight*: 20–30 kg (44–66 lb) – *Colour*: black and white, orange and white, tricolour (white, black, orange) – *Physical characteristics*: see Grand Anglo-français.

Breed: Petit Anglo-français (Petit Bâtard) – *Origin*: France – *Height*: 40–50 cm (16–20 in) – *Weight*: 16–20 kg (35–44 lb) *Colour*: tricolour (white, orange, black) – *Physical characteristics*: see Grand Anglo-français.

Breed: Griffon Fauve de Bretagne – *Origin*: France – *Height*: 48–55 cm (19–21½ in) – *Weight*: 25–30 kg (55–66 lb) – *Colour*: fawn – *Physical characteristics*: dark eyes; brown or black nose; pendulous ears covered in soft hair; tail of medium length, tapering to the tip and carried well; very hard coat of medium length.

Breed: Bayerischer Gebirgsschweisshund (Bavarian Schweisshund) – *Origin*: Germany – *Height*: dogs up to 50 cm (20 in); bitches no more than 45 cm (18 in) – *Weight*: not specified – *Colour*: fawn (various shades) with dark ears, muzzle, cheeks and lips – *Physical characteristics*: black nose; dark brown eyes; ears hanging close to the head; thick, smooth coat.

Breed: Steinbracke – *Origin*: Germany – *Height*: approximately 50 cm (20 in) – *Weight*: 25–30 kg (55–66 lb) – *Colour*: white with dark back, black and tan, tricolour – *Physical characteristics*: dark brown eyes; large ears hanging close to the head; tail set high; short, thick, hard coat.

Breed: Polish Hound (Ogar Polsky) – *Origin*: Poland – *Height*: 55–65 cm (21½–25½ in) – *Weight*: 25–32 kg (55–70½ lb) – *Colour*: black, dark grey, brown (all variously shaded) – *Physical characteristics*: dark nose; wrinkles on forehead; brown eyes; pendulous ears; thick tail which droops at rest; smooth coat.

Breed: Hungarian Hound (Erdelyi Kopo) – *Origin*: Hungary – *Height*: long-legged variety: 55–65 cm (21½–25½ in); short-legged variety: 45–50 cm (18–20 in) – *Weight*: 30–35 kg (66–77 lb) – *Colour*: long-legged variety: black with some white markings (on the forehead, chest, feet and tip of the tail) or tan markings (on the throat, legs and brows); short-legged variety: red brown shaded around the belly and legs, sometimes with not very large white markings (in the same areas as the other variety) – *Physical characteristics*: dark eyes; large ears hanging without folds; tail carried low (not in action); smooth coat (longer and rougher in the long-legged variety).

Breed: Slovakian Hound (Slovensky Kopov) – *Origin*: Czechoslovakia – *Height*: dogs 45–50 cm (18–20 in); bitches 40–45 cm (16–18 in) – *Weight*: approximately 18 kg (40 lb) – *Colour*: black and tan – *Physical characteristics*: dark eyes; black nose; drooping ears; tail carried sabre-like at work; rough coat 2–5 cm (¾–2 in) long.

Breed: Jugoslavenski Planinski Gonič (Yugoslav Mountain Hound) – *Origin*: Yugoslavia – *Height*: 45–55 cm (18–21½ in) – *Weight*: not specified – *Colour*: black and tan – *Physical characteristics*: dark eyes; pendulous ears without folds; tail carried sabre-like; short, thick coat.

Breed: Jugoslavenski Drobojni Gonič (Yugoslav Tricolour Hound) – *Origin*: Yugoslavia – *Height*: 45–55 cm (18–21½ in) – *Weight*: not specified – *Colour*: tricolour – *Physical characteristics*: well-developed, black nose; dark eyes; straight or slightly curved tail carried low (less in action); smooth coat.

Breed: Basanski Ostrodlaki Gonič-Barak (Rough-haired Bosnian Hound) – *Origin*: Yugoslavia – *Height*: 46–56 cm (18–22 in) – *Weight*: 16–24 kg (35–53 lb) – *Colour*: yellow, reddish, grey, black (sometimes with white flecking or all combined) – *Physical characteristics*: brown eyes; pendulous ears; long, coat.

Balkan Hound

Rauhaarlaufhund

Swiss Short-legged Hound

Swiss Hound

Austrian Hound

Sabueso Hound

Hellenic Hound

Black and Tan Coonhound

Tennessee Treeing Brindle

Redbone Coonhound

Treeing Walker Coonhound

Breed: Balkan Hound (Balkanski Gonič) – *Origin*: Yugoslavia – *Height*: 44–54 cm (17½–21 in) – *Weight*: approximately 20 kg (44 lb) – *Colour*: reddish or russet with black back – *Physical characteristics*: brown eyes; ears hanging close to the cheek; tail thick at the root, tapering to the tip; strong, thick coat with undercoat.

Breed: Rauhaarlaufhund (Rough-coated Swiss Hound) – *Origin*: Switzerland – *Height*: 40–50 cm (16–20 in) – *Weight*: 27–30 kg (59½–66 lb) – *Colour*: any, excluding black or brown (chocolate) – *Physical characteristics*: thick, fine undercoat, hard, wiry coat.

Breed: Swiss Short-legged Hound (Schweizer Niederlaufhund) – *Origin*: Switzerland – *Height*: 30–38 cm (12–15 in) – *Weight*: not specified – *Colour*: the same as in the corresponding large breed – *Physical characteristics*: dark eyes; long, pendulous ears; tail carried low without any appreciable curve; belly drawn up.

Breed: Swiss Hound (Schweizer Laufhund) – *Origin*: Switzerland – *Height*: 40–55 cm (16–21½ in) – *Weight*: 27–30 kg (59½–66 lb) – *Colour*: orange and white – *Physical characteristics*: pronounced stop; long muzzle with slight curve of foreface; black nose; dark eyes; long ears, set low and falling in folds; tail not too long, with a slight downward curve; hard, smooth and profuse coat.

Breed: Austrian Hound (Österreichischer Bracke or Brandlbracke) – *Origin*: Austria – *Height*: 46–52 cm (18–20½ in) – *Weight*: not specified – *Colour*: black and tan, fawn (small, white patch allowed on the chest) – *Physical characteristics*: pendulous ears; long, slightly curved tail; smooth, glossy coat.

Breed: Sabueso Hound (Sabueso Español) – *Origin*: Spain – *Height*: dogs 51–56 cm (20–22 in); bitches 49–52 cm (19½–20½ in) – *Weight*: not specified – *Colour*: black and white, orange and white – *Physical characteristics*: brown eyes; pendulous flews; long, drooping ears; fine, smooth coat.

Breed: Hellenic Hound (Ellinikós Ichnilátis) – *Origin*: Greece – *Height*: 47–55 cm (18½–21½ in) – *Weight*: 17–20 kg (37½–44 lb) – *Colour*: black and tan – *Physical characteristics*: brown eyes; pendulous ears; tail not too long, carried sabre-like; dense, short coat.

Breed: Black and Tan Coonhound – *Origin*: United States – *Height*: dogs 63–68 cm (24½–26½ in); bitches 58–63 cm (23–25 in) – *Weight*: not specified – *Colour*: black and tan – *Physical characteristics*: brown eyes; long ears hanging in folds, long tail set slightly below the level of the back; dense, short coat.

Breed: Tennessee Treeing Brindle – *Origin*: United States – *Height*: 40–61 cm (16–24 in) – *Weight*: 13–22 kg (28½–48 lb) – *Colour*: black striped – *Physical characteristics*: pendulous ears; tail carried fairly horizontally; short, soft, slightly curled coat.

Breed: Treeing Walker Coonhound – *Origin*: United States – *Height*: 50–68 cm (20–26½ in) – *Weight*: 18–34 kg (40–75 lb) – *Colour*: white with black and brown markings – *Physical characteristics*: drooping ears; tail carried high; smooth coat.

Breed: Redbone Coonhound – *Origin*: United States – *Height*: 53–66 cm (21–26 in) – *Weight*: 20–32 kg (44–70½ lb) – *Colour*: red – *Physical characteristics*: long, pendulous ears; long tail; smooth, soft coat.

Breed: Trigg Hound – *Origin*: United States – *Height*: 51–64 cm (20–25 in) – *Weight*: 16–25 kg (35–55 lb) – *Colour*: any – *Physical characteristics*: drooping ears; long legs set true; tail curved like a hook; fine, soft coat.

Breed: Plott Hound – *Origin*: United States – *Height*: 53–63 cm (21–25 in) – *Height*: 18–29 kg (40–64 lb) – *Colour*: tan-pied with black saddle – *Physical characteristics*: large, drooping ears; long tail; smooth, soft coat.

Breed: Rastreador Brasileiro – *Origin*: Brazil – *Height*: approximately 65 cm (25½ in, even less in bitches) – *Weight*: not specified – *Colour*: brown and black, white flecked with blue and brown, white with black or brown markings – *Physical characteristics*: dark eyes; long, drooping ears; long, sabre-like tail; smooth coat.

Trigg Hound

Rastreador Brasileiro

Plott Hound

Other Earth Dogs

Breed: American Staffordshire Terrier – *Origin*: United States – *Height*: 44–46 cm (17½–18 in); bitches 40–42 cm (16–16½ in) – *Weight*: 17–20 kg (37½–44 lb) – *Colour*: all varieties (white should not cover more than 80 per cent of the body surface) – *Physical characteristics*: dark eyes; cropped ears; short tail carried horizontally; short, thick coat.

Breed: Český Terrier (Bohemian Terrier) – *Origin*: Czechoslovakia – *Height*: 27–35 cm (10½–14 in) – *Weight*: 6–9 kg (13–20 lb) – *Colour*: blue grey, light coffee brown (yellow, white or grey shading allowed) – *Physical characteristics*: small ears hanging close to the head; tail carried low at rest (sabre-like in action), 18–20 cm (7–8 in) long; thick, wavy coat (requiring to be clipped for show purposes).

Breed: Glen of Imaal Terrier – *Origin*: Ireland – *Height*: 33–35 cm (13–14 in) – *Weight*: 13–16 kg (28½–35 lb) – *Colour*: bluish grey, wheaten – *Physical characteristics*: brown eyes; drop ears; long, rough coat.

Breed: Tibetan Terrier – *Origin*: Tibet – *Height*: 35–40 cm (14–16 in) – *Weight*: 6–7 kg (13–15½ lb) – *Colour*: white, golden, black grey, cream (parti-colour and tricolour also allowed, excluding chocolate) – *Physical characteristics*: dark eyes; heavily feathered ears lying close to the head; tail curled over the back, with feathering; long, fine coat.

American Staffordshire Terrier

Glen of Imaal Terrier

Český Terrier

Tibetan Terrier

Other Greyhounds

Breed: Sloughi – *Origin*: North Africa – *Height*: 60–70 cm (23½–27½ in) – *Weight*: 30–32 kg (66–70½ lb) – *Colour*: sandy, fawn (all shades), brindle, black and tan, off-white – *Physical characteristics*: large, dark eyes; short, drooping ears; drawn-up belly; thin tail, curved towards the tip, reaching to the hocks and carried low in repose (not above the level of the back in action); smooth, fine coat.

Breed: Hungarian Greyhound (Magyar Agár) – *Origin*: Hungary – *Height*: 65–70 cm (25½–27½ in) – *Weight*: 22–31 kg (48½–68½ lb) – *Colour*: grey, black, brindle, white, pied, isabella – *Physical characteristics*: semi-drop ears; long tail, curled at the tip; short, smooth coat.

Sloughi

Hungarian Greyhound

COMPANION DOGS

This category covers a vast number of breeds which vary greatly and frequently have no shared characteristics. Poodles, Griffons, small Spaniels, Pomeranians, toy breeds, all belong to this group. Some are dogs which – for reasons either of particular physical beauty or special qualities, such as friendliness, an affectionate disposition, intelligence, the ability to adapt easily to confined spaces – tend to be kept as pets rather than for their original function. Others may be toy breeds which have developed naturally in the course of evolution. Finally there are those dogs which are the result of artificial "miniaturization", an art at which the Chinese and Japanese excel. An example of this in a different sphere is their creation of the miniature bonsai trees.

Poodle

Although everybody is familiar with the Poodle, its origins are not so well known. Although officially considered a French dog, one of its ancestors is thought to be the North African Barbet, first imported to the Iberian Peninsula where it was crossed with Portuguese water dogs. From there it arrived in Gaul, where it was much admired for its hunting ability in water, being a naturally good swimmer and retriever. The French name for the Poodle, Caniche, derives from its being used to hunt duck. Its German name, Pudel, is also a reference to its fondness for water. In the seventeenth century, the Poodle became a prestige companion and came to be primarily known as a "ladies' dog". It soon began to gain popularity far and wide both because it was not too large and for its many positive features. It is a very intelligent animal, quick to learn, naturally clean, friendly, docile, obedient, affectionate and patient with children. The unfortunate repercussion of the Poodle being adopted by fashion-conscious society is that its appearance is spoiled. Its thick, abundant curly fur is trimmed in accordance with the latest fashion, often making the dog look ridiculous, so much so that it has become necessary to fix strict standards for trimmings. Even so, with the possible exception of the so-called modern trim, the Poodle almost invariably looks affected and unnatural, far removed aesthetically from its hunting ancestry. There are three varieties of Poodle, differing only in size. The head is long and straight, with a well-formed skull, fairly prominent occiput, poorly defined stop, and long but not snipy muzzle. The eyes are of medium size, dark or black in white or black dogs and dark amber in brown dogs. The ears, set fairly low, are quite long and broad, hanging close to the head. The neck is strong, slightly arched and free from dewlap. The body is marginally longer than the height at the withers. The back is level and there is reasonable tuck-up of the underline. The tail is set high at the level of the loins, docked to about one third of its length and carried high and erect. In the corded variety the tail is docked by half or left intact. The legs are thin, sinewy and perfectly straight, with relatively small, solid, arched, oval-shaped feet. The coat can be one of two kinds, either profuse, woolly, luxuriant, fine in texture and evenly distributed, or corded and considerably longer, with cords of at least 20 cm (8 in) in length. The Poodle's skin colour depends on the colour of the coat; in white dogs it has a characteristic silver hue.

Weight: from 25–40 kg (55–88 lb) according to size. Height: standard: 45–55 cm (18–22 in); miniature: 35–45 cm (14–18 in); toy: under 35 cm (14 in). Colour: black, brown, white, grey.
Country of Origin: France.

Standard Poodle

Miniature Poodle

Toy Poodle

173

King Charles Spaniel

This small English spaniel is probably an offshoot of the large spaniels, developed through crosses with the Cocker, Pug and perhaps the Tibetan Spaniel. The King Charles certainly does not have the spaniel build, both in terms of its compact, cobby body and its Molossian-like face. The current type, officially recognized in 1892, differs from the dog which lived in the English courts of Charles I and Charles II, whose face was not as flat nor its hair as long. With the fall of the Stuarts, the King Charles Spaniel went through a period of decline but was preserved and bred by some of the noble houses, each of which concentrated on developing its own particular variety distinguished by the colour of the coat. It has a gentle and affectionate disposition, loves affection, is of equable temperament and devoted to its owner, making an excellent pet. The head is fairly large, with a massive, dome-shaped skull, very marked stop, and a short, square, broad, blunt muzzle with a wide lower jaw. The eyes are large, dark and spherical, and the ears, set low, are very long and pendulous. The neck is short and strong and the body long and massive. The legs are short and straight.

Weight: 3–6 kg (6½–13 lb). Height: 26–32 cm (10–12½ in). Colour: King Charles: glossy black with mahogany markings on the cheeks, linings of the ears, under the tail and over the eyes. Prince Charles: pearly white ground with evenly distributed black markings and tan markings on ears, cheeks and under the tail. Ruby: solid mahogany. Blenheim: pearly white ground with large, evenly distributed chestnut markings.
Country of Origin: Great Britain.

Cavalier King Charles Spaniel

Clearly a relative of the King Charles, this spaniel is nevertheless classified as a separate breed and therefore possesses its own standard. Like the King Charles, it was given its name by Charles II. It is still not clear whether the King Charles derived from the Cavalier or vice versa, but the Cavalier King Charles is the more popular of the two and makes an excellent pet, being lively and affectionate, friendly, docile and obedient. The Cavalier King Charles is more slight in build than the King Charles. The head is fairly large, with a longer muzzle and a flat, not domed, skull. The eyes are large, dark and round, but never prominent, and the ears are long, set high and hang close to the cheek. The neck is of medium length and slightly arched. The body is short, sturdy and well proportioned, set on reasonably long, straight, sinewy, sturdy legs. The coat is long, silky, soft to the touch, slightly wavy but free from curl, with feathering on the neck, chest, ears, tail and backs of the legs. The tail can either be left intact or docked, but by no more than a third. Selective breeding has again produced four varieties of this spaniel, corresponding exactly to those of the King Charles, with the same variation in coat colour.

Weight: 5–8 kg (11–18 lb). Height: 25–34 cm (10–13½ in). Colour: as in the King Charles.
Country of Origin: Great Britain.

Pug

This small dog – of not altogether attractive appearance, although it does have a certain charm – is a Chinese creation, brought over to Holland from the East in the sixteenth century and then crossed with the Bulldog. The fashion for small dogs prevalent in the European courts, where the nobles took pride in possessing animals of high commercial value, led to an influx of dogs from China and Japan, where miniature forms are a speciality. The Pug enjoyed a period of great popularity in England under the reign of William III, and from there spread further afield. The Pug looks like a small Bullmastiff, and is athletic in build, with its compact form and powerful muscles. In exchange for the comfort in which it was kept and the favours of the ladies, this small dog, with its characteristic face, had to allow itself to be dressed up in the most bizarre and sometimes ridiculous fashion and

to be treated like a toy. Nowadays the Pug has diminished in popularity in favour of more attractive dogs. It has a lively, friendly disposition, and is clean, even-tempered and exclusive in its affections, but has the unfortunate habit of snoring. The head is broad and round, with a wide forehead and no indentation, a pronounced stop and very short, square muzzle. The eyes are large, globular and prominent, and the "button" ear is preferred. The skin is slack, forming wrinkles on the forehead and dewlap on the neck. The tail is set very high and carried tightly curled. The coat is fine, soft and glossy.

Weight: 6–8 kg (13–17½ lb). Height: 26–33 cm (10–13 in). Colour: silver, fawn, apricot, always with black mask. Black variety. Country of Origin: Great Britain.

Papillon
Continental Toy Spaniel

Papillon

Phalene

The Papillon is a lively and irrepressible pet, affectionate but sometimes intrusive, and in need of strict training if it is not to become a nuisance. The breed may be considered French or Belgian, although there are the usual conflicting opinions over its ancestry. Some say that it is a native of China, the result of crossbreeding between the Chihuahua and Chinese and Tibetan spaniels; others that, as its name suggests, it is a miniature variety of continental spaniel. The breed enjoyed a period of great popularity during the Renaissance and in the seventeenth century, a favourite not only of noble ladies but also of kings such as Louis XIV and Henry III, and of painters such as Rubens, Titian, Veronese, Van Dyck and others. At that time only the so-called Phalene ("moth"), drop-eared variety was known, whereas there is now a more modern representative of the breed (dating back to the end of the nineteenth century), with erect, open ears resembling the wings of a butterfly – hence the name of Papillon, by which the entire breed is known in Great Britain and America. It is not clear how this new characteristic came into being, whether it was the result of crossbreeding or of a mutation. The general structure is sturdy in spite of the breed's size. The smaller specimens are the more highly valued, provided that the constitution remains hardy, the standard is complied with and the dogs are not too delicate. The head is small, with a slightly rounded skull, a straight, finely pointed muzzle and a well-defined stop. The eyes are quite large, almond-shaped, dark and should not bulge. The two varieties are differentiated by their ears, which are set high and dropped but very mobile in the Phalene, and set well back but very open with ear-tips pointing outwards in the Papillon. The neck is slightly arched and fairly short, and the body is of good length. The legs are short, straight and fine-boned, with hare-like feet. The tail is long and set high. The coat is abundant, long, glossy and wavy, longer on the neck and chest, with ears, legs, thighs and tail well-fringed.

Weight: large size 2.5–5 kg (5–11 lb); small size 1.5–2.5 kg (3–5 lb). Height: 15–28 cm (6–11 in). Colour: any colour admissible.
Country of Origin: France.

French Bulldog

The French Bulldog is a small dog, closely related to the English Bulldog and possibly also to the Manchester Terrier. Like its English counterpart, it was originally developed for fighting (with other dogs), but its appearance and character were subsequently refined so that it is now an ideal companion, whose gentle and affectionate character, obedience, responsiveness and patience with children have made it very popular. In addition it makes a willing guard dog and will attack intruders. Its only drawback is that it snores, due to the fact that the lower jaw is undershot. It has a look of alertness and intelligence. The head is massive, square and broad, with a wide, nearly flat skull, domed forehead, well-defined stop, and a short, pug-face with a turned-up nose. The jaws are wide and powerful with thick, pendulous flews which always cover the teeth when the mouth is closed. The eyes are large, dark, round and quite protuberant beneath prominent orbital arches. The medium-sized ears are bat-shaped, broad at the base and rounded at the top, high and erect. The neck is short, strong and thick; the body is short and cobby with a broad, deep chest, strong rump and moderate belly tuck-up. The forelegs are short, wide apart, straight and sturdy, while the hind legs are slightly longer. The feet are small and compact and turned slightly outwards, the hind feet being slightly longer. The coat is short, thick, smooth, glossy and close to the body.

Weight: dogs minimum 8 – maximum 14 kg (17½–30 lb); bitches minimum 7 – maximum 13 kg (15½–28½ lb). Height: 30–35 cm (12–14 in). Colour: brindle (a mixture of black and dark red hair), white with brindle markings, white (with black eyelashes and eye-rims).
Country of Origin: France.

French Bulldog

Boston Terrier

Boston Terrier

The Boston Terrier is actually closer to the Bulldog family than to the Terriers both in appearance and temperament, being descended from the French Bulldog (with a possible contribution from the Bull Terrier). It was developed in America as a companion dog about one hundred years ago, and appeared in Europe about 1930. It is intelligent, clean, good-natured, faithful and affectionate, well suited to living in a flat. In general appearance it is sturdy but not massive, with a certain elegance in its movements. The head is large but in proportion, with a broad, flat skull, well-defined stop, a short, square muzzle, free from wrinkles, and wide jaws with the lower one slightly undershot. The flews are large and thick, but not pendulous. The eyes are big, dark, round and wide apart, with a kind, alert expression, and the ears set high and either cropped short to a point, or (compulsory in Britain) carried erect. The neck is slightly arched, of fair length, without dewlap. The body is fairly short but not chunky, with a broad, deep chest and ribs well sprung, and moderate tuck-up of the belly. The loins are muscular with a slightly curved rump. The legs are strong and straight with small, compact, round feet. The coat is short, fine, glossy and quite soft.

Weight: lightweight: under 7 kg (15 lb); middleweight: 7–8.5 kg (15–19 lb); heavyweight: 8.5–12 kg (19–26 lb). Colour: dark brindle, with large white markings as defined by the standard.
Country of Origin: U.S.A.

177

English Toy Terrier
Black and Tan

This small dog is no more than the toy variety of the Manchester Terrier. Created primarily for the purpose of catching vermin in the home, the strain degenerated to such an extent that animals were produced weighing less than 2.5 kg (5 lb) and less than 20 cm (8 in) high, with foetal-type heads, spherical, pop-eyes, a round skull, very week limbs and almost no coat. Nowadays the English Toy Terrier is more of a family pet and companion. Restored to its former shape and size, it is an elegant, well-proportioned, intelligent and lively animal, endowed with the fiery temperament typical of terriers. Its standard is very similar to that of the Manchester Terrier, except it is lighter in body structure and has large, flared ears, set high on the head and carried erect. The English Toy Terrier is not nowadays a common breed.

Weight: 2.7–3.6 kg (6–8 lb). Height: approximately 25 cm (10 in). Colour: black and tan like the Manchester.
Country of Origin: Great Britain.

Yorkshire Terrier

This dog was bred in Yorkshire with the aim of creating a dog small enough to live in cramped, working-class houses, and which would also kill rats and mice. It probably evolved through the crossing of the Manchester with the Skye Terrier, and possibly the Dandie Dinmont. Originally known as the Rough Toy Terrier, the breed was much more rugged in appearance than it is now, and it was certainly not the intention of the workers of Halifax, Bradford and Huddersfield to produce the pet it has become today. Its pretty, charming appearance combined with a lively, intelligent and affectionate nature has made it a highly desirable pet and ensured its popularity practically everywhere. The Yorkie retains the impetuous temperament typical of the terrier and likes its independence, which can make it wilful and unruly if it is not properly trained. It is still a fierce enemy of vermin which it attacks furiously. The head is small, with a slightly flattened skull, well-defined stop, wide muzzle and black nose. The eyes are of medium size, dark, lively and sparkling, and the ears small, triangular and carried erect or semi-erect. The body is sturdy, compact and long, set on short, straight legs well covered with hair; the feet should be very round. The tail is docked at half its original length. The coat should be as long as possible, smooth, silky and glossy, with a parting from the head to the root of the tail.

Weight: 1.5–3.2 kg (3–7lb). Height 19–22 cm (7½–8½ in). Coat: steel blue with golden tan markings on head and legs.
Country of Origin: Great Britain.

Bichon Frise

Maltese

Bichon Frise

Maltese

The Bichon Frise was derived from the Maltese in the fifteenth century and belongs to a group of small dogs all of which have the name of Bichon, a contracted form of *Barbichon* or *Petit Barbet*. Its current name was adopted after a controlled breeding programme, and refers to the curly coat characteristic of the breed. The Bolognese is an Italian strain very similar to the Bichon Frise. The smallest of the Bichon varieties, it was a great favourite at the European courts, particularly in Spain (under Philip II) where it was immortalized in several of Goya's paintings, and Russia (under Catherine the Great). It is a bold, affectionate animal, lively, happy and alert. As it is also beautiful to look at it makes a charming pet. The head is large but not massive, with a broad, slightly arched skull, a well-defined stop and pronounced occiput. The muzzle is square and straight, with a black nose and strong jaws. The eyes are round, dark brown and full of expression; the drop ears are set high. The neck is slender and the length of the body more or less equal to the height. The legs are straight with oval feet. The tail is very thick and carried curved over the back.

Weight: maximum 4 kg (9 lb). Height: approximately 25 cm (10 in). Colour: pure white.
Country of Origin: France.

The Maltese is a dog of ancient origin, and although the breed is considered Italian it was almost certainly imported, probably from Asia Minor. Indeed the name it was given in the first century BC by Strabo – Canis Melitei or Melitensis – is derived from the town of Melita in Asia Minor. Malta cannot therefore be considered the birthplace of the Maltese, even though the dog has been named after the island it has made its home and where it has always been highly prized. A popular pet among the aristocratic ladies of ancient Rome and Greece, the Maltese is a dog which has always been admired for its attractive appearance. Quiet, happy and sociable by nature, it is very affectionate towards its owner but does not take easily to strangers, with whom it may well be snappy. It is strong, hardy and tough, despite its modest size. The skull is broad and flat, the stop very well defined, and the muzzle short and straight with a black nose. The eyes are large, round, dark and not protuberant. The ears are set high, wide and drooping. The neck is of medium length and the body approximately 8 cm (3 in) longer than it is high. The legs are short with round feet, and the high tail well arched over the back. The coat is dense, silky, glossy and a good length.

Weight: 3–4 kg (6½–9 lb). Height: average 25 cm (10 in) and never more than 30 cm (12 in). Colour: pure white, pale ivory.
Country of Origin: Italy.

Italian Spitz
Volpino Italiano

The Volpino Italiano has the same ancient origins as the Spitz dogs, and in many respects closely resembles the Pomeranian. At one time very popular in Italy, it was considered both a pet for the gentry and a working dog for poorer people, who used it as a guard dog, a role in which it excelled because of its acute hearing and loud, shrill bark. Nowadays it is only a pet and is less common, partly because it is becoming increasingly difficult to find pure animals due to crossbreeding with other Spitz breeds. Lively, intelligent and friendly, it makes an excellent pet, its main drawback being that it barks too much. It has an egg-shaped skull, more rounded than the Pomeranian's, with a pronounced occipital crest and well-defined stop. The muzzle is long and wedge-shaped, like that of a fox, with a black nose. The eyes are round and dark ochre in colour, and the ears are small, triangular, set high and held erect. The neck is of medium length and free from dewlap. The body is compact, cobby and square in outline. The coat is thick, smooth and close, very long all over, except on the front of the legs, with feathering on the legs and tail and a full mane and frill.

Weight: approximately 4 kg (9 lb). Height: dogs 27–30 cm (10$\frac{1}{2}$–12 in); bitches 25–28 cm (10–11 in). Colour: all-white or all-red; champagne, less popular.
Country of Origin: Italy.

Pomeranian

The Pomeranian is a dog of Spitz origin. The Germans began the process of producing a miniature breed and this was continued by the English so successfully that by the end of the nineteenth century dogs were produced weighing only 7 kg (15$\frac{1}{2}$ lb). When it became a favourite at the court of Queen Victoria, the Pomeranian's popularity soon escalated and it was further bred down to satisfy the demands of a fashionable society that liked smaller and smaller dogs. Some very small specimens, however, began to show signs of degeneration, clear traces of dwarfism being excessively domed skulls, spherical, bulging eyes and frail limbs; official minimum proportions were established as a result. The Pomeranian is a very lively, happy, sociable and intelligent dog, clean and easy to train. Its only drawback is its tendency to yap. The head is small, with a slightly flat skull, very pronounced stop and sharp muzzle. The eyes are dark, oblique and bright; and the ears triangular, smaller than in the Italian variety, high and erect. The tail is one of the characteristics of the breed and is set high, turned over the back and carried straight so that the feathery plume touches the ruff. The coat is thick, very soft, fluffy and long, forming feathering, ruff and frill.

Weight: maximum 3 kg (7 lb). Height: maximum 28 cm (11 in). Coat: pure white, black, brown, wolf grey, orange.
Country of Origin: Germany.

Spitz

The members of the Spitz family are nowadays all classified as companion dogs, although the larger variety (Gross Spitz) is still used as a guard dog. The Wolf Spitz (so called because of the colour of its coat), long known by Dutch sailors as the Keeshond, is one of the best guard dogs in the world and is also a member of this family. The Spitz are an extremely ancient breed, bearing a marked resemblance to the fossilized remains of *Canis Familiaris Palustris*. Natives of Russia and the Baltic regions, they rapidly spread throughout Europe, gaining favour both by virtue of a proud and elegant demeanour and a friendly, unselfish and highly affectionate disposition. They have very keen hearing and a loud, piercing, all too frequent bark. The head is of medium size and wedge-shaped, with an almost flat skull, pronounced stop and moderately long, straight, tapering muzzle, with a small, black nose. The eyes are medium-sized, dark and

obliquely set; the ears are small, triangular, set high and close together, erect and pricked forward. The neck is of medium length and the body fairly short, compact and sturdy, with a straight back and slight tuck-up of the belly. The legs are sturdy with small, round, solid feet. The tail is set high, held erect at the root and carried curled over one side of the back. The coat is long and luxuriant, neither close-lying nor parted down the middle, with profuse feathering on the legs and belly and a dense ruff and mane. The hair is shorter on the face and ears.

Weight: depending on size. Height: Wolf Spitz: 45–55 cm (17½–21½ in). Large: 40–50 cm (15½–19½ in). Medium: 29–36 cm (11½–14 in). Small: 25–28 cm (10–11 in). Miniature: maximum 25 cm (10 in). Colour: black, grey, white, brown, orange. Country of Origin: Germany.

181

Pinscher and Miniature Pinscher

The Pinscher is a German breed which was created by crossing the Schnauzer and the Dobermann (which it closely resembles), with a contribution from the Manchester Terrier. From the Pinscher a smaller version was then developed through a further contribution of Manchester blood, so that the Miniature Pinscher bears some resemblance not only to the Dobermann but also to the Black and Tan Toy Terrier. Although not identical and classified under two different standards, these two German terrier-type dogs share a number of characteristics. Both were originally bred for hunting and were very useful for destroying vermin; their cheerful, friendly natures and considerable intelligence then led to their adoption as household pets. However, they have retained the typically proud and fearless terrier temperament and will automatically unleash their fury upon rats and mice. They also make willing guard dogs and are endowed with acute hearing and a loud, piercing bark. In general appearance both dogs are sturdy, well built and elegant, with a very well-balanced muscle structure and no trace of dwarfism in the miniature variety. The head is sturdy and rather long and narrow, never round. The skull is flat, with only a slight stop; the muzzle is tapering and wedge-shaped with a black nose. The eyes are dark and oval and the ears set high and cropped (in countries where this is allowed), and carried erect. The length of the body is equal to the height. The tail is set high and docked at the third joint. The coat is short, smooth and glossy.

Weight: Miniature Pinscher: 3–4 kg (6½–9 lb); Pinscher: 13–16 kg (28½–35 lb). Height: Miniature Pinscher: 25–30 cm (10–12 in); Pinscher: 45–48 cm (17½–19 in). Colour: Miniature Pinscher: black and tan, yellow, brown, blue, with or without tan markings, stag-red variety known as "Reh Pinscher". Pinscher: black and tan, black, brown (varying to red), grey-blue with tan markings, pepper and salt. Country of Origin: Germany.

Miniature Pinscher

Affenpinscher

The Affenpinscher is a very rare breed of dog which, despite its name, does not share any characteristics with the Pinscher. The Affenpinscher, also known as the "monkey terrier", probably sprang from a union between the Miniature Schnauzer and the Belgian Griffon, and bears a close resemblance to the latter. It is a small dog, almost a mixture of Griffon and Terrier, bred to kill mice and rats in the home, but also good at hunting small game. Nowadays it is primarily a pet, though it is not common. It is lively, unpredictable (terrier heritage), very affectionate, and automatically assumes the role of guard dog. Its characteristic feature is its overall tousled appearance, created by the untidy coat and the mass of hair which frames its face and forms thick, shaggy eyebrows and beard. The Affenpinscher is the smallest of the Schnauzer family. It is sturdy in build, with fine but not delicate bones, strong and tough for its size. The head is large and round with a short, broad forehead, very well-defined stop and short muzzle – but not turned upwards as in the Griffon. The lower jaw is slightly longer than the upper. The eyes are large, dark, round and prominent and the ears set high and wide apart, cropped to a point and carried erect. The length of the body equals the height at the withers and looks cobby and compact. The legs are sturdy and well proportioned, with round, cat-like feet. The tail is docked to a third of its length. The coat is long, profuse, wiry and shaggy, with a crisp undercoat.

Weight: maximum 4 kg (9 lb). Height: 25–28 cm (10–11 in). Colour: black, blue-grey, fawn.
Country of Origin: Germany.

Schipperke

Schipperke

The Schipperke is a small dog of wolf-like appearance, used as a guard dog by Flemish sailors. As regards its origins, some would call it a miniature version of the Belgian Shepherd Dog, while others claim it is descended from crosses between Keeshonds and Belgian sheepdogs. Affectionate, gentle and patient with children, the Schipperke makes an admirable pet. It is, however, rather restless by nature, continually darting about, full of curiosity, wanting to join in every household activity and expressing its reactions by barking shrilly and raising its ruff. But if well trained, it makes a delightful pet. It makes a very useful guard dog and rat and mouse catcher too. If suitably trained, it can also be made into a good hunting dog for small game. It is known for its love of horses. The head is fox-like, with a slightly rounded skull, gentle stop and tapering muzzle of moderate length, with a small, black nose. The eyes are dark, lively and sharp; the high-set ears are triangular, erect and parallel. The neck is strong and sturdy and the body powerful, short, thick-set and cobby, with considerable tuck-up at the loins. The legs are thin but solid, well proportioned with hocks well let down, and the feet small, compact and rounded. The dog is sometimes born without a tail, but if not the tail is docked at the root. The coat is abundant, thick, dense and harsh, long from the ears down to the neck – where it forms a ruff – and chest, short on the head and the front of the legs, and smooth on the ears.

Weight: Different for the three sizes; small: 3–4 kg (6½–9 lb); medium: 4–5 kg (9–11 lb); large: 5–9 kg (11–20 lb). Height: 25–35 cm (10–14 in) according to size. Colour: solid black. Other whole colours are permissible.
Country of Origin: Belgium.

Griffon Bruxellois

Petit Brabançon

Griffon
Bruxellois, Brabançon, Belge

The term Griffon refers to three different dogs, namely the Griffon Bruxellois, the Petit Brabançon and the Griffon Belge, the last being recognized mainly on the Continent. Although classified as separate breeds, they are actually almost identical, the only variation being the texture and colour of the coat. The three "breeds" can appear in a single litter, so it would be more accurate to consider them varieties of the same breed. The Griffon made its first appearance in 1883 and was such a success that Dutch and German as well as Belgian breeders were anxious to claim responsibility for its creation. But it was the Belgians who developed this breed by crossing the old Stable Griffon with the Pug and the King Charles, from which it has inherited its characteristic pug-face. Relatively rare and not very well known, these small, rather comical-looking animals make intelligent, affectionate and faithful pets and are easy to train. They make good guard dogs and are natural enemies of rats and mice. Their build is that of a compact, cobby dog of elegant appearance and proud, smart carriage. The head is broad and round, with domed skull and forehead, deep stop and very short muzzle with slightly undershot chin. The eyes are large, black, round, protruding and set well apart. Together with the ears, which are set high and carried semi-erect (or cropped in some countries), this gives the dog a slightly owl-like appearance. The tail is docked.

Weight: small size maximum 3 kg (6½ lb); large size 3–5 kg (6½–11 lb). Height: small size 21 cm (8 in); large size 28 cm (11 in). Colour: Bruxellois (rough-coat): clear red. Brabançon (smooth-coat): reddish, black and rich tan. Belge (rough-coat): black, black and red, black and reddish-brown mixed.
Country of Origin: Belgium.

Griffon Belge

Hairless Dog

The Hairless Dog originated in the tropics, although its exact country of origin has never been fully established. It is a very unusual animal, its skin being completely devoid of hair except for a few thin, bristly tufts on the skull, lips, ears, tail and along the back. As it can only live in countries where the climate is consistently hot, for this reason it is extremely rare in Europe, despite having been known for a long time. Not only is it particularly subject to colds, but it has little to recommend it aesthetically. The "hairless" feature probably established itself as a direct result of the torrid climate (environmental mutation) and has now become hereditary, so that Hairless Dogs crossed with other breeds will produce hairless young. Teeth have the same embryological origin as hair and are also sometimes affected, giving rise to delicate, sometimes fragile teeth, and stronger milk teeth than in other dogs. Slight tremors almost invariably run through the skin of the Hairless Dog, probably due to a congenital weakness of the nervous system or to an imperfect adaptation of the body's heating system to the total absence of hair. It has come to have a certain prestige as a pet primarily because of its rarity value and the difficulty in rearing it. It resembles the Italian Greyhound in appearance, but is less elegant and lithe. The head is well chiselled, with a slightly domed skull, moderate stop and long muzzle. The eyes are sad and rather lifeless, and the ears large and erect, sometimes rose-shaped.

Weight: 4–8 kg (9–17½ lb). Height: 25–40 cm (10–16 in). Colour: hairless, elephant grey, slate grey, flesh-coloured (without pigment) with grey or black markings.
Country of Origin: not established.

Xoloitzcuintli
Mexican Hairless Dog

The Xoloitzcuintli, or Mexican Hairless Dog, derives its name from the god Xoloth, and is the only hairless breed recognized in Mexico. In ancient times it was bred by the Indians for food. Gradually this custom died out and the Mexican Hairless Dog developed into a companion and pet. It is found almost exclusively in its own country due to the same problems of adaptability and breeding experienced with the Hairless Dog. The limited information which is available regarding its character and behaviour tends to be subjective and unreliable. It is described as a fairly intelligent and lively animal, an excellent watch dog because of its alert temperament and effective bark. This may be why it enjoys a certain popularity in Mexico, having little to recommend it in appearance. It is somewhat similar in build to the Manchester Terrier, though sturdier and less refined in appearance. The head is long, with a broad skull, definite stop, long, tapering muzzle and a black or flesh-coloured nose. The eyes are of medium size and oval, the colour ranging from yellow to black; the ears are set high, are large and held erect, and are "bat" shaped. The neck is long, slender and elegant and the body sturdy, with a broad, deep chest and moderate tuck-up of the belly. The young are pink all over at birth and remain so for the whole of their first year.

Weight: 6–10 kg (13–22 lb). Height: 30–50 cm (12–20 in). Colour: reddish-grey hairless skin with dull black mask.
Country of Origin: Mexico.

Mexican Hairless Dog

Chihuahua

The Chihuahua is an ancient breed which originated in Mexico and is named after the city of the same name in the Sierra Madre. The Aztecs considered it a sacred animal and it was eaten by priests as sacrificial food. The Americans were responsible for making it popular round 1850. The Chihuahua is the world's smallest dog, but is nevertheless strong and hardy, easily acclimatized and resistant to illness. It is affectionate, faithful and fearless, refusing to be intimidated by other dogs. It is also intelligent, loyal and very lively. The general conformation is dainty and elegant, with fine but solid bone and a well-balanced muscle structure. The skull is rounded, with a definite stop, and the muzzle moderately long and tapering. The colour of the nose depends on that of the coat. The eyes are large, very dark, spherical and slightly prominent, and the ears – set high and far apart – are large and broad at the base, carried erect when the dog is alert and at a 45° angle in repose. The neck is of medium length and arched, and the body sturdy and compact, longer than it is high. The chest is very broad and deep, and the underline level. The tail is set at medium height, is not too long and carried in a loop over the back. There are two varieties of Chihuahua, the Smoothcoat, which has fine, thick, soft, glossy hair, evenly distributed over the body, but short and smooth on the head and ears, with a collar of longer hair; and the Longcoat, with flat or slightly wavy, soft hair, which has an undercoat, a profuse collar and feathering on the ears and legs. The tail is long and very furry.

Weight: Smoothcoat, approximately 1.5 kg (3½ lb); Longcoat, approximately 3 kg (6½ lb). Weight: 16–20 cm (6–8 in). Colour: all colours permitted,.
Country of Origin: Mexico.

Pekingese

The Pekingese is a dwarf spaniel of ancient origin, depicted in recognizable form in remains dating from 2000 BC. A symbol of power, bred and carefully guarded in the imperial palaces as sacred animals, exportation of the Pekingese was forbidden until 1860 and not until 1864 was a live one to be seen in England and in France. The Pekingese has an unmistakable appearance and whether or not it is found pleasing is largely a question of personal taste. At all events, despite its small size, it is a dignified and proud looking animal with a distinguished bearing. Haughty, detached, independent and sometimes bad-tempered, it is slow to bestow its friendship, although it displays devotion, faithfulness and affection towards its owner. The head is massive, with a broad, flat skull, never domed, and a deep stop. The muzzle should be as short as possible, wide, flat and well wrinkled, with the nose very close to the skull. The jaw is turned upwards, sometimes undershot, but the teeth are always well covered by the lips. The eyes are large, dark, lustrous and slightly prominent, and the ears, set at medium height, are pendant. The neck and body are short but the chest is broad and the ribs well sprung. The forelegs are short, thick and bowed at the shoulder, giving the Pekingese a rolling gait, while the hind legs are lighter and close together. The feet are large and flat, the front ones turned slightly outwards. The coat is very long and straight, neither wavy nor curly, with a thick, soft undercoat to give it body. A profuse mane extends to form a frill around the neck, and there is extensive feathering on the legs, tail and ears.

Weight: dogs not over 5 kg (11 lb), bitches 5.5 kg (12 lb). Height: 18–25 cm (7–10 in). Colour: black, fawn, sable, white (all with black mask), solid or parti-coloured.
Country of Origin: China.

Lhasa Apso

The Lhasa Apso is an ancient Tibetan breed, which originated from crosses between Tibetan spaniels and small Chinese terriers, from which it has inherited its coat. It bears a strong resemblance to the drop-eared variety of the Skye Terrier, and the two might easily be confused at first glance. It is a member of the group of highly esteemed small Oriental dogs that were held sacred. Like the other sacred dogs, the Lhasa Apso was for many years hidden away in palaces and especially in monasteries, and it was not until 1922 that the first specimens were brought to Europe by travellers. The Lhasa Apso is a lively, alert, gay and sociable dog, playful and fond of children, making an ideal pet. The head is large, with thick, abundant hair falling over the eyes and a good beard and moustache. The skull is relatively narrow, almost flat, with a well-defined stop, a long muzzle (inherited from the terrier), and a level or slightly undershot jaw. The eyes are dark, medium-sized and round but not globular, and the ears pendant and profusely covered in hair. The neck is short and strong and the body very long with powerful hindquarters. The legs are short, sturdy, and straight with rounded feet. The tail is set high, is long and carried curved over the back. The coat is thick, straight, soft, but not silky, long, but does not touch the ground, and parted down the spine from the head to the root of the tail.

Weight: dogs 6–7 kg (13–15½ lb); bitches 5–6 kg (11–13 lb). Height: 21–25 cm (8–10 in). Colour: One colour: golden, honey, sandy, liver, slate. Parti-coloured: black and white, brown and white. Country of Origin: Tibet.

Lhasa Apso

Shih Tzu

Shih Tzu

The Shih Tzu was also known at one time by the name of Lion Dog because of the distinctive way in which it was clipped. A native of China, it is often confused with the Lhasa Apso, which is of Tibetan origin. To the inexpert eye the two dogs could indeed appear identical, partly because the long, flowing hair hides their actual physical features. The two breeds in fact differ significantly and are therefore justifiably kept separate. The Shih Tzu used to live in the imperial palaces where, like the Pekingese, it was held in high esteem and enjoyed privileges reserved for animals considered sacred. Jealously guarded within its homeland, it made its first appearance in England in 1930, where it was greatly admired by many small-dog lovers. The Shih Tzu has a lively, alert, noble and proud character; affectionate and devoted to its owner, it makes an ideal pet. The head is broad and round, with abundant, untidy hair creating a characteristic chrysanthemum-like effect. The stop is very distinct and the muzzle short and square, but not wrinkled. The jaw may either be level or slightly undershot. The eyes are large, very dark and round but not prominent and the ears large and pendant. The neck is short and the body longer than it is high, compact and strong, set on short, straight, sturdy, muscular legs. The tail is set high and carried curled over the back. The coat is long, thick and dense but not curly, with a good, thick undercoat.

Weight: maximum 9 kg (20 lb). Height: approximately 28 cm (11 in). Colour: all colours permissible.
Country of Origin: China.

Tibetan Spaniel

Tibetan Spaniel

The Tibetan Spaniel is a small dog, equal in height to the Shih Tzu and the Lhasa Apso. Although there is some uncertainty over its ancestry, it is probably descended from the Lhasa Apso crossed with Chinese spaniels and then with continental spaniels, which increased its original size. It does in fact bear a certain resemblance to the Phalene variety of Papillon. The Tibetan Spaniel was another of the breeds considered sacred and precious, living in the palaces and monasteries and jealously guarded from the eyes of strangers. It first appeared in Europe in the fifteenth century but it was only in 1921, when it had already lost some of its original features, that it captured the attention of small-dog lovers. It is a quiet, somewhat aloof and unfriendly animal, though not ill-tempered or aggressive. The head is of medium size, with a domed skull, slight but defined stop, a straight, relatively long muzzle, and a slightly undershot jaw. The eyes are dark and oval in shape, the ears well feathered and falling forward. The neck is moderately short and the body longer than it is high, set on legs which look straight but are actually slightly bowed. The feet are of medium size, and the richly plumed tail is set high and carried up and curled over the back. The coat is dense, profuse, of moderate length and lies flat, with a mane of longer hair round the neck and shoulders and shorter hair on the head (except on the ears).

Weight: dogs 5–7 kg (11–15½ lb); bitches 4.5–5 kg (10–11 lb). Height: dogs 27 cm (10½ in); bitches 25 cm (10 in). Colour: One colour: golden, fawn, cream, white, brown, black. Parti-coloured: markings in the above-mentioned colours.
Country of Origin: Tibet.

Japanese Chin
Japanese Spaniel

It would appear that this small Spaniel, which is classed as Japanese, was actually imported from China. It probably sprang from a union between the Tibetan Spaniel and the Pekingese, with contributions from other Oriental small dogs, but in its present form the Chin is a Japanese creation. Bred for a life of luxury and a favourite of all the aristocratic Japanese families, the Chin was first to be found outside its homeland around 1865. An elegant and dainty animal, the Japanese Chin makes an ideal companion, being good-natured and affectionate towards its owner, though not towards strangers; it is extremely clean, cheerful by nature and has the amusing characteristic of rapidly twirling around almost as if dancing. The general appearance is of a small, stylish dog with unmistakable features. The head is rather large with a broad skull and rounded, prominent forehead, clearly defined stop, a very short, wide muzzle and strong, rounded jaws. The eyes are dark, very large, almond-shaped, set wide apart and protruding. The ears are small, V-shaped, well feathered and carried forward. The neck is moderately short and the body square and compact in build, with a wide, deep chest and a tucked-up belly. The legs are fine but with solid bone, and the feet small, oval and hare-like. The tail is set high and not very long, carried curved over the back to form a fine feathery plume. The coat is long, straight, silky and not close, shorter on the head and the lower half of the legs.

Weight: 2–6 kg (4½–13 lb). Height: 18–28 cm (7–11 in). Colour: white with black or red patches.
Country of Origin: Japan.

Japanese Chin

Bichon Bolognese

Harlequin Pinscher

Kromfohrländer

Coton de Tuléar

Lowchen

Bichon Havanais

Japanese Spitz

Telomian

Chinese Imperial Ch'in

Shiba Inu

Chinese Crested Dog

Chinese Temple Dog

Other Companion Dogs

Breed: Lowchen (Little Lion Dog or Petit Chien Lion) – *Origin*: France – *Height*: 20–35 cm (8–14 in) – *Weight*: 2–4 kg (4½–9 lb) – *Colour*: white, black, and lemon are most common – *Physical characteristics*: black nose, dark eyes, drooping ears with feathering; tail of medium length; fairly long, wavy coat.

Breed: Bichon Bolognese – *Origin*: Italy – *Height*: approximately 25 cm (10 in) – *Weight*: not specified – *Colour*: pure white – *Physical characteristics*: round, dark eyes; drop ears; tail curled over the back; long, thick coat.

Breed: Harlequin Pinscher (Harlekinpinscher) – *Origin*: Germany – *Height*: 30–35 cm (12–14 in) – *Weight*: not specified – *Colour*: pied on a white background or grey or grey dappled with black markings, or brindle – *Physical characteristics*: black nose; dark eyes; small, erect ears, or with the tips slightly folded; docked tail; short, dense coat.

Breed: Kromfohrländer – *Origin*: Germany – *Height*: 38–46 cm (15–18 in) – *Weight*: not specified – *Colour*: white with light or dark brown markings (and shades in between) – *Physical characteristics*: black nose; dark eyes; ears hanging close to the head; tail slightly curved or even curled; coat distinguishes the three varieties: rough; short and rough; long and rough.

Breed: Dutch Smoushondje – *Origin*: Holland – *Height*: 37–42 cm (14½–16½ in) – *Weight*: 9–10 kg (20–22 lb) – *Colour*: fawn, yellowish brown – *Physical characteristics*: pronounced stop; black nose; short muzzle; dark eyes; drooping ears; docked tail carried high; long, hard coat.

Breed: Coton de Tuléar – *Origin*: Madagascar – *Height*: 28–31 cm (11–12 in) – *Weight*: 3.5–4 kg (7½–9 lb) – *Colour*: white with slight yellowish shading on the ears – *Physical characteristics*: drooping ears; black nose; tail of medium length; long, cottony coat.

Breed: Telomian – *Origin*: United States – *Height*: 38–48 cm (15–19 in) – *Weight*: 10–13 kg (22–28½ lb) – *Colour*: sandy with white ticking on the chest, feet and tip of the tail – *Physical characteristics*: erect ears; tail carried sickle-like; short, soft coat.

Breed: Bichon Havanais – *Origin*: remote, unknown – recent, Cuba – *Height*: 25–35 cm (10–14 in) – *Weight*: up to 6 kg (13 lb) – *Colour*: beige; white; light brown; grey (also combined) – *Physical characteristics*: black nose; drooping ears; tail held high and curled; long, rather flat coat.

Breed: Shiba Inu – *Origin*: Japan – *Height*: 35–41 cm (14–16 in) – *Weight*: not specified – *Colour*: fawn, pepper and salt, red pepper, black pepper, black, white, brindle – *Physical characteristics*: dark nose; small, dark eyes; erect, triangular ears; thick tail, carried curled over the back towards the flank; thick, hard coat.

Breed: Japanese Spitz – *Origin*: Japan – *Height*: dogs 30–40 cm (12–16 in); bitches 25–35 cm (10–14 in) – *Weight*: not specified – *Colour*: white – *Physical characteristics*: black nose; dark eyes; small, erect ears; tail covered with long hair curled over the back; thick, straight coat.

Breed: Shar-Pei (Chinese Fighting Dog) – *Origin*: China – *Height*: 40–50 cm (16–20 in) – *Weight*: 16–25 kg (35–55 lb) – *Colour*: fawn, black, cream – *Physical characteristics*: small, drooping ears; tail carried high; fairly soft coat; skin forms large wrinkles.

Breed: Chinese Imperial Ch'in – *Origin*: China – *Height*: large 22–25 cm (8½–10 in); medium 10–15 cm (4–6 in); miniature 10 cm (4 in); sleeve 7 cm (2¾ in) – *Weight*: large 7 kg (15½ lb); medium 2 kg (4½ lb); miniature 1.5 kg (3½ lb); sleeve 0.6–0.9 kg (1½–2 lb) – *Colour*: black and white, black, fawn – *Physical characteristics*: short muzzle; long, drooping, feathered ears; tail curled over the back; profuse, cottony coat.

Breed: Chinese Temple Dog – *Origin*: China – *Height*: large 30–35 cm (12–14 in); medium 25–30 cm (10–12 in); miniature 10–12 cm (4–5 in); sleeve 7 cm (2¾ in) – *Weight*: large 9 kg (20 lb); medium 4–7 kg (9–15½ lb); miniature 2 kg (4½ lb); sleeve 0.6–0.9 kg (1½–2 lb) – *Colour*: black and white – *Physical characteristics*: short muzzle; flattened nose; drooping ears; very long, silky coat.

Breed: Chinese Crested Dog – *Origin*: China – *Height*: approximately 30 cm (12 in) – *Weight*: not specified – *Colour*: no coat, except for a tuft of hair on the skull and tip of the tail; pinkish grey skin – *Physical characteristics*: long muzzle; dark eyes; erect ears.

Mongrels

A section on those dogs which belong to no particular breed but are a result of casual mating makes a fitting conclusion to a book devoted entirely to the pedigree dog. All too often deprived of the recognition it deserves, the mongrel has proved itself the equal of its pedigree cousins in terms of physical and moral stamina. Having described and illustrated the different canine breeds it seemed appropriate to dedicate a few words to the common dogs which make up the majority of our four-legged friends. The dogs illustrated show, albeit in a limited way, some of the possible physical variations which can occur through spontaneous cross-breeding. Despite the evident mixture of characteristics of different breeds, the result is often attractive and well put together, not to mention the fact that the temperament of these dogs is often mellow and flexible, all of which combines to make them trusted, irreplaceable friends in spite of their dubious pedigree.

Conformation of the dog

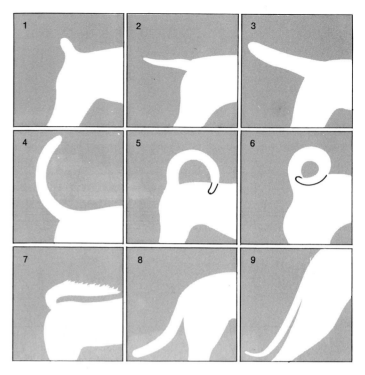

Shape and position of the tail

1 – set high and carried erect (usually docked)
2 – set high and carried horizontally, low in repose
3 – otter tail of medium length, rounded without feather
4 – long, set high and carried sickle-like, low in repose
5 – of medium length and set high, curved over one side
6 – ring tail, set high
7 – set high, folded along the back
8 – medium set-on, carried sabre-like
9 – long, set low and curved at the tip

Shape and fall of the ears

1 – bat ears, set high and broad at the base
2 – folded ears, drooping forward
3 – pendulous ears, set low
4 – erect ears with medium-high set-on (sometimes cropped to give this erect effect)
5 – semi-erect ears
6 – rose ears, set back

The aim of this section is to clarify some of the terms which have been used to describe the different breeds of dog and illustrate their exact meaning. There are diagrams of the main ear and tail conformations, which are often the distinguishing characteristics of a breed. The diagram of the dog is designed to show the exact location of the different parts of the body, which is particularly helpful when measuring a dog to ensure it complies with the breed standard. The illustrations below this show the underside and profile of the two types of foot most frequently found: the compact, rounded, arched cat foot, with pads very close together; and the more elongated hare foot, with toes further apart and less arched.

The final set of diagrams gives the terminology of the different parts of the skull and shows the different ways in which the upper and lower jaws fit together. When the upper and lower jaws develop normally, the top teeth meet the corresponding bottom teeth with only a very slight overlap of the upper incisors.

A so-called overshot jaw occurs when there is underdevelopment of the mandible or lower jaw, causing it to lie further back than the upper jaw, which gives the dog's muzzle a snipy appearance. An undershot jaw, on the other hand, occurs when there is overdevelopment of the lower jaw, causing it to project beyond the upper jaw, often curving upwards, giving the dog a typical mastiff appearance.

Other deviations, not illustrated here, may be found in the angle of insertion of the lower molars; if the lower molars lean towards the inside of the mouth, the area of contact is limited to their outside edge.

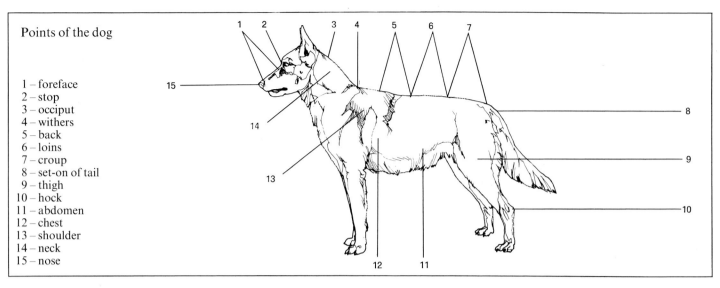

Points of the dog

1 – foreface
2 – stop
3 – occiput
4 – withers
5 – back
6 – loins
7 – croup
8 – set-on of tail
9 – thigh
10 – hock
11 – abdomen
12 – chest
13 – shoulder
14 – neck
15 – nose

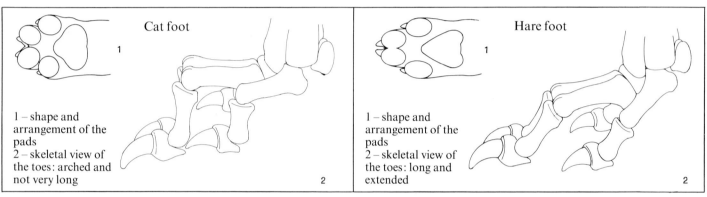

Cat foot

1 – shape and arrangement of the pads
2 – skeletal view of the toes: arched and not very long

Hare foot

1 – shape and arrangement of the pads
2 – skeletal view of the toes: long and extended

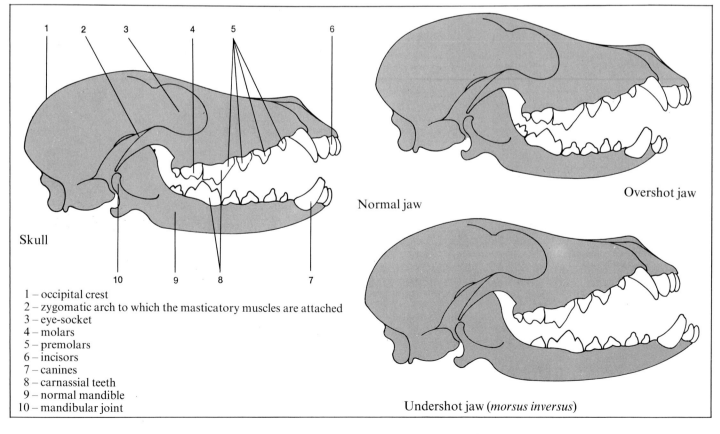

Skull

1 – occipital crest
2 – zygomatic arch to which the masticatory muscles are attached
3 – eye-socket
4 – molars
5 – premolars
6 – incisors
7 – canines
8 – carnassial teeth
9 – normal mandible
10 – mandibular joint

Normal jaw

Overshot jaw

Undershot jaw (*morsus inversus*)

193

Qualities and defects of breeds

Breed	Physical constitution	Main physical defects	Qualities	Defects	Note
LEONBERGER page 12	Well proportioned in spite of its size.	Head resembling a St Bernard; tail curled over the back; white markings on the coat.	Fond of its owner, highly intelligent.	Wary of strangers, cannot bear to be chained up.	Avalanche dog.
ST BERNARD page 13	Sturdy, strong and muscular.	Sway back; tail curled over the back; curly or excessively long coat; self-coloured coat or lack of white.	Docile, faithful, courageous and generous.	Sometimes irritable in hot climates.	Mountain rescue.
NEWFOUNDLAND AND LANDSEER page 14	Elegant in appearance, agile in movement.	Sway back; weak loins; tail curled over the back in action; cow hocks; presence of dew claws; feet turning outwards.	Faithful and courageous.	None.	Sea rescue.
PYRENEAN MOUNTAIN DOG page 16	Strong and muscular.	Excessively heavy head; pronounced stop; round, prominent eyes; undershot jaw; cow hocks; absence of two sets of dew claws at the back.	Gentle, calm, affectionate, courageous.	None.	Excellent guard dog.
BOXER page 18	Strong and hardy. Agile in movement, proud of bearing.	Heavy appearance; light nose; light eyes; haw showing; tongue and teeth visible when the mouth is shut; missing teeth; tail set low; white markings on the coat covering more than one-third of the total surface area.	Obedient and intelligent, easy to train.	Wary of strangers.	Excellent guard dog.
DOBERMANN (Dobermann Pinscher) page 20	Elegant and lithe in build, well muscled.	Heavy appearance; excessively large head; pronounced stop; light eyes; overshot or undershot jaw; presence of dewlap; incorrect stance; straw-coloured coat; white markings on the chest; tan markings not clearly defined.	Intelligent, lively, courageous, faithful, easy to train.	Reacts aggressively to provocation.	Excellent bodyguard.
SCHNAUZER page 22	Strong and hardy, compact in build.	Wrinkles on the forehead; light eyes; undershot jaw; presence of dewlap; cow hocks; wavy coat; atypical colouring.	Lively, faithful, easily trainable.	Sometimes restless and dangerous with strangers.	Resistant to adverse weather conditions, killer of vermin.
GREAT DANE page 25	Strong and elegant, proud of bearing.	Snipy muzzle; missing teeth; overshot or undershot jaw; even bite; short neck; presence of dewlap; sway back; incorrect stance; curled tail; colour not conforming to the standard.	Obedient and faithful to its owner, docile and even-tempered.	Suspicious of strangers.	The poorly developed sense of smell does not allow it to recognize even its owner in the dark.
HOVAWART page 28	Strong and hardy.	Undershot or overshot jaw; ears wide apart; sway back; hind legs not well angled; tail curled over the back, curly coat.	Intelligent and obedient.	Retains its happy-go-lucky puppy temperament too long.	Excellent guard dog.
ROTTWEILER page 29	Strong but of rather heavy build.	Long muzzle with excessively drooping lips; narrow skull; light eyes; light build; thin tail.	Intelligent, faithful to its owner.	Aggressive and dangerous with strangers.	Good guard dog, even used by the police in some states.
DOGUE DE BORDEAUX page 30	Muscular and powerful, structurally well-balanced.	Small head; lack of stop; undershot jaw; sway back; presence of dew claws; white coat; white markings in areas other than the chest and legs.	Faithful to its owner.	Dangerous and uncontrollable when roused.	Excellent guard dog.
BULLDOG page 31	Powerful and muscular despite its lack of stature.	Black or black and tan in colour.	Quiet and docile, faithful to its owner.	Sometimes aggressive ancestral tendencies emerge.	Guard dog, police dog.
MASTIFF (Old English Mastiff) page 32	Heavy overall build, majestic and powerful.	Heavily undershot jaw; cow hocks.	Aware of its own strength.	If attacked, becomes violent and ferocious.	Guard and watch dog.
BULLMASTIFF page 33	Heavy build but agile and powerful.	Yellow or light eyes; strongly undershot jaw; uneven teeth; cow hocks; tail carried high, above the level of the back; white markings on the coat (allowed on the chest, if small).	Intelligent, cheerful, lively.	Intimidating if well trained.	Strong ownership instinct, used by the British police.
AIREDALE page 34	Sturdy and muscular, compactly built.	Undershot jaw; tail curled or drooping over the back; white markings on the head and body.	Lively and intelligent, faithful to its owner, affectionate.	If attacked, turns vicious.	Very versatile, excellent watch dog, very good swimmer.
NEAPOLITAN MASTIFF page 35	Strong and hardy, agile for its size.	Long, narrow head; snipy muzzle; nose lacking pigment; light or wall eyes; uneven teeth; strongly undershot jaw; overshot jaw; lack of dewlap; incorrect stance; extensive white markings on the coat.	Quiet and even-tempered, affectionate towards its owner.	Dangerous when chained up.	Excellent guard and watch dog. Avoid changing owners.
CHOW CHOW page 36	Sturdy and compactly built, refined in bearing.	Ears not erect; pink mucous membranes; tail not curled over the back; markings on the coat.	Very intelligent.	Haughty and even sometimes dangerous with strangers.	Guard dog, but also used for hunting sable in China.
DALMATIAN page 37	Strong and hardy.	Lack of pigmentation in the eye-rims and nose; folds of skin on the forehead; presence of dewlap; cow hocks; white hairs in the markings on the coat.	Intelligent, courageous and very faithful. Rarely barks.	Independent nature.	Excellent guard dog, good with horses, very sensitive nose.

Qualities and defects of breeds

Breed	Physical constitution	Main physical defects	Qualities	Defects	Note
AUSTRIAN PINSCHER page 38	Compactly built, sturdy and muscular.	Snipy muzzle; undershot or overshot jaw; sway back or roached back; white or glossy black and harlequin colours to be avoided.	Alert, courageous, tenacious, lively.	Barks frequently.	Excellent guard dog.
KYŪSHŪ page 38	Well built, sturdy and muscular, with a certain overall elegance.	Undershot jaw; incorrect stance; any deviation from the standard.	Intelligent, patient and silent, easy to train, docile and affectionate.	None discernible.	Good guard dog, also useful for hunting.
AINU DOG (Hokkaido Dog) page 38	Strong and well muscled.	Undershot jaw; monorchidism; cryptorchidism (disqualifies); incorrect stance.	Courageous, faithful, obedient.	Timidity in some dogs (serious fault).	Guard dog and used for bear hunting, also as a draught dog.
TOSA page 38	Sturdy and well built, solid and majestic in appearance.	Missing teeth (more than 5); undershot jaw; monorchidism; cryptorchidism (disqualifies); delicate build.	Courageous and aggressive, patient, obedient, reflective.	None discernible.	Excellent guard dog and pet.
JAPANESE AKITA page 38	Well built, strong and hardy, attractive appearance, elegant bearing.	Nose light or lacking pigmentation (with the exception of white dogs); undershot jaw; drop ears; short or drooping tail; long or smooth coat.	Courageous and full of fighting spirit, docile, intelligent, affectionate.	None discernible.	Used to be a fighting dog, now a guard dog and pet.
SANSHU page 38	Strong and well built, elegant bearing.	Undershot jaw; incorrect stance.	Affectionate, sensitive, docile, very clean (even outside the home).	None discernible.	Useful guard dog, excellent pet.
AIDI page 38	Strong and muscular, solidly built, rugged in appearance but not without a certain elegance.	Narrow skull; pointed muzzle; nose lacking pigmentation; short and erect or excessively long ears; bird of prey eyes; malicious or shifty look; poorly or too well defined stop; undershot jaw; monorchidism; cryptorchidism; curled tail; incorrect stance, dew claws on hind legs.	Alert, active, affectionate.	None discernible.	Excellent guard and watch dog.
TIBETAN MASTIFF page 38	Strong and sturdy, of elegant bearing.	Light build; incorrect stance.	Obedient and affectionate, courageous but docile and quiet.	None discernible.	Excellent guard dog.
PYRENEAN MASTIFF (Mastin de los Pirineos) page 38	Strong and well built, elegant in movement, aesthetically pleasing.	Nose not black; muzzle too pointed; sway back; tail short or carried above the level of the back; incorrect stance; coat too long and woolly.	Intelligent and affectionate.	None discernible.	Very versatile: guard and watch dog, sheepdog, hunting dog, draught dog.
SPANISH MASTIFF (Mastin Español) page 38	Strong and sturdy.	Nose not black; muzzle too pointed; sway back; short tail or carried above the level of the back; incorrect stance; long or woolly coat.	Obedient and affectionate, intelligent and easy to train.	Wary of strangers.	Very versatile: can be used as a guard dog, to hunt wild boar, as a sheepdog and draught dog.
PORTUGUESE WATER DOG (Cão d'Agua) page 38	Strong and well muscled, aesthetically pleasing appearance.	Long, narrow head; flesh-coloured nose or lacking in pigmentation; light eyes; ears set badly or with folds; tail missing or docked; presence of dew claws on the hind legs; albinism.	Cheerful, affectionate, persevering.	None discernible.	Excellent swimmer, good at retrieving fish and objects from the water.
FILA BRASILEIRO page 38	Strong and well muscled, streamlined shape, of elegant bearing.	Flesh-coloured nose; bulging eyes; overshot or undershot jaw; poorly developed flews; cropped ears; docked tail; monorchidism; cryptorchidism; white coat.	Docile and affectionate with its owner.	Wary of strangers and aggressive, timidity in some dogs (considered a fault for showing purposes).	Excellent guard dog, needs open spaces.
GERMAN SHEPHERD DOG (Alsatian) page 40	Strong and elegant, very agile.	Ears not erect; undershot or overshot jaw; uneven teeth; tail curled or carried badly; height at the withers above or below the standard; white or albino in colouring.	Intelligent and of equable temperament.	Excessive nervousness or listlessness in some dogs (serious faults).	Highly developed sense of smell, excellent watch dog and bodyguard.
BELGIAN SHEPHERD DOG (GROENENDAEL) page 42	Presents a picture of strength and elegance.	Ears not erect; light eyes; undershot or overshot jaw; incorrect stance; tail curled or carried to the side.	Tenacious, alert, untiring and obedient (if well trained).	Excessive timidity in some dogs; a nervous temperament sometimes makes training difficult.	Watch dog and bodyguard.
BRIARD (Chien Berger de la Brie) page 44	Strong and hardy, of elegant, well-proportioned appearance.	Nose lacking pigmentation; wall eye; absence of double dew claws on the hind legs; tail missing or docked; curly coat; white markings on the legs.	Lively and intelligent, willing, easy to train.	Often timid with strangers.	Endowed with very sharp hearing, loves water.
BEAUCERON (Beauce Shepherd Dog) page 45	Strong and sturdy.	Light nose; small or almond-shaped eyes; badly carried tail; absence of dew claws on the hind legs; white markings on the chest; coat not smooth or very short.	Faithful and courageous.	Originally too aggressive.	Strong instinct for rounding up and defending the flock.
PICARDY SHEEPDOG page 46	Muscular and well built, very rugged appearance.	Long, pointed muzzle; black nose; light or wall eyes; ears not erect; strongly undershot jaw; double dew claws; excessively large white markings.	Lively and faithful.	Sometimes too docile.	Highly developed guarding instinct.

195

Qualities and defects of breeds

Breed	Physical constitution	Main physical defects	Qualities	Defects	Note
PYRENEAN (Berger des Pyrénées) page 47	Sturdy and hardy, agile in movement.	Pronounced stop; light eyes; undershot jaw; erect ears; dew claws on the forelegs; tail carried sabre-like and not hooked at the tip; black and tan in colour.	Highly intelligent, faithful to its owner.	Suspicious of strangers.	Excellent guard.
BERGAMASCO SHEEPDOG page 48	Strong and hardy, well-proportioned.	Foreface not straight; nose lacking pigmentation; light, wall or small eyes; undershot or overshot jaw; badly shaped or incorrectly angled legs; black or white coat (exceeding one-fifth of the total surface area).	Very intelligent, docile and courageous.	Rather stubborn.	Excellent guard dog.
MAREMMA SHEEPDOG page 49	Strong and hardy, refined of bearing.	Concave or too convex foreface; nose completely lacking in pigmentation; wall eye; heavily undershot jaw; overshot jaw; incorrect stance; dew claws on the hind legs; tail missing or curled over the back; curly coat.	Lively and courageous, intelligent and reflective, docile and affectionate with its owner.	Very aggressive, sometimes dangerous with strangers.	Excellent guard dog, suffers from the heat and needs open spaces.
KARST page 50	Strong and hardy.	Nose lacking pigmentation; wall eye; heavily undershot jaw; overshot jaw; incorrect stance; tail too short or with stiffened joints; coat too short.	Quiet and cheerful, faithful to its owner, very courageous.	Suspicious of strangers.	Guard and watch dog.
SAR PLANINA page 51	Strong and sturdy.	Light eyes; white, yellow or brown coat.	Courageous and full of life.	Often vicious with strangers.	Excellent sheepdog.
COLLIE (Scotch Collie) page 52	Powerful and well built, agile of movement.	Round, light eyes; pronounced stop; nose not black; undershot or overshot jaw; missing teeth; erect or pendulous ears; incorrect stance; tail short or carried curled over the back or to the side.	Intelligent and quiet; should not be harshly trained.	Often stubborn and lazy.	Excellent sheepdog, suited as a guard dog and as a guide dog for the blind; suffers from the heat.
SHETLAND SHEEPDOG page 54	Powerful and swift, a miniature version of the Collie.	No stop; undershot or overshot jaw; weight and height exceeding the standard; forelegs not straight, cow hocks; tail curled over the back or short.	Quiet and affectionate.	Suspicious of strangers and stubborn.	Excellent sheepdog, suitable pet.
BEARDED COLLIE page 55	Strong and hardy.	Narrow skull; cow hocks; short tail; lack of hair on the legs.	Docile and affectionate, courageous and intelligent.	None outstanding.	Valiant sheepdog, excellent pet.
OLD ENGLISH SHEEPDOG (Bobtail) page 56	Strong and muscular, agile in movement.	Long, narrow head; brown or sandy coat.	Intelligent, docile and patient.	None discernible.	Ambling gait; excellent sheepdog and pet; characteristic bark.
WELSH CORGI page 57	Long in body, despite the short legs, a powerful and agile mover.	Undershot or overshot jaw; forelegs turned outwards; tail curled over the back; all white coat.	Good-natured, lively and intelligent.	None discernible.	Considerable adaptability.
SWEDISH VALLHUND (Västgötaspets) page 58	Muscular and energetic despite the short legs.	Too short tail; white markings on the coat covering more than 30 per cent of the total surface area.	Faithful and courageous.	Independent, may experience problems adapting to city life.	Herding dog.
PULI AND PUMI page 58	Powerful and hardy.	Light brown eyes; erect ears (Puli), drooping ears (Pumi); strongly undershot or overshot jaw; tail carried straight; short, smooth coat; speckled coat or with excessively large markings.	The Puli is quieter, the Pumi more lively, both intelligent.	The Pumi barks a lot; the Puli has nomadic tendencies.	Splendid sheepdogs.
KUVASZ page 59	Strong and sturdy, elegant appearance.	Pronounced stop; nose lacking pigmentation; light eyes; erect ears; heavily undershot or overshot mouth; lack of height; yellow or spotted coat.	Faithful and courageous, affectionate with its owner.	None outstanding.	Strong sense of ownership; needs open spaces.
KOMONDOR page 60	Sturdy and muscular.	Nose lacking pigmentation; wall eye; short or excessively curved tail; spots on the coat; smooth coat.	Intelligent and courageous, very faithful.	Aloof.	Excellent house guard and watch dog.
RAFEIRO DO ALENTEJO (Alentejo Herder) page 61	Strong and hardy, heavy in appearance.	Long narrow head; nose not black; light eyes; undershot or overshot jaw; tail short (even if docked) or missing; very short coat.	Quiet, a tireless worker.	None discernible.	Good guard and watch dog.
APPENZELL MOUNTAIN DOG (Appenzell Sennenhund) page 62	Muscular but not of heavy appearance.	Excessively long, thin muzzle; stop too pronounced; light eyes; short, pointed ears.	Intelligent and courageous, agile and untiring.	None discernible.	Excellent herder; needs open spaces.
GREAT SWISS MOUNTAIN DOG (Great Swiss Sennenhund) page 63	Strong and powerful, of heavy build, lacking agility of movement.	Light eyes; imperfect teeth; badly carried ears; sway back; badly carried tail; unsymmetrical markings on the coat.	Faithful, courageous, intelligent and very patient.	Sometimes timid or, conversely, vicious.	Needs open spaces; makes an excellent guard dog and watch dog.
BERNESE MOUNTAIN DOG (Bernese Sennenhund) page 64	Solid and well proportioned.	Heavy head; wall eyes; overshot jaw; tail curled over the back; curly coat.	Intelligent and affectionate, very attached to its owner.	Does not accept a change of owner.	Also used as a police dog.

196

Breed	Physical constitution	Main physical defects	Qualities	Defects	Note
BOUVIER DES FLANDRES page 65	Majestic, compactly built.	Nose lacking pigmentation; light or wall eyes; undershot or overshot jaw; incorrect stance; chocolate brown coat or with excessively large white markings.	Determined and energetic, faithful and intelligent.	None discernible.	Highly developed sense of smell; makes a fine guard and watch dog, used as a police dog.
ESKIMO DOG page 66	Sturdy and hardy.	Feet small and toes too closely set.	Docile and faithful, tireless.	Sometimes slightly timid and suspicious.	Does not bark but howls; used for pulling sledges.
SIBERIAN HUSKY page 67	Sturdy and hardy, swift and agile in movement.	Ears too large and drooping; weak hindquarters; shaggy coat; height exceeding the maximum allowed by the standard.	Particularly attached to man.	None discernible.	Sledge dog.
ALASKAN MALAMUTE page 68	Powerful and well built.	Dew claws on the hind legs; irregular markings on the coat.	Docile and affectionate towards its owner, does not bark.	None discernible.	Used for pulling sledges.
SAMOYED page 70	Strong and well built; elegant appearance.	Cow hocks; wavy or curly coat.	Quiet and obedient, very intelligent.	Barks too much.	Sledge dog.
CÃO SERRA DE AIRES page 71	Strong and hardy, rather rugged in appearance.	Long, narrow head; pointed nose; convex or straight foreface in profile; pendulous flews; light eyes; stop not clearly defined; tail docked or missing from birth, set low, short, curled over the back (not in action); white nails; coat with white markings on the chest or lower legs; curly or woolly coat.	Very intelligent, lively, fond of its owner.	Very suspicious of strangers.	Sheep and cattle herder.
ESTRELA MOUNTAIN DOG (Cão Serra da Estrela) page 71	Sturdy and well built, rugged in appearance.	Light nose or lacking in pigmentation; wall eyes; ears too large or badly set; undershot jaw; tail docked or with congenital defects; albinism.	Intelligent, docile with its owner, full of fighting spirit.	Vicious with strangers.	Excellent guard dog and sheepdog.
CÃO DE CASTRO LABOREIRO page 71	Strong and hardy, of noble bearing.	Head too large or long and narrow; nose not black; wall eyes; ears set badly or too large; undershot or overshot jaw; tail missing or docked; markings on the coat; albinism.	Courageous, docile, affectionate.	None discernible.	Excellent guard dog and sheepdog.
GOS D'ATURA CERDA page 71	Strong and sturdy, well built.	Nose not black; light eyes; lack of belly tuck-up; curled tail.	Courageous, intelligent.	None discernible.	Herding dog which, close up, resembles the Catalonian Sheepdog and is now very rare, even in its country of origin.
HOLLANDSE HERDERSHOND (Dutch Shepherd Dog) page 71	Strong and well muscled, well proportioned and slender in build.	Nose not black; ears not erect; wall eyes; undershot or overshot jaw; tail short or curled; incorrect stance; white markings and streaks or excessive black in the coat.	Lively, intelligent, obedient, docile.	None outstanding.	Fine sheepdog resistant to bad weather and fatigue.
BOUVIER DES ARDENNES page 71	Strong and sturdy, rugged in appearance.	Nose not black; yellow or wall eyes; flat ears; dew claws on the hind legs; incorrect stance.	Intelligent, affectionate, obedient.	Suspicious of strangers.	Excellent herder.
BORDER COLLIE page 71	Well built, strong, of elegant bearing.	Not clearly defined.	Intelligent, alert, willing.	None discernible.	Sheepdog resistant to fatigue.
KEESHOND page 71	Sturdy and well muscled.	Any deviation from type.	Alert, lively, gay, intelligent.	Somewhat intrusive.	At one time a Dutch barge dog, now a pet.
ENTLEBUCH SENNENHUND (Entlebuch Mountain Dog) page 71	Strong and sturdy, agile in movement.	Long, thin muzzle; light eyes; short, pointed ears; undershot or overshot mouth; coat too long; excessive white in the coat.	Good-natured, intelligent, faithful, docile.	None discernible.	Tireless herder.
CROATIAN SHEEPDOG (Hrvatški Ovčar) page 71	Strong and sturdy.	Light eyes; nose not black; undershot or overshot jaw; dew claws on the hind legs; white markings on the head, trunk or tail.	Lively, obedient, alert, easy to train.	None outstanding.	Excellent guard dog and sheepdog.
MUDI page 71	Strong and sturdy, staunch in bearing.	Nose lacking pigmentation; light brown eyes; ears not erect or with short hair; undershot or overshot jaw; dew claws on the hind legs; short hair on the trunk and long on the head.	Courageous, energetic, docile, obedient.	None outstanding.	Herding dog; makes a suitable pet and house guard.

197

Qualities and defects of breeds

Breed	Physical constitution	Main physical defects	Qualities	Defects	Note
POLISH SHEEPDOG (Polski Owczarek Nizinny or Lowlands Shepherd Dog) page 71	Strong and well muscled, elegant appearance.	Concave or convex foreface; erect ears; undershot or overshot jaw; incorrect stance; curly and insubstantial coat.	Lively, steady, intelligent, alert, easy to train, good memory.	Laziness or nervousness (disqualification in shows) in some dogs.	Excellent sheepdog, guard dog and pet.
POLISH SHEEPDOG (Owczarek Podhalanski or Tatra Mountain Dog) page 71	Strong and well built, staunch in bearing.	Light eyes; haw showing; nose not black; presence of dewlap; barrel chest; tail carried high; curly coat, lack of undercoat; colours other than white or cream.	Lively, active, intelligent, courageous.	Nervousness or aggressiveness (disqualification in shows) in some dogs.	Excellent sheepdog, suitable guard dog.
SLOVAKIAN KUVASZ (Slovensky Cuvač or Tsuvatch) page 72	Strong and sturdy, well muscled, solidly built.	Short muzzle; pendulous lips; wall eye; dew claws on the hind legs; coat too long and trailing with a parting along the back; markings on the coat.	Faithful, alert, courageous, affectionate, lively.	Aggressiveness (significant fault in shows) in some dogs.	Splendid sheepdog, also makes a suitable guard dog and pet.
LAPPHUND (Lapland Spitz) page 72	Strong and muscular, compactly built.	Incorrect stance, any deviation from the standard.	Faithful, obedient, affectionate, alert.	Suspicious of strangers.	Excellent guard dog.
NORRBOTTENSPETS page 72	Well built and fairly compact in outline, elegant bearing.	Incorrect stance, dew claws on the hind legs.	Alert, faithful, affectionate, lively.	None discernible.	Guard dog and draught dog.
ICELAND DOG page 72	Sturdy and well muscled.	Undershot or overshot jaw; incorrect stance.	Intelligent, lively, affectionate.	None discernible.	Sheepdog and guard dog.
LAPPONIAN HERDER (Lapland Vallhund) page 72	Sturdy and well muscled.	Drooping ears; dew claws on the hind legs; incorrect stance.	Courageous, quiet, obedient, loves working.	Barks frequently.	Herder of reindeer.
GREENLAND DOG page 72	Sturdy and well muscled.	Incorrect stance, albinism.	Affectionate, gay, loyal.	None discernible.	Guard dog and sledge dog.
NORWEGIAN BUHUND (Norsk Buhund) page 72	Well muscled and compactly built.	Nose not black; undershot or overshot jaw; incorrect stance.	Energetic, courageous, faithful, obedient.	None discernible.	Sheepdog, also makes a suitable guard and watch dog.
RUSSIAN OWTSCHARKA (Russian Sheepdog) page 72	Strong and sturdy, rugged in appearance, well balanced.	Incorrect stance, any deviation from the standard.	Lively, intelligent, courageous.	None discernible.	Splendid sheepdog.
CANAAN DOG page 72	Well muscled, well balanced.	Undershot or overshot jaw, incorrect stance.	Lively, alert, faithful, docile, full of fighting spirit.	Suspicious of strangers.	Guard and watch dog, sheepdog.
ANATOLIAN KARABASH (Anatolian Sheepdog or Turkish Shepherd Dog) page 72	Strong and well muscled, agile in movement.	Undershot jaw; incorrect stance.	Sensitive, faithful, intelligent, easy to train.	Suspicious of strangers	Sheepdog, makes a suitable guard dog.
CATAHOULA LEOPARD DOG page 72	Well built, well proportioned.	Incorrect stance, any deviation from type.	Faithful, fond of its owner, easy to train.	Very aggressive.	Sheepdog and herder.
AUSTRALIAN CATTLE DOG page 72	Well built, well proportioned.	Ears not erect; undershot jaw; incorrect stance.	Intelligent, cunning, obedient.	None discernible.	Herder and guard dog.
AUSTRALIAN KELPIE page 72	Sturdy and well muscled, rugged appearance.	Ears not erect; incorrect stance.	Intelligent, obedient, active, trainable.	None discernible.	Fine sheepdog, needs open spaces.
AUSTRALIAN SHEPHERD page 72	Sturdy and well muscled, rugged appearance.	Incorrect stance; any deviation from type.	Courageous, affectionate, cheerful, active.	None discernible.	Sheepdog, also makes a suitable pet.
POINTER page 74	Strong and well built, elegant appearance, noble bearing.	Short muzzle or roman nose; poorly defined stop; nose lacking pigmentation; wall eye; undershot or overshot jaw; dew claws on hind legs; tail missing or docked or carried over the back.	Intelligent, obedient, quiet and reserved; tenacious and enthusiastic in work.	Mediocre retriever.	Tireless galloper; ambling and continual trotting while working mean disqualification; excellent nose.
GORDON SETTER page 76	Sturdy and well muscled, elegant appearance.	Light head; topline of muzzle concave or arched; nose lacking pigmentation; wall eye; undershot or overshot mouth; drawn-up belly; incorrect stance; dew claws on the hind legs; tail the wrong length or badly carried.	Intelligent and diligent, not impulsive in work, affectionate and docile.	None discernible.	Ambling and continual trotting while working mean disqualification.

Breed	Physical constitution	Main physical defects	Qualities	Defects	Note
IRISH SETTER (Red Setter) page 76	Well balanced and slimly built, elegant bearing.	Heavy head; topline of muzzle concave or convex; nose lacking pigmentation; wall eye; over-developed lips; undershot or overshot mouth; incorrect stance; dew claws; tail missing, docked or carried badly and incorrectly set.	Sensitive, agile and swift at work, energetic.	Sometimes restless and over-fond of freedom.	Ambling and continual trotting during work bring disqualification.
ENGLISH SETTER page 78	Powerful but not heavy, elegant build, lively and agile in movement.	Topline of muzzle concave or arched; no stop; nose lacking pigmentation; wall eye; heavily undershot jaw; overshot jaw; dew claws; tail missing or docked or carried over the back.	Affectionate and obedient though exuberant, very attached to its owner.	Cannot tolerate living in a confined space.	Ambling and continual trotting while working bring disqualification; excellent over any terrain, even marshland.
FRENCH POINTER (Braque Français) page 79	Sturdy and powerful, without presenting a picture of excessive heaviness.	Head too short; nose black or lacking pigmentation; light eyes; dew claws; black markings on the coat.	Quiet and obedient (if well trained).	Does not retrieve in water and sometimes bites the game too fiercely.	Motionless, impeccable point.
AUVERGNE POINTER (Braque d'Auvergne) page 80	Sturdy and powerful but not massive, elegant appearance.	Topline of muzzle too short or arched; nose lacking in pigmentation; undershot or overshot jaw; long or sway back; incorrect stance; dew claws; tail short or missing; excessive white in the coat.	Affectionate, obedient, lively and very active.	None outstanding.	Suited to any terrain.
ARIÈGE POINTER (Braque de l'Ariège) page 81	Sturdy and powerful, yet of elegant appearance.	Nose too dark; small eyes; sway back; tail set high; incorrect stance; excessive markings on the coat.	Lively and tenacious, very intelligent, hunts by instinct.	Often independent and not very easy-going (particularly in old age).	Suited to any terrain, splendid retriever.
BRITTANY SPANIEL page 82	Compactly built and sturdy, of elegant appearance.	Pronounced stop; nose lacking pigmentation; ears set low; narrow chest; long sway back: long tail; curly coat.	Quiet and intelligent; sensitive and reserved but also demonstrative, easy to train.	None discernible.	Excellent nose, suited to any terrain; resistant to cold and damp.
FRENCH SPANIEL page 82	Strong and sturdy, majestic in appearance yet presenting a picture of elegance.	Light or yellow eyes; dew claws on the hind legs; tan markings on the cheeks and around the eyes.	Intelligent and obedient, a very keen worker, easy to train.	Lacks speed.	Excellent in water, suited to any terrain.
PICARDY SPANIEL page 83	Compactly built, elegant appearance.	Pointed nose; eyes too light; short, narrow ears without any feathering; sway back; thin forelegs without any feathering; incorrect stance; tail carried sabre-like; thin, curly coat; too much brown in the coat.	Quiet, responsive, intelligent.	None discernible.	Hardy and suited to any terrain.
PONT-AUDEMER SPANIEL page 84	Strong and compactly built.	Short foreface; nose black or lacking pigmentation; sway back; tail carried sabre-like or plumed; black and white or black coat; tan markings.	Quiet, an energetic worker, faithful and affectionate.	None discernible.	Excellent on marshland, poorly developed nose.
KORTHALS (Pointing Wire-haired Griffon) page 85	Solid and rugged.	Small or broad head; curled ears; pink or black nose; dewlap; badly carried tail.	Lively and intelligent, fond of its owner, an active worker.	If not trained at a very early age, it becomes stubborn and independent.	Very versatile and able to endure a long time in water.
BOULET (Pointing Long-coated Griffon) page 85	Powerful and fairly compactly built.	Pink nose; absence of moustache; eyes any colour except yellow; ears set high; plumed tail; hard, curly coat; extensive white markings.	Docile, lively and intelligent.	None discernible.	Resistant to heat and fatigue, suited to any ground.
ITALIAN SPINONE page 86	Sturdy and powerful, rugged in appearance, but graceful in movement.	Concave foreface; nose black or lacking pigmentation; wall eye; undershot or overshot jaw; lack of dew claws on the hind legs; no tail; coat tricoloured or self-coloured (except white); black markings in the coat; coat-type not conforming to the standard.	Docile and patient, quiet and very friendly.	None outstanding.	Splendid retriever, skilled swimmer; galloping and continual ambling during the hunt bring disqualification.
BRACCO ITALIANO (Italian Gundog) page 87	Sturdy and powerful, well balanced, of distinguished bearing.	Double nose; light or too dark eyes; undershot or overshot mouth; tail curved upwards or missing; colour: black, black and white, tricolour, fawn, hazel-brown, with tan markings.	Docile and diligent, quiet, easy to train.	None discernible.	Suited to any type of hunting.
GERMAN SHORT-HAIRED POINTER (Kurzhaar) page 88	Graceful, powerful and well built, of noble bearing, agile in movement.	Heavy build; flesh-coloured nose; ears too long; dewlap; tail set too low, dew claws.	Intelligent and obedient, even-tempered and energetic, easy to train.	None discernible.	Suited to any climate and all terrains, hardy, swift.
GERMAN WIRE-HAIRED POINTER (Drahthaar) page 89	Well proportioned, agile in movement, proud of bearing.	Pendulous flews; undershot jaw; incorrect stance.	Lively and even-tempered, energetic and courageous.	None discernible.	Agile, swift and hardy.
GERMAN LONG-HAIRED POINTER (Langhaar) page 90	Sturdy and muscular but of noble bearing.	Black or pink nose; dew claws; incorrect stance; black or red coat.	Lively and even-tempered, faithful and obedient, easy to train.	None discernible.	A tenacious hunter.
WEIMARANER (Weimar Pointer) page 91	Medium-heavy build, aesthetically pleasing appearance.	Concave foreface; pronounced stop; sway back; dew claws.	Lively, loyal, fond of its owner.	None discernible.	Highly developed sense of smell, active in the hunt, safe retriever.

Qualities and defects of breeds

Breed	Physical constitution	Main physical defects	Qualities	Defects	Note
LARGE AND SMALL MUNSTERLANDER page 92	Strong and well built, cleanly cut, of noble bearing.	Eyes too light; overshot jaw; dewlap; barrel chest; sway back; incorrect stance; black coat (large); curly or shaggy coat.	Obedient, courageous, intelligent, easily trainable.	None discernible.	The small variety loves hunting in water.
SPANISH POINTER (Perdiguero de Burgos) page 93	Strong and sturdy.	Black nose, cow hocks.	Docile and affectionate, loves hunting, easy to train.	None discernible.	Not very fast but suited to any climate and any terrain.
IBIZAN HOUND page 94	Greyhound type, agile in movement.	Dark eyes; ears not erect; undershot or overshot jaw; breast-bone not very prominent; incorrect stance.	Lively and intelligent, shrewd, docile and affectionate.	Males fight among themselves.	Gets bored with rabbits and cannot be used for a time, possibly a long time, when it has hunted too many.
PORTUGUESE POINTER (Perdigueiro Português) page 95	Solidly built, well-balanced appearance.	Nose lacking pigmentation or any colour except black (black or white dogs); undershot or overshot jaw; deafness; tail missing; dew claws; albinism.	Lively, shrewd, intelligent, loves hunting.	Unfriendly towards other dogs.	Excellent for pointing, seeking out game and retrieving.
HUNGARIAN VIZSLA page 96	Sturdy but not heavy, elegant bearing.	Nose black or slate-grey; light eyes; undershot or overshot mouth; barrel chest; dew claws.	Intelligent, even-tempered and obedient.	None discernible.	Quick at the hunt and a splendid retriever, suited to any terrain.
ČESKÝ FOUSEK page 97	Strong and sturdy, of noble bearing.	Ears too long; neck too long and thick; breast-bone not very prominent; coat too long or too short; predominance of white in the coat.	Intelligent and attached to its owner, a tireless worker.	Impulsive.	Suited to any climate and any terrain.
LABRADOR RETRIEVER page 99	Well built, solid and sturdy.	Ears too large; undershot or overshot mouth; wrinkles on the head; tail curved above the back; cow hocks.	Lively, intelligent, affectionate.	None discernible.	Exceptional nose, excellent retriever in water.
FLAT-COATED RETRIEVER page 100	Well built, powerful and strong, without presenting a picture of heaviness.	Round, bulging eyes; dewlap; incorrect stance.	Intelligent and obedient, affectionate, easy to train.	None discernible.	Exceptionally good at working in water.
CURLY-COATED RETRIEVER page 100	Sturdy and powerful, agile and elegant in movement.	Excessively broad skull; light eyes; curled tail.	Lively, intelligent, affectionate, easy to train.	None discernible.	Excellent retriever over any ground and in water.
GOLDEN RETRIEVER page 101	Sturdy and powerful, flowing gait.	Cow hocks; white markings on the face and neck or feet.	Intelligent and affectionate.	None discernible.	Excellent nose, also retrieves in water.
CHESAPEAKE BAY RETRIEVER page 101	Solid and powerful.	Dew claws on the hind legs; curly coat.	Gay, lively, affectionate, easy to train.	None discernible.	Loves water, resistant to any climate.
ENGLISH COCKER SPANIEL page 102	Sturdy and compactly built.	Small or bulging eyes; undershot or overshot jaw; wavy or hard, curly coat.	Cheerful and friendly, affectionate and obedient.	Sometimes neurotic and aggressive.	Excellent nose, splendid retriever, even in water.
AMERICAN COCKER SPANIEL page 104	Powerful and well muscled, compactly built.	White markings in the solid colours (allowed on the throat and chest with black), base colour covering more than 90 per cent of the total surface area in the parti-coloureds; tan markings covering more than 10 per cent of the surface area in the black and tans (white markings allowed on the chest and throat).	Cheerful and easy-going, affectionate, faithful, obedient.	None discernible.	Careful and tireless hunter, perfect pet.
ENGLISH SPRINGER SPANIEL page 105	Sturdy and well built, compact outline.	Light eyes; undershot or overshot jaw; dewlap; tail carried above the level of the back.	Courageous, gay, affectionate.	None discernible.	Swift and hardy, excellent nose.
WELSH SPRINGER SPANIEL page 105	Sturdy and rather compactly built.	Short, heavy head; undershot or overshot jaw; tail carried above the back; incorrect stance; long, curly coat.	Responsive, lively, cheerful.	Independent spirit.	Very hardy.
SUSSEX SPANIEL page 106	Strong and sturdy, of elegant appearance despite its size.	Hind legs shorter than forelegs; dark liver colour.	Quiet and even-tempered in the home, active and energetic at work.	Not easy to train, sometimes unfriendly towards other dogs.	Suited only to easy terrains.
CLUMBER SPANIEL page 106	Massive build, solid and sturdy.	Light eyes; undershot or overshot mouth; incorrect stance.	Intelligent, cheerful, friendly.	Lack of speed.	Hunts in packs of 5 to 10; very hardy.
IRISH WATER SPANIEL page 107	Compact in outline, sturdy and well built.	Pronounced stop; undershot or overshot jaw; white markings on the chest.	Intelligent, obedient and tenacious.	None discernible.	Loves water, tireless.
FOXHOUND page 109	Compactly built, well muscled, well proportioned.	Heavy head; ears set too high; arched loins; incorrect stance; tail carried low.	Quiet and obedient, courageous and tenacious.	None discernible.	Very swift and tireless.

Breed	Physical constitution	Main physical defects	Qualities	Defects	Note
BEAGLE page 110	Compact in outline, solid and well built.	Eyes small or too close together; "V"-shaped or curled ears; undershot jaw; crooked elbows; tail curled over the back; tan markings too clear or flecked with black.	Quiet and affectionate, cheerful.	None discernible.	Active and hardy, hunts in packs.
HARRIER page 110	Strong and well built, elegant appearance.	Massive head; rounded ears; nose lacking pigmentation; overshot jaw; straight shoulders and hocks; coat too short and fine.	Lively and intelligent.	None discernible.	Swift and hardy, excellent nose.
OTTERHOUND page 111	Rather massive appearance, sturdy.	Short ears; sway back; straight hocks.	Quiet and intelligent, faithful and courageous.	None discernible.	Hunts otter; well-developed sense of smell, resistant to cold.
GRAND GASCON SAINTONGEOIS or VIRELADE page 112	Well built, elegant appearance, noble bearing.	Eyes too light; undershot or overshot jaw; colour of the coat deviating from the standard.	Willing, tenacious, courageous, quiet and affectionate in the home.	None discernible.	Excellent sense of smell, hunts wolf and roe.
BILLY page 112	Well built, well proportioned.	Excessively long and narrow foreface; incorrect stance; traces of black in the coat.	Shrewd, bold, obedient.	Picks fights with other dogs, unfriendly.	Hunts roe.
ARIÉGEOIS page 113	Lightly built, noble in appearance, proud of bearing.	Excessively rounded head; dewlap or wrinkles formed by the skin; colour not conforming to the standard.	Active, quiet and affectionate in the home.	None discernible.	Swift and hardy, hunts hare.
CHIEN FRANÇAIS page 113	Well built, elegant appearance.	Nose lacking pigmentation; pronounced stop; short ears; undershot or overshot jaw; incorrect stance; coat colour not conforming to the standard.	Quiet and obedient, active and courageous in a shooting-party.	None discernible.	Hunts deer and roe.
GRAND BLEU DE GASCOGNE page 114	Noble appearance, solid and well built.	Short head; light eyes; ears short or barely curled; visible mucous membranes pink; absence of any trace of tan in the coat.	Courageous and tenacious, quiet and affectionate in the home.	Barks frequently and sometimes turns vicious.	Not very fast but hardy.
PETIT BLEU DE GASCOGNE page 114	Well built, elegant appearance, proud bearing, agile in movement.	Light eyes; short ears; incorrect stance.	Courageous and tenacious, shrewd and determined, quiet and affectionate in the home.	None outstanding.	Exceptional sense of smell.
POITEVIN page 116	Strong and elegant in build, refined bearing.	Strongly undershot jaw; dewlap; black and white coat.	Quiet, courageous, faithful.	None discernible.	Hardy and suited to any terrain, hunts wolf.
GRIFFON NIVERNAIS page 117	Well built, rather rugged in appearance, agile in movement.	Eyes too light; pink nose; incorrect stance; long pasterns; woolly or curly coat; colours: black, orange, wheaten, tricolour with bright, sharply defined colours.	Courageous, active, a keen hunter.	Slightly stubborn.	More hardy than swift.
BASSET BLEU DE GASCOGNE page 118	Well structured and of noble bearing.	Pointed muzzle; light eyes; undershot jaw; coat colour not conforming to the standard.	Courageous and affectionate.	None discernible.	Excellent nose, very useful and rarely gets in the way.
BASSET ARTÉSIEN-NORMAND page 119	Rather long in body, solid and well muscled, proud of bearing.	Wide forehead; ears set low; overshot jaw; short neck; sway back; out at elbows; cow hocks; tail too long; too much black flecking in the coat.	Bold and tenacious, docile and quiet in the home.	None discernible.	Hunts fox and wolf; forces its way into lairs.
BASSET FAUVE DE BRETAGNE page 120	Solid and well muscled.	Short, pointed muzzle; ears set low and of the wrong length; drawn-up belly; long coat; colour not conforming to the standard.	Quiet and affectionate.	None discernible.	Very hardy.
BASSET GRIFFON VENDÉEN page 120	Not very long in body, dignified in bearing.	Light eyes; pointed muzzle; nose lacking pigmentation; sway back; incorrect stance; coat silky or woolly and curly.	Tenacious and courageous, gentle and affectionate in the home.	None discernible.	Hunts wild boar and roe; swifter than the other bassets.
SICILIAN HOUND (Cirneco dell'Etna) page 121	Strong and hardy despite its light build, dignified in bearing.	Short muzzle; pronounced stop; nose lacking pigmentation; hazel or dark brown eyes; ears not erect; incorrect stance; tail set high or curled over the back; colours: brindle, brown, liver, black or brown markings.	Intelligent, faithful, obedient and active.	None discernible.	Hunts wild rabbit.
ITALIAN HOUND page 122	Solid and well built, muscular and clean-cut in outline.	Short muzzle; pronounced stop; concave foreface; nose lacking pigmentation; light or wall eye; undershot or overshot jaw; short ears; incorrect stance; atypical coat colouring or type.	Intelligent, faithful, obedient, active, dignified and unobtrusive.	None discernible.	Swift and hardy, ambling or continual trotting during the hunt means disqualification; dog of great versatility.
BERNESE HOUND page 123	Well built, streamlined structure, powerful.	Poorly defined stop; incorrect stance; dew claws on the hind legs; tail carried like a hunting-horn.	Lively and intelligent, tenacious, quiet in the home.	None discernible.	Very hardy, suited to any terrain.
LUCERNESE HOUND page 124	Well built, streamlined structure, sturdy and well muscled.	Poorly defined stop; incorrect stance; dew claws on the hind legs; tail carried like a hunting-horn.	Lively, intelligent, tenacious, quiet in the home.	None discernible.	Very hardy.

Qualities and defects of breeds

Breed	Physical constitution	Main physical defects	Qualities	Defects	Note
BRUNO DE JURA page 124	Well built, fairly long in body, powerful.	Poorly defined stop; incorrect stance; dew claws on the hind legs; tail carried like a hunting-horn.	Lively, intelligent, tenacious, quiet in the home.	None discernible.	Very hardy.
BLOODHOUND page 125	Sturdy and of massive build, long-bodied, slow in movement.	Light constitution; incorrect stance; tail carried too much curled over the back; white markings on the coat (small ones allowed on the chest and legs).	Obedient, affectionate, docile, does not bark.	Rather timid, vicious and vindictive if badly treated.	Excellent sense of smell enabling it to be used to track down lost people.
STYRIAN MOUNTAIN HOUND page 126	Sturdy and powerful, well muscled, rather rugged in appearance.	Curled ears; undershot or overshot jaw; tail too short; curly coat; colour not conforming to the standard.	Tenacious, intelligent and affectionate	None discernible.	Resistant to fatigue.
TYROLEAN HOUND (Tyroler Bracke) page 127	Sturdy and well muscled, long in body.	Yellow eyes; curled ears; undershot or overshot jaw; missing teeth; legs not straight; too much white on the collar and legs.	Determined, lively, obedient.	None discernible.	Excellent sense of smell, hardy and swift.
HANOVERIAN SCHWEISSHUND page 128	Sturdy and rather long in body.	Forehead arched and not broad; ears too long; long legs with incorrect stance; traces of white or light yellow in the coat.	Tenacious, affectionate and obedient.	None discernible.	Very good at seeking out the quarry.
WESTPHALIAN DACHSBRACKE page 128	Sturdy and muscular, long in body.	Short ears; undershot jaw; dewlap; incorrect stance; tail curled over the back; wavy coat.	Intelligent, reflective, lively, tenacious and full of fighting spirit.	None discernible.	Suited to difficult, mountainous terrain.
WACHTELHUND (German Spaniel) page 129	Sturdy and well muscled, long in body, elegant appearance.	Undershot jaw; incorrect stance.	Affectionate and obedient, courageous.	Sometimes too cruel and merciless with the quarry.	Very hardy, good over any terrain.
HAMILTON HOUND (Hamiltonstövare) page 129	Well structured, powerful, of elegant appearance.	Imperfect teeth; incorrect stance.	Courageous, intelligent, obedient.	None discernible.	Can hunt large game over difficult terrain.
DREVER page 130	Sturdy and muscular, very long in body.	Pronounced stop; dewlap; dew claws on the hind legs; tail curled over the back.	Courageous and obedient.	None discernible.	Hunts fox and hare but is not afraid of wild boar.
FINNISH SPITZ (Suomenpystykorva) page 130	Compactly built, proud of bearing.	Light eyes; dew claws; long, wavy or curly coat.	Lively, faithful, courageous and friendly.	None discernible.	Fairly versatile, highly developed nose and vision.
FINNISH HOUND (Suomenajokoira) page 131	Sturdy and well structured, agile in movement.	Incorrect stance.	Quiet, friendly, energetic, obedient.	None discernible.	Hunts fox and hare.
KARELIAN BEAR DOG page 131	Strong and sturdy, well built.	Light or wall eyes; dewlap; barrel chest; curly or wavy coat; colour not conforming to the standard.	Tenacious and courageous.	Aggressive towards man.	Strong fighting spirit.
ELKHOUND (Norsk Elghund) and SWEDISH ELKHOUND (Jämthund) page 132	Sturdy and well muscled, rather compactly built.	Light eyes; undershot jaw; dew claws on hind legs; incorrect stance; tail set low and with feathering.	Courageous and even-tempered, energetic, not impetuous.	None discernible.	Also used as a sledge dog.
POSAVASKI GONIČI page 133	Solid and well built.	Light eyes; ears too short; undershot jaw; tail curled or carried to the side; markings on the coat (except white).	Even-tempered and obedient, affectionate.	None discernible.	Excellent nose, very hardy.
ISTRIAN HOUND page 133	Well proportioned, of refined bearing.	Wall eyes; strongly undershot jaw; ears too short; tail curled or carried to the side; markings on the coat (except orange).	Quiet and affectionate, a keen hunter.	None discernible.	Suited to difficult terrain.
PODENGO PEQUEÑO (Small Portuguese Warren Hound) page 134	Well muscled and rather long in body.	Ears not erect; dew claws; tail curled over the back.	Lively and intelligent.	None discernible.	Hunts wild rabbit.
BASENJI page 135	Well proportioned, of elegant bearing.	Incorrect stance; cream coloured coat.	Even-tempered, affectionate, patient, does not bark.	Few hunting skills.	Extended trot.
RHODESIAN RIDGEBACK page 136	Sturdy and well muscled.	Nose any colour except black or brown; undershot mouth; dewlap; tail curled over the back; white markings on the belly and legs.	Lively, obedient, quiet in the home, very courageous.	None discernible.	Swift and hardy.
BASSET HOUND page 138	Very long in body, sturdy, agile in movement.	Ears set high; height at the withers exceeding 38 cm (15 in); sway or roach back; long coat.	Sweet, gentle, very faithful, reserved.	Sometimes stubborn.	Ideal pet.
DACHSHUND (Teckel) page 140	Powerful and well muscled, of elegant appearance.	Undershot or overshot jaw; dewlap; sway back; flawed tail; cow hocks; toes turned inwards; cryptorchidism; monorchidism.	Very intelligent, tenacious, courageous, strong personality.	Not always obedient, rather independent.	Makes a nice pet.

202

Breed	Physical constitution	Main physical defects	Qualities	Defects	Note
GERMAN HUNT TERRIER (Deutscher Jagdterrier) page 142	Strong and well muscled, of elegant appearance.	Erect ears; undershot or overshot jaw; short back; very short or woolly coat.	Lively and full of fighting spirit.	Often stubborn, sometimes aggressive and vicious.	Ill-advised pet.
FOX TERRIER page 143	Powerful and well balanced, elegant appearance.	Light nose; erect ears; undershot or overshot jaw; incorrect stance.	Very active, likes to play, affectionate.	Quarrels with other dogs; frequently nervous.	Swift and hardy; hunts vermin.
IRISH TERRIER page 144	Well proportioned, bold in carriage.	Light nose; undershot jaw; tail curled or curved over the back; incorrect stance; curly coat; flecking or white markings on the coat.	Active, courageous, impulsive, quiet and dignified in the home.	Fights with other dogs.	Very agile and an excellent swimmer; versatile.
WELSH TERRIER page 144	Sturdy and well built, elegant appearance.	Light nose; erect ears; undershot mouth; tail curved over the back; white or black markings on the feet.	Obedient, gay, lively, affectionate.	Rather independent, unfriendly with strangers.	Splendid worker in water.
LAKELAND TERRIER page 145	Sturdy and well built, elegant appearance.	Head too long; incorrect stance; tail curved over the back.	Active, tenacious, courageous, gay and affectionate.	None discernible.	Hunts otter, badger and fox.
SCOTTISH TERRIER page 146	Sturdy and rather compactly built, of dubious proportions but agile and nimble in movement.	Light eyes; folded ears; undershot jaw; no undercoat; white markings on the coat (except for very small ones on the chest).	Courageous, lively, intelligent and responsive, rarely barks.	Independent.	Kept as a pet but often intolerant with children.
KERRY BLUE TERRIER page 146	Compactly built but well proportioned in appearance.	Light eyes; undershot or overshot jaw; sway back; tail curved over the back; cow hocks; hard or woolly coat.	Determined and courageous, fond of its owner.	Sometimes stubborn.	Very versatile.
SEALYHAM TERRIER page 147	Solid and powerful, of dubious proportions but agile in movement.	Light eyes; light nose; erect ears; undershot or overshot jaw; black markings in the coat.	Courageous, lively, gay, intelligent, lovable.	None discernible.	Pet.
WEST HIGHLAND WHITE TERRIER page 147	Sturdy and well muscled, agile in movement.	Nose lacking pigmentation; light eyes; ears not erect; undershot jaw; incorrect stance; tail curved over the back; curly coat.	Active, courageous, proud.	Suspicious of strangers.	Pet.
DANDIE DINMONT TERRIER page 148	Of dubious proportions, aesthetically pleasing overall appearance.	Undershot or overshot mouth; curled tail.	Determined, lively, intelligent, friendly, affectionate.	None outstanding.	Ratter.
CAIRN TERRIER page 148	Sturdy and powerful, fairly compactly built.	Light eyes; light nose; heavy jaw; undershot or overshot mouth; curly coat.	Courageous, lively, gay, lovable, very faithful.	None discernible.	Pet.
NORWICH TERRIER page 149	Sturdy and muscular, solid despite its small stature.	Light eyes; undershot or overshot jaw; long back; incorrect stance; soft, wavy or curly coat.	Faithful, very energetic, lively.	Rather independent nature, very occasionally rebellious.	Pet.
SKYE TERRIER page 149	Very long in body, elegant overall appearance despite its unique proportions.	Yellow eyes; light nose; undershot or overshot jaw; tail curved over the back.	Gentle, intelligent, very attached to a single owner.	None discernible.	Pet.
MANCHESTER TERRIER or BLACK AND TAN TERRIER page 150	Well built, elegant appearance.	Tail docked; incorrect stance; tan markings on the outside of the hind legs.	Active, faithful, intelligent.	Quite vicious.	Ratter.
SOFT-COATED WHEATEN TERRIER page 150	Sturdy and well built, fairly rugged in appearance.	Long muzzle; undershot or overshot jaw; dew claws; hard or rough coat; colour not conforming to the standard.	Active, lively, courageous.	None discernible.	Versatile.
NORFOLK TERRIER page 151	Sturdy and solid despite its small size.	Light eyes; undershot jaw.	Gentle, even-tempered, courageous.	None discernible.	Hunts fox and otter.
BORDER TERRIER page 151	Well built, agile in movement.	Undershot jaw; tail docked or curved over the back; white markings on the coat.	Lively, courageous, affectionate.	None discernible.	Hunts fox and marten.
STAFFORDSHIRE BULL TERRIER page 152	Sturdy and well muscled, agile in movement.	Light eyes; pink nose; erect or drooping ears; undershot or overshot jaw; tail curled or too long.	Active, tenacious, courageous, faithful, obedient.	Vicious with strangers.	Awesome guard dog.
BULL TERRIER page 152	Solid and well built, proud of bearing.	Light nose; wall eye; deafness; undershot jaw; dewlap; incorrect stance; soft or long coat.	Docile, obedient, very active, very affectionate towards its owner.	Aggressive with strangers.	Ratter.

Qualities and defects of breeds

Breed	Physical constitution	Main physical defects	Qualities	Defects	Note
BEDLINGTON TERRIER page 153	Sturdy and well muscled, springy gait.	Tail curved over the back; rough coat.	Intelligent, faithful, affectionate, hardly ever barks.	Reacts strongly to provocation.	Very swift at the gallop.
AUSTRALIAN TERRIER page 153	Sturdy and well muscled, fairly long in body.	Flesh-coloured nose; undershot or overshot jaw; woolly or curly coat; black in colour, white markings on the chest and feet.	Active, lively, gay, affectionate.	None discernible.	Ratter.
SILKY TERRIER page 154	Fairly long in body, solid in spite of the light appearance.	Light eyes; nose not black; undershot or overshot jaw; tail curved over the back; coat short and rough, wavy or curly; colour not conforming to the standard.	Active, lively, gay, friendly, intelligent.	None discernible.	Pet.
AFGHAN HOUND page 156	Well built, proud and noble bearing.	Short muzzle; large, round eyes; heavy constitution; short neck.	Intelligent, courageous, sensitive.	Cannot tolerate ill-treatment and bears grudges.	Pet.
SALUKI (Gazelle Hound) page 158	Well muscled, well proportioned, agile in movement.	Incorrect stance; brindle colouring.	Sensitive and affectionate.	None discernible.	Swift and hardy.
BORZOI page 159	Well proportioned, noble bearing.	Undershot or overshot jaw; tail curled or carried to the side; incorrect stance; black and tan coat (with or without white markings).	Courageous, docile, quiet.	Stubborn, bad-tempered and aloof with strangers.	Pet.
DEERHOUND (Scottish Deerhound) page 160	Sturdy and well built, elegant appearance, agile in movement.	Light eyes; straight back; curled or ring tail; cow hocks; woolly coat; white markings on the coat.	Quiet, reflective, obedient, affectionate.	Sometimes too timid.	Very swift, not snappy by nature.
IRISH WOLFHOUND page 161	Sturdy and well muscled, majestic but not heavy in appearance.	Nose not black; very light eyes; large, drooping ears; short neck; straight or sway back; weak hindquarters with insufficient musculature.	Bold and energetic, very faithful but becomes attached to only one person.	None discernible.	Needs open spaces, cannot tolerate the heat, fearsome if trained.
GREYHOUND page 162	Muscular and well built, elegant bearing.	Straight ears; incorrect stance.	Courageous, faithful, sensitive, reserved.	Does not like to be disturbed.	Unrivalled as a racing dog, not very good with children.
WHIPPET page 163	Powerful and well muscled, elegant appearance.	Short muzzle; undershot or overshot jaw; erect ears; curled or short tail; rough, woolly coat.	Docile, lively, obedient, affectionate, intelligent.	Rather timid.	Needs open spaces; delicate health.
ITALIAN GREYHOUND (Levrette) page 163	Very elegant in appearance and graceful in movement, noble bearing.	Short muzzle; light or wall eyes; erect ears; pronounced stop; undershot or overshot jaw; sway back; incorrect stance; dew claws on the hind legs; tail missing or curled over the back.	Intelligent, lively, faithful, affectionate.	Sometimes timid.	Pet.
PHARAOH HOUND page 164	Slender outline, well muscled, agile in movement.	Incorrect stance.	Very active.	Not very docile and rather snappy; difficult to train.	Very swift; excellent nose.
SPANISH GREYHOUND (Galgo Español) page 165	Well muscled, slender outline, noble bearing.	Pronounced stop; undershot or overshot jaw; incorrect stance.	Quiet and obedient.	None discernible.	Racing dog.
BRAQUE DUPUY page 166	Strong and well muscled, noble appearance, elegant bearing.	Undershot or overshot mouth; incorrect stance.	Intelligent, lively, active.	None discernible.	Swift and very sensitive nose.
BRAQUE DU BOURBONNAIS page 166	Well built, compactly built.	Black nose; light eyes; sway back; tail too long or docked; incorrect stance; white or black coat; large markings on the coat.	Faithful, affectionate, quiet.	None discernible.	Well-developed sense of smell, impeccable point, hunts over difficult terrain.
BRAQUE SAINT-GERMAIN page 166	Well built, elegant outline, well balanced.	Black or speckled nose; arched or short foreface; undershot or overshot jaw; black eyes; incorrect stance; dew claws.	Intelligent, affectionate, quiet.	Stubborn	Diligently seeks out the quarry at a gallop.
DRENTSE PARTRIDGE DOG (Drentse Patrijshond) page 166	Well built, rather long in body.	Definite roman nose; dewlap; incorrect stance.	Intelligent, active, obedient, faithful, easy to train.	None discernible.	Splendid nose.
GERMAN ROUGH-HAIRED POINTER (Stichelhaar) page 166	Sturdy and well built, elegant outline.	Black or flesh-coloured nose; sway back; incorrect stance; excessively large.	Intelligent, faithful to its owner.	Aggressive with strangers and merciless with the quarry.	Rarely found even in Germany.

Breed	Physical constitution	Main physical defects	Qualities	Defects	Note
POODLE POINTER (Pudelpointer) page 166	Sturdy and well built.	Incorrect stance; white or black in the coat.	Intelligent, faithful, obedient, affectionate.	None discernible.	Created to fill numerous hunting requirements.
WETTERHOUN (Dutch Water Spaniel) page 166	Strong and sturdy.	Heavy ears; sway back; incorrect stance.	Courageous, active.	Rather aggressive.	Also used as a guard dog.
STABYHOUN page 166	Sturdy and well built, streamlined shape.	Yellow eyes; dewlap; sway back; incorrect stance; curly coat.	Intelligent, faithful, quiet, obedient, docile.	None discernible.	Pointing dog, makes a suitable pet.
BARBET page 166	Well built, rugged appearance.	Incorrect stance; any deviation from type.	Cheerful, obedient, intelligent.	None discernible.	Now very rare.
DROTSZORUVIZSLA (Rough-haired Hungarian Vizsla) page 166	Strong and well built, noble appearance.	Black or speckled nose; pendulous lips; undershot or overshot mouth; dew claws on the hind legs; markings or speckling on the coat; curly hair; height above or below the limits of the standard.	Intelligent, active, energetic.	None discernible.	Very resistant to fatigue.
OLD DANISH POINTER (Gammel Dansk Honsehund) page 167	Strong and well muscled, streamlined shape.	Sway back; incorrect stance.	Quiet, affectionate, tenacious.	None discernible.	Not common outside its country of origin.
AMERICAN WATER SPANIEL page 167	Sturdy and well muscled, distinguished carriage.	Yellow eyes; rat tail or tail devoid of hair; hocks turning outwards.	Intelligent, active, obedient, easy to train.	None discernible.	Excellent nose.
FIELD SPANIEL page 167	Sturdy and well muscled, agile in movement.	Incorrect stance; uneven coat colouring; curly coat.	Docile, affectionate, quiet, intelligent, active.	None discernible.	Suited to hunting over not too difficult terrain.
REDTICK COONHOUND page 167	Well built and well proportioned.	Incorrect stance; any deviation from type.	Affectionate, obedient, gentle.	None discernible.	Hunts raccoon; guard dog.
BLUE TICK COONHOUND page 167	Well built, distinguished bearing.	Incorrect stance; any deviation from type.	Gentle, quiet, patient.	None discernible.	Hunts raccoon.
WEST COUNTRY HARRIER page 167	Strong and sturdy, distinguished bearing.	Sway back; incorrect stance.	Intelligent, lively, gay, cunning.	None discernible.	Swift and hardy, hunts fox.
DUNKER (Norwegian Hound) page 167	Strong and muscular.	Sway back; curled tail; incorrect stance; predominance of white in the coat.	Docile, quiet, even-tempered.	None discernible.	Endowed with stamina rather than speed.
HALDEN HOUND (Haldenstövare) page 168	Sturdy and well built.	Short or pointed muzzle; light eyes; undershot or overshot jaw; incorrect stance; badly carried tail; coat not conforming to the standard.	Intelligent, docile, active.	None outstanding.	Swift and suited to hunting over difficult terrain.
HYGEN HOUND (Hygenhund) page 168	Solidly built, elegant appearance.	Wall eye; visible haw; dewlap; drawn-up belly; tail curled over the back; double dew claws on the hind legs; incorrect stance.	Lively, active, intelligent.	None discernible.	Very hardy.
LUNDEHUND (Puffin Dog) page 168	Sturdy and well muscled.	Incorrect stance; any deviation from the standard.	Lively, careful, intelligent.	None discernible.	Furnished with five toes and seven or eight pads.
SCHILLER HOUND (Schillerstövare) page 168	Strong and sturdy, noble in appearance.	Incorrect stance.	Intelligent, lively, active.	None discernible.	Hunts on snow-covered land.
SMALANDS HOUND (Smalandsstövare) page 168	Sturdy and muscular.	Nose not black; pointed muzzle; incorrect stance.	Intelligent, affectionate, even-tempered.	None outstanding.	Hunts fox and hare.
GRÄHUND (Swedish Grey Dog) page 168	Compactly built, well muscled, noble carriage.	Yellow eyes; incorrect stance; coat colouring other than grey.	Careful, energetic, obedient, even-tempered.	None discernible.	Hunts elk, lynx and bear.
GRAND GRIFFON VENDÉEN page 168	Well built, distinguished carriage.	Incorrect stance; woolly coat.	Active, courageous, intelligent.	Too impetuous and easily tires.	Excellent nose but lacks stamina.

205

Qualities and defects of breeds

Breed	Physical constitution	Main physical defects	Qualities	Defects	Note
PORCELAINE page 168	Well muscled, elegant appearance.	Light nose; light eyes; herring-bone tail; incorrect stance; rough coat; height at the withers above or below the limit set by the standard.	Energetic, tenacious, active.	None discernible.	Hound endowed with a superb nose.
GRAND ANGLO-FRANÇAIS (Grand Bâtard) page 168	Well muscled, elegant appearance.	Standard not yet drawn up.	Energetic, tenacious, active, intelligent.	None discernible.	Hound endowed with a superb nose.
ANGLO-FRANÇAIS (Bâtard) page 169	Well built, elegant appearance.	Standard not yet drawn up.	Shrewd, obedient, tenacious.	None discernible.	Hound endowed with an excellent nose and speed.
PETIT ANGLO-FRANÇAIS (Petit Bâtard) page 169	Well built, elegant appearance.	Standard not yet drawn up.	Quiet, active.	None discernible.	Hound highly suited to apartment life.
GRIFFON FAUVE DE BRETAGNE page 169	Strong and muscular.	Short or pointed muzzle; pendulous lips; drawn-up belly; delicate constitution.	Intelligent, courageous, active.	None outstanding.	Hunts hare and fox.
BAYERISCHER GEBIRGSSCHWEISS-HUND (Bavarian Schweisshund) page 169	Well muscled, streamlined form.	Narrow head; flesh-coloured nose; yellow eyes; ears set high or curled; undershot or overshot jaw; sway back; incorrect stance.	Courageous, lively, obedient, affectionate.	None discernible.	Agile hound suited to difficult ground.
STEINBRACKE page 169	Well built, refined bearing.	Undershot jaw; bad angulation of forelegs.	Courageous, active, full of fighting spirit, docile in the home.	None outstanding.	Hound rarely found outside Germany.
POLISH HOUND (Ogar Polsky) page 169	Strong and sturdy.	Pointed muzzle; black nose; light eyes; tail thin, sparsley covered with hair or too short.	Affectionate, tenacious, obedient.	None discernible.	Excellent sense of smell.
HUNGARIAN HOUND (Erdelyi Kopo) page 169	Sturdy and muscular.	Sway back.	Courageous, easy to train, obedient, tenacious, affectionate.	None outstanding.	Hound suited to difficult ground; endowed with a good sense of direction.
SLOVAKIAN HOUND (Slovensky Kopov) page 169	Solidly built, rather long in body.	Light eyes; small ears; pendulous lips; undershot or overshot jaw; dewlap; tail carried above the level of the back (not in action); incorrect stance; coat colouring other than black or with white markings.	Lively, active, tenacious, intelligent.	Rather independent nature.	Hunts wild boar.
JUGOSLAVENSKI PLANINSKI GONIČ (Yugoslav Mountain Hound) page 169	Sturdy and muscular.	Light eyes; semi-pendulous ears; undershot jaw; faulty stance; white markings not allowed by the standard.	Quiet, intelligent, tenacious, courageous, reflective.	None discernible.	Excellent nose.
JUGOSLAVENSKI DROBOJNI GONIC (Yugoslav Tricolour Hound) page 169	Strong and well built.	Light eyes; erect ears; undershot or overshot jaw; sway back; incorrect stance; monorchidism; cryptorchidism; no white markings in the coat.	Courageous, affectionate, even-tempered.	None outstanding.	Suited to any climate and any terrain.
BASANSKI OSTRODLAKI GONIC-BARAK (Rough-haired Bosnian Hound) page 169	Strong and sturdy.	Light eyes; nose and visible mucous membranes lacking pigmentation; wrinkled ears, not hanging close to the head; little dewlap; sway or roach back; weak bone and muscle; dew claws; curly or wavy coat.	Courageous, tenacious, affectionate.	None outstanding.	Very resistant to fatigue.
BALKAN HOUND (Balkanski Gonič) page 170	Strong and sturdy, nimble in movement.	Light eyes; pointed muzzle; undershot or overshot jaw; short or badly carried tail; incorrect stance; monorchidism; cryptorchidism; atypical colouring; size above or below the established limits.	Intelligent, energetic, tenacious.	None discernible.	Hound suited to difficult terrain.
RAUHHAARLAUF-HUND (Rough-coated Swiss Hound) page 170	Strong and well built, noble in appearance, quite long in body.	Undershot or overshot jaw; dewlap; sway back; tail carried like a hunting-horn; dew claws on the hind legs; incorrect stance; black or chocolate colouring.	Intelligent, affectionate, a keen hunter.	None discernible.	Hound with an exceptional nose, suited to hunting in any climate and over any terrain.
SWISS SHORT-LEGGED HOUND (Schweizer Niederlaufhund) page 170	Strong and well built, noble appearance, very long in body.	Any deviation from the standard.	Intelligent, affectionate, a keen hunter.	None discernible.	There are four varieties: the Schweizer, the Bernese, the Lucernese and the Jura, considered separate breeds with a single standard.

Breed	Physical constitution	Main physical defects	Qualities	Defects	Note
SWISS HOUND (Schweizer Laufhund) page 170	Strong and well built, noble appearance, rather long in body.	Undershot and overshot jaw; dewlap; sway back; tail carried like a hunting-horn; dew claws on the hind legs; incorrect stance.	Intelligent, affectionate, a keen hunter.	None discernible.	Hound of exceptional scenting powers, suited to hunting in any climate and over any terrain.
AUSTRIAN HOUND (Österreichischer Bracke or Brandlbracke) page 170	Sturdy and well muscled, long in body.	Ears curled or pointed at the tip; bite not level; undershot or overshot jaw; short or curled tail; weak limbs; colours not conforming to the standard; greater height than length.	Obedient, quiet, responsive.	None outstanding.	Hound endowed with an excellent sense of smell.
SABUESO HOUND (Sabueso Español) page 170	Strong and sturdy.	Lack of pigmentation in the eye-rims; undershot or overshot jaw; tricoloured coat with tan markings over the eyes; albinism; bone malformation.	Faithful, affectionate, lively.	None discernible.	Does not suffer from the heat.
HELLENIC HOUND (Ellinikós Ichnilátis) page 170	Strong and well built.	Nose not black; eyes of any colour other than brown; lack of pigmentation in the visible mucous membranes; semi-erect ears; undershot or overshot mouth; curled tail; incorrect stance; dew claws; monorchidism; cryptorchidism; colours not conforming to the standard.	Lively, shrewd, very active.	None outstanding.	Suited to hunting over impassable, mountainous land.
BLACK AND TAN COONHOUND page 170	Well built, noble carriage.	Any deviation from the original type.	Careful, intelligent, obedient to its owner.	Generally aggressive; timidity or nervousness (faults which lead to disqualification in a show) in some dogs.	Hunts raccoon.
TENNESSEE TREEING BRINDLE page 170	Strong and sturdy.	Any deviation from type.	A keen hunter, very attached to its owner.	None discernible.	Recently developed breed.
TREEING WALKER COONHOUND page 170	Well built, refined bearing.	Any deviation from type.	A keen hunter, courageous, careful, affectionate.	None discernible.	Recently developed breed.
REDBONE COONHOUND page 170	Sturdy and muscular.	Any deviation from type.	A keen hunter, lively, cheerful, docile.	None discernible.	Recently developed breed for raccoon-hunting.
TRIGG HOUND page 171	Sturdy but slender in build.	Any deviation from type.	Tenacious, obedient, diligent.	None discernible.	Swift and hardy.
PLOTT HOUND page 171	Strong and muscular.	Any deviation from type.	Courageous, tenacious, determined.	None outstanding.	Not a common breed though it has been recognized in the United States since 1946.
RASTREADOR BRASILEIRO page 171	Strong and sturdy.	Pronounced stop; short ears; undershot or overshot jaw; curled tail; light bone.	Cheerful, lively, courageous, intelligent, obedient.	None outstanding; lack of vitality is considered a fault in shows.	Hunts jaguar.
AMERICAN STAFFORDSHIRE TERRIER page 171	Sturdy and muscular.	Any deviation from type.	Courageous, lively, trainable, obedient.	None outstanding.	Guard dog and pet.
ČESKÝ TERRIER (Bohemian Terrier) page 171	Well built, very long in body, dignified bearing.	Nose any colour other than the standard; eyes too large or cow-like; short or pointed muzzle; undershot or overshot mouth; sway or roach back; tail carried over the back.	Tenacious, courageous, obedient, patient, faithful.	None discernible.	Ratter; friendly towards other domestic animals.
GLEN OF IMMAL TERRIER page 171	Well muscled, well proportioned.	Any deviation from type.	Intelligent, tenacious, full of fighting spirit, affectionate.	Aggressive towards other animals.	Ratter.
TIBETAN TERRIER page 171	Well proportioned, well built.	Pointed muzzle; very heavily undershot jaw; chocolate-coloured coat.	Full of fighting spirit, intelligent, lively, reserved with strangers.	None discernible.	Makes a nice pet.
SLOUGHI page 171	Well muscled, elegant appearance, noble bearing.	Light eyes; badly carried ears; undershot jaw; hard or medium-long coat, feathering on the tail and legs; markings on the coat.	Reserved, obedient, docile, affectionate.	None discernible.	Not very common, now kept mainly as a pet.

Qualities and defects of breeds

Breed	Physical constitution	Main physical defects	Qualities	Defects	Note
HUNGARIAN GREYHOUND (Magyar Agár) page 171	Slender in build, well muscled, dignified carriage.	Erect ears; pronounced stop; straight back; coat longer and rougher on the croup and tail.	Faithful, affectionate, quiet.	None discernible.	Poorly developed nose.
POODLE page 173	Well built, well proportioned, elegant bearing.	Roman nose; short, narrow ears; no tail; monorchidism; cryptorchidism; dew claws on the hind legs; coat not self-coloured; white markings on the coat.	Very intelligent, lively, affectionate, sensitive, courageous.	Sometimes neurotic and timid (especially the toys).	Strongly imitative nature.
KING CHARLES SPANIEL page 174	Compactly built but of elegant appearance.	Long or pointed muzzle; light eyes; ears short or without feather; white hair on the muzzle; white markings in the coat (in black and tan dogs).	Lively, cheerful, friendly, affectionate, rarely barks.	Sometimes timid with strangers, does not like to be alone.	Very delicate.
CAVALIER KING CHARLES SPANIEL page 174	Well built, well proportioned.	Nose lacking pigmentation; light eyes; undershot or overshot mouth; white markings in self-coloured coats.	Lively, easy-going, loves hunting.	None discernible.	Hunts small game, makes a suitable pet.
PUG page 175	Compactly built, well muscled.	Long, tapering muzzle; light eyes; badly carried tail; excessively long body; mask not definite (in fawn dogs); white hairs (in black dogs).	Affectionate and demonstrative.	Wary of strangers.	Pet.
PAPILLON (Continental Toy Spaniel) page 176	Well proportioned, elegant in movement.	Foreface not straight; nose any other colour than black; light eyes; tongue showing; undershot or overshot mouth; sway or roach back; incorrect stance; dew claws on the hind legs; tail curled over the back.	Lively and obedient.	None discernible.	Ratter.
FRENCH BULLDOG page 177	Muscular and powerful in spite of its small size.	Nose any colour other than black; light or wall eyes; ears not erect; hare-lip; tongue or teeth showing; strongly undershot jaw; overshot jaw; dewlap; dew claws on the hind legs; colours: black, black and tan, mouse grey, brown, coffee-coloured.	Active, bold, determined, intelligent, affectionate.	None discernible.	Enemy of mice and rats, splendid guard dog for the home; snores.
BOSTON TERRIER page 177	Well proportioned, well built.	Wide nostrils or flattened nose; stop too shallow; light or wall eye; ears out of proportion or poorly carried; dewlap; tail docked or poorly carried; colours: black, black and tan, liver, mouse grey, white; absence of white markings.	Active, determined, lively, intelligent.	None discernible.	Pet, also makes a useful guard dog.
ENGLISH TOY TERRIER (Black and Tan) page 178	Well proportioned, agile and elegant in movement.	Light eyes; bulging eyes; large, pendulous ears; white markings in the coat.	Courageous, very lively, intelligent, affectionate.	Wary of strangers, sometimes neurotic.	Ratter.
YORKSHIRE TERRIER page 178	Well proportioned, bold carriage.	Nose any colour other than black; light eyes; bulging eyes; undershot or overshot jaw; sway back.	Lively, obedient, affectionate.	Wary of strangers, not very friendly towards other animals.	Enemy of rats and mice, also makes a useful guard dog for the home.
BICHON FRISE page 179	Well built, well proportioned, bold carriage.	Light eyes; nose lacking pigmentation; undershot jaw; strongly overshot jaw; curled tail; incorrect stance; cryptorchidism; black markings in the coat.	Cheerful, gay, lively.	None discernible.	Makes a nice pet.
MALTESE page 179	Fairly long in body, elegant appearance.	Nose any colour other than black or lacking pigmentation; light or wall eye; roman nose; heavily undershot jaw; overshot jaw; no tail; short tail; curly coat; monorchidism; cryptorchidism.	Lively, affectionate, reserved.	None outstanding.	Pet.
ITALIAN SPITZ (Volpino Italiano) page 180	Compactly built, well proportioned.	Roman nose; any colour other than black or lacking pigmentation; light or wall eye; tail missing, short, or hanging between the legs; markings on the coat.	Very lively, intelligent, affectionate.	Sometimes aggressive and suspicious of strangers; barks too much.	Strong sense of ownership.
POMERANIAN page 180	Well built, elegant appearance.	Nose lacking pigmentation; ears too long and not completely erect; undershot or overshot jaw; dew claws (should be removed).	Diligent, faithful, lively, intelligent.	Suspicious of strangers; possibly neurotic.	Pet.
SPITZ page 181	Well built, elegant appearance.	Nose lacking pigmentation; ears too long and not properly erect; undershot or overshot jaw; dew claws (should be removed); white markings (in the wolf grey colouring).	Faithful, lively, diligent, intelligent.	Suspicious of strangers; barks too much.	Pet, also makes a reasonable house guard.
PINSCHER and MINIATURE PINSCHER page 182	Sturdy and well muscled, well proportioned and elegant appearance.	Bulging eyes; undershot or overshot jaw; back not straight; incorrect stance; white markings in the coat, too light or too dark tan markings.	Diligent, courageous, docile, affectionate.	Wary of strangers.	Also makes a useful guard.

208

Breed	Physical constitution	Main physical defects	Qualities	Defects	Note
AFFENPINSCHER page 183	Well built, compact in outline, sturdy despite its size.	Light eyes; ears not erect; incorrect stance.	Courageous, lively, intelligent, very affectionate.	Aggressive with strangers; variable moods.	Exceptionally good ratter.
SCHIPPERKE page 183	Sturdy and well muscled, compact in outline.	Light eyes; ears too long and not erect; undershot or overshot jaw; coat wavy or too long; absence of ruff; white hairs in the coat.	Cheerful, lively, curious.	Very suspicious of strangers.	Excellent guard dog, loves horses.
GRIFFON (Bruxellois, Brabançon, Belge) page 184	Sturdy and well muscled, compactly built, elegant appearance.	Nose of any colour other than black; light eyes; overshot jaw; teeth and tongue showing; white markings in the coat.	Very lively, diligent, obedient.	None outstanding.	Ratter, useful as a guard.
HAIRLESS DOG page 185	Streamlined, well built, elegant appearance.	Incorrect stance.	Sensitive, lively, affectionate.	None discernible.	Pet.
XOLOITZCUINTLI (Mexican Hairless Dog) page 185	Well proportioned, well muscled.	Ears not erect, or cropped; docked tail; dew claws; albinism.	Quiet, reserved, cheerful, watchful temperament.	None discernible.	Good guard dog.
CHIHUAHUA page 186	Strong considering its minute size, graceful appearance.	Ears not erect, or cropped; docked tail; incorrect stance; absence of hair.	Careful, courageous, intelligent, fond of its owner.	Bad-tempered with strangers.	Pet.
PEKINGESE page 186	Quite long in body, noble carriage.	Overshot, wry mouth; tongue and teeth showing; albinism; liver colouring.	Dignified, courageous, affectionate, intelligent.	Rather independent, wary of strangers.	Pet.
LHASA APSO page 187	Long in body, elegant appearance.	Light eyes; square muzzle; tail carried low.	Cheerful, lively and self-assured.	None outstanding.	Good hearing.
SHIH TZU page 187	Long in body, haughty bearing.	Pink nose; pointed muzzle; light eyes.	Easy-going, lively, intelligent.	None discernible.	Pet.
TIBETAN SPANIEL page 188	Quite long in body, distinguished bearing.	Bulging eyes; pronounced stop.	Cheerful, lively, affectionate.	Suspicious of strangers.	Pet.
JAPANESE CHIN (Japanese Spaniel) page 188	Quite compactly built, distinguished carriage.	Nose any colour other than black (in black and white dogs); light eyes; overshot jaw; all-white coat; monorchidism, cryptorchidism.	Docile, cheerful and intelligent.	Sometimes timid.	Pet.
LOWCHEN (Little Lion Dog or Petit Chien Lion) page 189	Well built despite its small size.	Nose not black; small, light eyes; ears too short; incorrect stance; short or curly coat.	Gay, affectionate, intelligent.	None discernible.	Rarely found outside France.
BICHON BOLOGNESE page 189	Compactly built, elegant appearance.	Nose any colour other than black; light or wall eyes; concave or convex foreface; strongly undershot jaw; overshot jaw; back not straight; tail missing, docked or drooping; dew claws on the hind legs; curly coat.	Quiet, very attached to its owner.	Not very lively, sometimes lazy.	Ambling gait is a very serious fault.
HARLEQUIN PINSCHER (Harlekinpinscher) page 189	Well muscled and sturdy, agile in movement.	Nose not black; undershot or overshot jaw; short, narrow muzzle; incorrect stance.	Lively, attentive, affectionate.	None outstanding.	Excellent for apartment living.
KROMFOHRLÄNDER page 189	Strong and sturdy, elegant appearance.	Light eyes; missing or uneven teeth; undershot or overshot jaw; markings on the coat not conforming to the standard; monorchidism; cryptorchidism.	Lively, attentive, faithful, obedient.	None discernible.	Also a useful guard.
DUTCH SMOUSHONDJE page 189	Strong and compactly built.	Nose not black; light eyes; incorrect stance.	Cheerful, lively, intelligent.	None discernible.	Now very rare even in Holland; good with horses.
COTON DE TULÉAR page 189	Well proportioned, graceful appearance.	Any deviation from type.	Faithful, affectionate, good-natured.	None outstanding.	Recently imported to the United States.
TELOMIAN page 189	Strong and sturdy, rugged appearance.	Any deviation from type.	Gay, lively, intelligent.	None discernible.	Imported to the United States from Malaysia in 1963.

Qualities and defects of breeds

Breed	Physical constitution	Main physical defects	Qualities	Defects	Note
BICHON HAVANAIS page 189	Graceful appearance.	Nose not black; overshot or undershot jaw.	Lively, affectionate, good-natured.	Timidity in some dogs (considered a fault for show purposes).	Rarely found pet.
SHIBA INU page 189	Well built, agile in movement.	Light eyes; nose not toning with coat colour; flat ears; missing teeth; undershot jaw; monorchidism; cryptorchidism; drooping or short tail.	Cheerful, lively, faithful, obedient and courageous.	Timidity in some dogs (considered a fault for show purposes).	Pet, useful guard dog.
JAPANESE SPITZ page 189	Dignified carriage, elegant appearance.	Flat ears; undershot jaw; monorchidism; cryptorchidism; tail not curled; short coat.	Intelligent, cheerful, clever, courageous.	Suspicious of strangers.	Pet, useful as a guard dog.
SHAR-PEI (Chinese Fighting Dog) page 189	Strong and sturdy, unusual appearance.	Any deviation from type.	Quiet, affectionate and obedient.	None discernible.	Pet.
CHINESE IMPERIAL CH'IN page 189	Elegant appearance, noble bearing.	Any deviation from type.	Sensitive, intelligent, dignified.	None discernible.	Pet, once the exclusive property of the Chinese imperial family.
CHINESE TEMPLE DOG page 189	Elegant appearance, dignified carriage.	Any deviation from type.	Quiet, affectionate, gentle.	Wary of strangers.	Temple guardian in the past.
CHINESE CRESTED DOG page 189	Well proportioned, unusual appearance.	Any deviation from type.	Lively, gay, intelligent.	None discernible.	Hardly known.

The names of the dogs in the set of tables entitled "Qualities and defects of breeds" follow the order in which they appear in the book. To locate any specific breed, refer to the contents or index.

INDEX

Page references in italics denote illustrations